Heroes & Villains

of

Worcester

Heroes & Villains

of

Worcestershire

A Who's Who of Worcestershire Across the Centuries

Terry Wardle

The History Press

First published 2010

The History Press
The Mill, Brimscombe Port
Stroud, Gloucestershire, GL5 2QG
www.thehistorypress.co.uk

© Terry Wardle, 2010

The right of Terry Wardle to be identified as the Author
of this work has been asserted in accordance with the
Copyrights, Designs and Patents Act 1988.

British Library Cataloguing in Publication Data.
A catalogue record for this book is available from the British Library.

ISBN 978 0 7524 5515 0

Typesetting and origination by The History Press
Printed in Great Britain
Manufacturing managed by Jellyfish Print Solutions Ltd

CONTENTS

INTRODUCTION & ACKNOWLEDGEMENTS

It is hoped that these bite-sized chunks of biography will prove as addictive and endlessly fascinating to the reader as they have to the author. Taken together they provide a sweeping overview of the gifted, interesting, powerful, famous – and infamous – people from more than 140 Worcestershire towns and villages who have shaped Worcestershire's history, as well as those who have taken its name out into the wider world and achieved great things there.

The starting point for this collection was *Short Biographies of the Worthies of Worcestershire*, by Edith Ophelia Browne and John Richard Burton, published in 1916. *Worthies* stood out dramatically from the biographical standards of its time, notably eschewing, or at least attenuating, the obsequiousness and hagiology of many of its contemporaries – though it did betray the clerical prejudice of its main progenitor, Revd Burton (one-time headmaster of Kidderminster School, author of histories of Kidderminster and Bewdley, and former Rector of Dowles) by containing a surfeit of obscure clerics who had published their sermons. There were also some biographies of people with no Worcestershire connections, mostly included due to geographical confusion. But despite these quibbles, *Worthies* was still the best historical collection of Worcestershire biographies of its time, and has been the standard work for almost a century. For this collection, all *Worthies* entries were evaluated, and many discarded, while many new ones were added; all facts were checked from a wide variety of sources, both local and national; and all biographies were brought up to date, both in style and in keeping with the present state of our knowledge regarding the lives of these men and women. Many more illustrations have also been used, ninety in all.

One characteristic of Worcestershire which inevitably impacts on a collection such as this is the way in which its county boundaries have changed over the years, so that some villages, and even towns, have moved into or out of the county. Perhaps the oddest feature of Worcestershire, and other counties, during the eighteenth and early nineteenth centuries, was the existence of 'detached parts' within surrounding shires, often the result of past Church landholdings. Some of these were dealt with by the Counties (Detached Parts) Act of 1844, though others persisted until 1931. These changes mean that some people included here lived in locations that are not now part of the county, but they *were* Worcestershire people and have therefore been included. In making reference to place names it has been borne in mind that many readers will be fellow 'locals', so it has not been thought necessary to add 'upon-Severn' to names such as Upton or Stourport; but, since not everyone reading the book will have an intimate knowledge of the whole of Worcestershire, it has been thought desirable to add 'near somewhere-or-other' after some place names, with apologies to those readers who are irritated by this because they know full well where the place is. Whenever buildings are referred to, their fate, present use or status has been given wherever possible – but of course buildings continue to be demolished or to change use, so this information may change after publication. Where there are several entries for one family it mostly seemed sensible to place them in chronological, rather than strict alphabetical, order. Underlined names indicate that that person also has a biography.

Many thanks are due to the staff of the Worcestershire Local History Centre and Worcestershire Record Office, to John Jenkinson of the Evesham Hotel, and to the following people and organisations, for kindly providing and/or permitting use of pictures: Philippa Tinsley of Worcester City Library, Museums and Art Gallery for the picture of H.H. Lines; Michael Grundy of the *Worcester News* for the pictures of the Huxter brothers, Lord Nuffield and H.H. Martyn; Martyn Webb, Archivist of the Morgan Motor Company for the picture of 'Harry' Morgan and for assistance with information; Paul Griffith for the pictures of Vesta Tilley; Bernard J. Taylor of Quinton Local History Society for the picture of Francis Brett Young; Worcester City Council for the pictures of Alexander Clunes Sheriff, Richard Padmore, George Henry Williamson, Thomas Winnington, Samuel Sandys, Ellen Wood, G.A.S. Kennedy and William Laslett; Pam Bairstow and Friends of Claines Church for the picture of John Colley; Worcestershire County Cricket Club for the pictures of 'Tip' Foster; and Spartacus Educational at www.spartacus.schoolnet. co.uk for the picture of George Wyatt VC. Great care has been taken to try to ensure that copyright and ownership of images have been respected, and it is trusted that rights holders will forgive any inadvertent breach in the interests of attempting to illuminate Worcestershire's past. Claire Wardle and Dave Worrall have unearthed some fascinating material for me, and Marianne Wardle has been of enormous help throughout the research process.

Most of all, thanks are due to the many unnamed authors, past and present, whose works have been consulted during the research for this book, and who have played their part in preserving the memory of the Worcestershire people listed here. As John Aubrey wrote to Anthony Wood in 1680:

> … many worthy men's names and inventions are swallowed up in oblivion; as much of these also would have been, had it not been through your instigation.

Terry Wardle, 2010

An **A-Z**

of

WORCESTERSHIRE
Heroes & VILLAINS

ABELL (TILLEY), MARY (*c.* 1755-1788)

Servant girl whose downfall was, perhaps, to love the wrong man. At Worcester Assizes on 5 March 1785, she was sentenced to death for stealing a cloak and other clothing valued at thirty-one shillings, probably from her employer. The sentence was later commuted to seven years transportation, and she was transported to Australia in the first convict fleet in 1787. She was about 30 years old and unmarried, but had fallen in with Thomas Tilley, a 40-year-old labourer turned robber, and began to use his name. He was also sentenced to transportation for robbery, at Stafford, 27 July 1785, and they arrived in Australia in January 1788. Whilst imprisoned they must have contrived to be together, and on 13 April 1787, a month before they sailed, Mary had Tilley's child. They married soon after landing, on 4 May 1788; their child died on 19 May, and Mary died soon afterwards. Tilley's death was not recorded in Australia, suggesting he may have got back to England.

ADAM DE EVESHAM (d. 1189)

Abbot of Evesham from 1161, for almost thirty years. He was the first abbot allowed to wear the mitre, a ceremonial headdress normally reserved for bishops. Originally a monk of Notre Dame de la Charite-sur-Loire, he became Prior of Bermondsey, 1157. At Evesham he finished the nave and cloister and St Egwine's shrine, and made an aqueduct.

ADELAIDE, QUEEN OF ENGLAND (1792-1849)

European noblewoman who married the future William IV in 1818. She bore William two daughters but both died in infancy, so he was succeeded by his niece, Queen Victoria. As a widow she lived at Witley Court (1843-6), Great Witley, where her chaplains were Revd John Ryle Wood, Canon of Worcester, and Revd Thomas Pearson, Rector of Stockton-on-Teme. On arrival she insisted that all the pianos be tuned; the tuner was

Edward Elgar's father, William. While there she financed the first village school and was often seen driving out in her carriage.

AELFRIC (d. 1051)

Short-lived and controversial Bishop of Worcester, regarded as a malign influence over King Harthacnut (1040-2). Archbishop of York from 1023, he obtained the see of Worcester in 1040, when the well-liked incumbent, Lyfing, was removed by the King for political reasons. This change was very unpopular in the city, and the people blamed Aelfric, perhaps unfairly, when the city was sacked and burnt in May 1041 after two royal tax collectors were killed. The citizens saved their lives by taking refuge on the Bevereye, a sandbar island in the Severn at Bevere. Later that year Lyfing was restored. Aelfric helped crown Edward the Confessor in 1043. He was buried in Peterborough.

AELFWEARD (d. 1044)

Distinguished Abbot of Evesham who fell victim to the prejudices of his time. A monk of Ramsey, Isle of Man, he was promoted to Evesham in 1014 where he recovered plundered abbey estates, added a guesthouse and enriched the library. He became the Bishop of London in 1035, though he retained Evesham. Sadly, when he became a leper he was expelled from Evesham. He angrily took many of the abbey's relics with him back to Ramsey, where he was welcomed and remained until his death.

ALDRED (d. 1069)

Ambitious, acquisitive and talented Bishop of Worcester (1046-62) who crowned William the Conqueror. Politician, traveller, ambassador and soldier, he began as a monk at Winchester, becoming Abbot of Tavistock around 1027. At Worcester he arranged a peace with Gruffydd, King of North Wales, but was defeated by Gruffydd, King of South Wales, and Irish pirates, leading a scratch military force against them, 1049. His diplomatic skills were shown in 1050 when he brought back Swein, the errant, exiled son of Godwine (Earl of Wessex) and reconciled him with King Edward. In 1056 he took over the dioceses of Hereford and Ramsbury, Wiltshire, in addition to Worcester, and rebuilt St Peter's Church at Gloucester in 1058. Elected Archbishop of York in 1060, he visited Rome for the Pope's assent but was attacked on the return journey and robbed of everything but his clothes. There may have been mutterings at Rome about the many appointments he held, and he gave up Worcester to St Wulfstan II, though he kept twelve of the bishop's manors. He was ambassador to Emperor Henry III in 1064, and may have crowned Harold in 1066. After the Battle of Hastings he initially supported Anglo-Saxon rebels, but crowned William on Christmas Day 1066. He was regarded as a hard-working bishop and firm and courageous ruler. When Urse d'Abitot, first Norman Sheriff of Worcester, encroached on Church property, the archbishop is said to have met him with a bold reproof, albeit a fairly awful pun: 'Highest thou Urse, Have thou God's curse.' He was buried in York Minster.

ALDWIN

Eleventh-century holy hermit of Malvern Chase. On the advice of St Wulfstan II, he was made the first Prior of Great Malvern Priory when it was founded by Urse d'Abitot, later becoming a dependency of Westminster. He ruled with great success.

ALLCOCK, SAMUEL (1829-1910)

Victorian businessman. Allcock changed Redditch from a quiet village of 500 inhabitants into a thriving industrial town of 15,000 people, and the world centre of fishing tackle manufacturing. He was the youngest child of the third marriage of Polycarp Allcock, who began the family fishing-hook business in Redditch, 1803; at 13 he was accompanying his father on sales trips in a horse and gig, and by 15 was undertaking them alone. He also joined the Wesleyan Methodist Church, which is credited as inspiration for his industriousness. At 20 he became Superintendent of the Wesleyan Sunday school, a post he held for twenty-five years, and took over the family business. Just two years later he booked a stand at the Great Exhibition of 1851 and, having little money, spent just £5 on a modest display of

Samuel Allcock – business tycoon.

fishing tackle which nevertheless received an Honourable Mention, and the company's renown began to spread. He diversified into rod and tackle making, had produced his first illustrated catalogue by 1866, and expanded from the original works (between Unicorn Hill and Bates Hill) to a much larger site at Clive Road, Redditch, establishing a North American subsidiary in 1871. By 1880 the company was claiming to be the oldest and largest fishing tackle manufacturer in the world, employing about 700 people. A caring, generous employer, he gave much to good causes. He was also the first county councillor for East Redditch in 1888. Allcock died at his home, The Cedars, Redditch, now a care home. In 1965 the company was taken over by US firm Shakespeare, which still has a base in Redditch. Ironically, though Samuel Allcock sent fishing tackle from Redditch all over the world, it is believed he never fished himself.

ALLCROFT, JOHN DERBY (1822-1893)

MP for Worcester (1878-80) with a reputation as a philanthropist. The only son of a partner in J&W Dent (a Worcester glover's), he successfully built up the business in London, where he held several public positions. A devout evangelical Christian, he founded a mission room in Worcester and built three London churches. In 1869 he purchased a large estate in Shropshire, including the then uninhabited thirteenth-century Stokesay Castle, regarded as the finest fortified manor house in England, which he completely restored. It is now managed by English Heritage. He died in London and was buried in Shropshire.

ALLIES, JABEZ (1787-1856)

Worcestershire-born solicitor who became an important early researcher and writer on county history and folklore. The second son of William and Anne Allies, he was born at Lulsley (near Alfrick), where his family had lived for generations. He practised as a solicitor in London, but after marriage to Catherine, a Northamptonshire landowner's daughter, he came to live at Catherine Villa, Lower Wick (near Worcester), where he eagerly took up researches into Roman occupation of the county. His most important work, *On the Ancient British, Roman and Saxon Antiquities of Worcestershire*, was published in 1840, and as a much-extended second edition in 1852, but he also wrote on subjects as diverse as fossils and planetary motion. He was well known as an expert amateur archaeologist associated with many major Victorian 'digs' across the country, and his contribution, particularly to recognising the significance of evidence such as field names, is still regarded as important today. He died at Tivoli House, Cheltenham and was buried beside his wife in Leckhampton churchyard.

ALLSOPP, HENRY, LORD HINDLIP (1811-1887)

First Lord Hindlip of Hindlip Hall. Born into a wealthy Burton-on-Trent brewing dynasty founded by his father Samuel, he took over the firm in 1838 and managed it very successfully. He was a Conservative MP for East Worcestershire in 1874 until ennobled in 1880. Allsopp was greatly upset by claims that his firm misled the public over its 1887 stock market flotation, and died within weeks. He left six sons; the eldest succeeded to the Hindlip title, one was MP for Worcester and another Mayor of Worcester (1892-3). The firm of Samuel Allsopp & Sons did not thrive under his descendants, merging with Ind Coope in 1935.

AMPHLETT, SIR RICHARD PAUL (1809-1883)

Lord Justice of Appeal and Privy Councillor. Shropshire-born son of Revd Amphlett, of Wychbold Hall, Hadzor (near Droitwich), which he inherited. Called to the Bar in 1834, he rose steadily through the legal ranks, though maintaining Worcestershire links; he was Justice of the Peace and Deputy Lieutenant for the county, MP for East Worcestershire (1868-74) Lord Justice of Appeal (October 1876) and Privy Councillor (November 1876). He died in London and was buried at Hadzor.

ANDREWS, MILES PETER (1742-1814)

MP for Bewdley, 1796-1814. The wealthy son of a London merchant, he inherited a fortune in shares of a great gunpowder mill at Dartford, but preferred business interests in the theatre. His elections as member for Bewdley were never opposed, but corporation accounts were later found to show that after each election he paid the borough large sums of money; for example, in 1801 he paid £3,000 towards the £11,000 cost of building Bewdley bridge.

ANSON, AUGUSTUS HENRY ARCHIBALD (1835-1877)

Victoria Cross winner and MP for Bewdley. The third son of the first Earl of Lichfield, he married Amelia Maria, the daughter of Revd Claughton, Vicar of Kidderminster, in 1863. As a soldier he served with the Rifle Brigade (1853-6), and later the 10th and 7th Dragoons, retiring as a Major in 1861. He fought with distinction at Sebastopol in 1853, was wounded at the capture of Delhi, and again at the relief of Lucknow – where he was awarded the VC. He was MP for Lichfield (1859-68), then in Bewdley as a Liberal (1869-74).

ARTHUR, PRINCE OF WALES (1486-1502)

Eldest son of Henry VII, destined to become King until he died and was replaced by his younger brother, Henry VIII. Born at Winchester, and baptised by Bishop Alcock of Worcester, the young prince was always delicate, and was brought by his father to Malvern for his health. Henry presented a magnificent stained-glass window to the priory church, with images of himself, his queen and the young prince. In 1491 Henry rebuilt a manor house at Tickenhill, Bewdley, as a royal palace for his son, whom he had appointed President of the Council of the Marches. Arthur's proxy marriage to Spanish princess Catherine of Aragon took place there in 1499. The real marriage was in 1501, and Catherine's settlement included the manor of Salwarpe (near Droitwich), which she held all her life. Arthur died at Ludlow soon afterwards. His cortège passed through Bewdley, but in bad weather the oxen could not reach his palace, so he lay in state at the drafty, wooden Bewdley chapel. He was taken to Worcester for burial in the cathedral, and Henry erected a beautiful chantry chapel in the choir over his son's grave. Tickenhill Palace remained in Crown ownership until 1873.

ASGILL, JOHN (1659-1738)

Lawyer and MP whose life was blighted by debt. Born at Hanley Castle, he was called to the Bar in 1692. He helped found the first land bank in 1695, and in 1698 published a pamphlet advocating a registry of titles of land. In 1699 he became an MP for Bramber, Sussex. In 1700, however, he wrote a controversial religious book which caused him, by 1707, to be expelled from both the Irish and English Parliaments. Plunged into financial difficulties, he spent the rest of his life as a debtor in Fleet Prison, London, where he tirelessly penned books and pamphlets.

ASHWIN, JAMES COLLINS (1833-1855)

Gallant victim of the Crimean War; eldest son of James Ashwin of Bretforton (near Evesham). A Lieutenant in the 57th (Middlesex) Regiment, he was killed, aged just 21, before Sebastopol in the assault on the Great Redan on 18 June.

BACHE, SARAH (1771?-1844)

Enterprising schoolmistress with a literary bent. Sarah was born at Bromsgrove and brought up in Worcester. She kept the Islington School in Birmingham, was a friend of the pioneering scientist and radical thinker Joseph Priestley, and wrote the hymn 'See how He loved', published in 1812. She died in Birmingham.

BADBY, JOHN (d. 1410)

Worcestershire blacksmith (or tailor). Condemned by a Worcester church court because he denied the Roman Catholic doctrine of Transubstantiation, he was burnt as a heretic at Smithfield, London, 1 March 1410.

BADLAND, THOMAS (1634-1698)

Nonconformist pastor of the Presbyterian congregation at Worcester for thirty-five years. He drew up a declaration of its doctrines (1687). Buried in St Martin's Church.

BALDWIN (*c.* 1125-1190)

Bishop of Worcester, 1180, and supporter of Richard the Lionheart's ill-fated crusade. Appointed Archbishop of Canterbury in 1184, he crowned Richard in 1189 and accompanied the crusaders – but died in the Holy Land.

BALDWIN, ALFRED (1841-1908)

Stourport-born industrialist and MP; father of British Prime Minister Stanley Baldwin. Alfred was Chairman of Baldwins Ltd, ironmasters and coal owners; chairman of the Great Western Railway Company; and Conservative MP for West Worcestershire (Bewdley) from 1892 until his death. In 1866 he married Wesleyan minister's daughter Louisa, whose three sisters married the artists Sir Edward Burne-Jones and Sir Edward Poynter, and a relative of the writer Rudyard Kipling. He had a reputation as a philanthropist and funded the building and endowment of the church and schools at Wilden, Stourport, 1880. He died in London.

BALDWIN, STANLEY (1867-1947)

Worcestershire-born politician who dominated the inter-war years; three times British Prime Minister. Born at Lower Park House, Lower Park, Bewdley, Stanley was the son of industrialist Alfred Baldwin, cousin to author Rudyard Kipling and nephew of artists Sir Edward Burne-Jones and Sir Edward Poynter. Despite an indifferent performance in education – he achieved only a third class history degree at Trinity College, Cambridge, and was thrown out of the debating society because he never spoke – he proved very successful in the family business, helping his father turn it into one of Britain's largest coal and iron firms by 1902. The company banked

Stanley Baldwin – three times Prime Minister.

with the Old Bank in Worcester, and he was fulsome in his praise of its support for the business. Following his father, already an MP, he took his West Worcestershire (Bewdley) seat, which he held for twenty-nine years. His rise through the ranks was rapid. By 1921 he was in the Cabinet; by October 1922, Chancellor of the Exchequer. In May 1923, Baldwin became Prime Minister for the first time – though nor for long. In December he decided to call a General Election, but lost. However, a year later he was back for five years, during which the government faced down the General Strike of 1926. In 1935 he became Prime Minister again and dealt with the abdication of Edward VIII in January 1936. Though infuriated by Winston Churchill's continued calls for rearmament, he privately insisted that Churchill should lead the country if there was a war. In May 1937 he retired, becoming Earl Baldwin of Bewdley. He died in December 1947, at Astley Hall (near Stourport), now a nursing home. After cremation in London, his ashes were buried in Worcester Cathedral.

BARNSLEY, WILLIAM

English exile. He was born mid-sixteenth century, at Barnsley Hall (near Bromsgrove), into a family which had held land in the area since at least the fifteenth century. Established in Russia by the late sixteenth century, he reputedly earned the unfortunate distinction of being the first Englishman exiled to Siberia, probably in the early 1580s, by Tsar Ivan the Terrible. Apparently this was at the instigation of leading Russian and future Tsar Boris Godunov, immortalised by Mussorgsky's nineteenth-century opera, *Boris Godunov*, who suspected him of 'over-familiarity' with his wife, Maria. That might have been the last to be heard of him, but after twenty years this irrepressible character returned hale and hearty, joined the Russian Church, and made a rich marriage. The old hall where he was born was taken down in 1771 and replaced by a large farmhouse nearby, itself replaced, after 1900, by a new Barnsley Hall which opened in 1907 as a County Asylum, subsequently an NHS hospital, then closed in 1996, after which the site was redeveloped.

BARR, MARTIN (1758-1813)

Porcelain manufacturer. Because of his technical knowledge, he was in partnership in 1793 with the Flight family, who ten years earlier had purchased the porcelain factory founded by Dr John Wall. His sons, Martin Jr and George continued the partnership after his death, until the firm was merged in 1840 with that founded by Robert Chamberlain in the 1780s. *See* Flight, Thomas.

BARRY, ALFRED (1826-1910)

Churchman and educationalist; son of Sir Charles Barry, architect of the Houses of Parliament. Canon of Worcester (1871-81) he zealously promoted higher education in the city, and gave popular lectures on Church history. Previously headmaster of Leeds Grammar School (1854-62) and principal of Cheltenham College (1862-8). Afterwards principal of King's College, London (1868-83). Bishop of Sydney and Primate of Australia (1884-9); Canon of Windsor (1891-1910). He also wrote many books, including religious works for teachers.

BASKERVILLE, JOHN (1706-1775)

Famed as one of the finest printers of all time. Born at Sion Hill, Wolverley (near Kidderminster), he seems to have taught himself calligraphy, and by the age of 20 set up in Birmingham as a writing master and tombstone engraver. Around 1740 he established a business in Moor Street making superior japanned (enamelled) goods, from which he became very wealthy. In 1745 he took the lease of a small estate near Birmingham on which he built a handsome house: his 'little Eden', where the city council's Baskerville House now stands. Having made his fortune, he turned to the work that really interested him. In 1750 he started type-founding, and in 1757 produced a quarto edition of *Virgil;* 'the first of those magnificent editions which went forth to astonish all the librarians of Europe,' said Macaulay. In 1758, he undertook to

Printer John Baskerville.

supply the University of Oxford with a complete alphabet of Greek types, and became printer to the University of Cambridge. His masterpiece was a folio edition of the Bible (1763); one of the finest ever printed. He continued printing fine classical and religious books – around sixty in all – almost until his death. He made innovations in type – the Baskerville typeface is still much used – in printing, and in his use of paper, creating advances used for generations afterwards. A Worcester bookseller and contemporary of Baskerville, William Smart of 88 High Street, was so impressed that he named his home in Barbourne, Worcester, Baskerville House. Being an atheist, Baskerville insisted on being buried in his garden, but in 1826 his coffin got in the way of canal works and was moved to Christ Church, New Street, and when that church was demolished at the end of the century he was moved again to Warstone Lane Cemetery.

BAXTER, RICHARD (1615-1691)

Clergyman and gifted teacher. His views and prolific writings often got him into trouble during the Civil War and Restoration, but his ideas were influential long after his death. Shropshire-born, he supplemented his irregular education with wide reading, and in 1638 was ordained by Bishop Thornborough of Worcester, and became the first headmaster of Dudley Grammar School. Minister at Kidderminster (1641-60), he made pastoral counselling as important as preaching, and his programme became a model for many other parishes. Increasingly he found his sympathies lay with the Puritans, rather than the established religion, and after the Battle of Naseby in 1645, he acted as chaplain to the Parliamentary Army for the next two years, and was present in that capacity at the Siege of Worcester. Falling seriously ill, he stayed for a time with <u>Sir Thomas Rouse</u>, of

Kidderminster cleric Richard Baxter.

Rouse Lench (near Evesham), where he began his best known book, *The Saints' Everlasting Rest*, completed at his house in Kidderminster High Street. About sixty of his astonishing 168 published works were first issued in the town. Having assisted the Restoration of Charles II, he moved to London as King's Chaplain, but his lifelong distaste for religious hierarchies made him refuse the Bishopric of Hereford. His preaching was influential in London, but in 1662 he felt unable to comply with the Act of Uniformity, and being refused a licence to preach, retired to Middlesex and married. He wrote many more books, but was repeatedly arrested and jailed. In 1685 he was abused and heavily fined by Judge Jefferies on spurious allegations of libelling the Church and, aged 70, remained in prison for eighteen months. He died and was buried in London. Proof of his continuing influence in Britain and America was the unveiling, almost two centuries after his death, of his statue in Kidderminster Bull Ring in 1875. The statue was moved to St Mary's parish church in 1967.

BAXTER, THOMAS (1782-1821)
Worcester-born porcelain painter. Thomas Baxter was instructed by his father in painting and gilding Worcester china. After art school in London, he worked for both Flight & Barr and Chamberlains, and painted a rich dessert service for Lord Nelson. He died in London.

BAYLIES, WILLIAM (1724-1787)
High-living Evesham-born doctor. The only son of an apothecary, he married the daughter of Evesham attorney Robert Cookes. Contested Evesham in 1761. He practised at Bath and London, but fled the country in 1766 to escape creditors and rumours that he had poisoned his wife's brother for his inheritance. Appointed physician to Frederick the Great, he settled in Berlin, where he died.

BEAUCHAMP, WALTER DE (*c.* 1065-1130)
Keeper of Worcester Castle and sheriff of the county, 1114-30. He married a daughter of the first Norman sheriff <u>Urse d'Abitot</u>, whose lands he inherited after Urse's son was exiled. He held other royal offices, and Henry I granted him the rights to breed pheasants and hunt wolves in royal forests in Worcestershire.

BEAUCHAMP, SIR JOHN DE, BARON OF KIDDERMINSTER (1319-1388)

Son of Richard Beauchamp, of Holt. He fought in the French and Scottish wars; Justice of North Wales. MP for Worcestershire (1352, 1355, 1377, 1380); Steward of the King's Household. Created Baron of Kidderminster in 1387, he fell from grace and was beheaded on Tower Hill, London in 1388. His son, John de Beauchamp, regained his father's honours in 1398, but forfeited them again on the accession of Henry IV. Buried in Worcester Cathedral.

BEAUCHAMP, RICHARD DE, EARL OF WARWICK (1382-1439)

Earl of Warwick and a noted military commander in the reigns of Henry IV and Henry V. Born at Salwarpe Manor House (near Droitwich); son of Thomas, Earl of Warwick. Knighted at the Coronation of Henry IV and succeeded to the earldom soon after 1400. He was involved in the defeat of Welsh rebel Owen Glendower and the Percys at Shrewsbury, 1403. One of the defeated lords was Richard Beauchamp, Earl of Worcester, who was executed, and Richard subsequently married his widow, Isabella. He made an ostentatious pilgrimage to the Holy Land, and visited Venice, Poland and Germany around 1408-10. He was Lord High Steward at the Coronation of Henry V in 1413 and helped suppress the Lollard rising in 1414. He joined the invasion of France, was present at the capture of Harfleur, and in 1419 received the surrender of Rouen. Henry V bequeathed to him the care of his infant son, Henry VI. Appointed Lieutenant Governor of France and Normandy in 1437, he died at Rouen in 1439 and was buried at Warwick.

BEAUCHAMP, HENRY DE, DUKE OF WARWICK (1425-1446)

Son of Richard de Beauchamp. Born at Hanley Castle, he succeeded his father in 1439; created Premier Earl in 1444, and Duke of Warwick, in recognition of his father's service, and no doubt because of his boyhood friendship with Henry VI. Antiquary Leland said Henry also crowned him King of the Isle of Wight. He died at Hanley and was buried at Tewkesbury. As he had no male heir, the dukedom expired.

BEAUCHAMP, SIR JOHN DE, BARON BEAUCHAMP OF POWYK (c. 1400-1475)

Son of Sir William de Beauchamp of Powick and Alcester. In 1439 he became guardian of the lands of his cousin Henry, Earl of Warwick. This was a substantial estate and he acquired increasing importance. By 1440 he had become Master of the King's Horse; he was knighted in 1445 on succeeding to his father's estates; created Baron Beauchamp of Powyk, 1447; and was Lord Treasurer of England, 1450-2. He remained a leading figure in the royal household, avoiding the partisan pitfalls of the Wars of the Roses, and retired in 1462. He was buried at the Dominican Friary, Worcester, which was founded by his ancestor.

BEDDOE, JOHN (1826-1911)

Doctor who became a leading Victorian anthropologist. Born at Bewdley, he was such a delicate boy that he was not taught to read until he was 8 years old. After private education in Stourport, he attended Bridgnorth Grammar School, and entered a solicitor's office at Ledbury, Herefordshire, but had a breakdown. He decided instead to train as a doctor, and went into practice at Clifton, Bristol in 1857. He had by then already published his

first anthropological paper, on the subject of ethnology – the study of the physical characteristics of races – on which he was to become an acknowledged authority. He assiduously collected ethnological material from almost every part of the United Kingdom, and Brittany, and in 1885 he published his best known work, *The Races of Britain: A Contribution to the Anthropology of Western Europe*, which was highly regarded by contemporaries and republished until 1971 – but his ideas on race are now very much out of fashion. He was buried in Edinburgh.

BELL FRANCIS (1590-1643)

An English Jesuit. Born at Temple Broughton, Hanbury (near Droitwich), he attended the College of English Jesuits at St Omer, and was ordained priest in 1618. He began his English mission in 1634, but was arrested as a spy by the Parliamentary soldiers at Stevenage, Hertfordshire, 1643, and hanged at Tyburn, London.

BELL, JOHN (d. 1556)

Worcestershire-born Bishop of Worcester, 1539-43. He was previously chaplain to Henry VIII, and much employed by him in relation to the King's divorce from his first wife, Catherine. He resigned his see in 1543 and retired to London, where he was buried. He provided in his will for maintenance at Oxford of two scholars born in Worcester diocese.

BELLAMY (BLOODWORTH), SARAH (1770-1843)

Transported to Australia on the first convict fleet in 1787, at the tender age of 17. She fared better there than most, despite perhaps being wrongly convicted. A spirited girl with striking red hair, one of seven children of Richard and Elizabeth Bellamy of Queens Hill, Belbroughton (near Bromsgrove), she became servant to a weaver – Benjamin Haden, of Dudley (then in Worcestershire) – but she appeared in court at Worcester on 9 July 1785, charged with stealing 630 shillings cash and promissory notes from him. The accusation may have been suspect, since it provided Haden with a convenient excuse for his recent bankruptcy. Sentenced to transportation for seven years, she begged in vain for public whipping instead. In Australia she fell in with convict bricklayer James Bloodworth, who built many of the colony's early buildings, and they became a much respected couple, having eight children, though four died in infancy. They never married because he already had a wife in England, but she used the name Bloodworth until her death in Australia, and it was on her tombstone.

BELLOMONT, EARL OF *see* <u>Coote, Richard</u>

BERKELEY, HERBERT BOWYER (1851-1890)

Early photographer and innovative chemical engineer. Born at Cotheridge Court (near Worcester), he became interested in chemistry at public school and by the 1870s was a keen amateur photographer, basing much of his work on landscapes around Cotheridge. He became a member of the Royal Photographic Society, and regularly exhibited his work between 1874 and 1889. During the 1870s he experimented with the developer then available, and produced a better formulation, details of which he published in 1881. He moved to London in that year and his new developer was marketed by the Platinotype Company. By 1889 his health was deteriorating, and, in need of a drier climate, he travelled to Algiers, where he died.

BERKELEY, SIR ROBERT (1584-1656)

Worcester-born lawyer of a wealthy family. He was born in St Martin's parish, the second son of wealthy clothier Rowland Berkeley, who was MP for Worcester (1593-1604). Called to the Bar in 1608, he became High Sheriff of Worcestershire (1613), Recorder of Worcester (1621), and MP (1620-2, 1624-5). He was Justice of King's Bench in 1632, but his strong Royalist views were not popular with Parliament, and he was imprisoned in 1641, deprived of his position and sentenced to a massive fine of £20,000. When freed he retired to the estate at Spetchley which his father had purchased. When Scottish troops burnt his mansion before the Battle of Worcester, 1651, he converted the stables and lived there. Buried in Spetchley church where there is a memorial figure of the judge in his robes. His grandson founded Berkeley's Hospital in Worcester.

BERKELEY, SIR ROWLAND (1613-1696)

Only son of William Berkeley of Cotheridge Court (near Worcester), and Margaret, daughter of Thomas Chettle of Worcester. He was knighted in 1641 and became sheriff of the county, but suffered in the Civil War and was fined around £2,000 afterwards. On 3 September 1651, according to his later account, he was taken from his home by Royalists keen to force him to fight for them in the Battle of Worcester. He claimed to have declined and escaped from the city later in the day, but was then taken by Roundheads the next day for having fought – though he was soon released. The historian Nash later claimed that the wily knight had two identical horses, one of which he rode in the battle and stabled at a neighbour's home, whilst the other was found at his home the next day, having clearly not been in a battle. Whatever the truth of this, he wrote a graphic account of the Battle of Worcester in personal letters, published by John Noake in *Worcestershire Nuggets*. He fared better after the Restoration, but in 1669 his only son died in Greece on a diplomatic mission.

BERNARDI, JOHN (1657-1736)

Colourful soldier, born at Evesham, son of a Genoese count. Unhappy at home, he left at 13, later enlisting as a soldier under the Prince of Orange, and rising to Captain. He lost an eye, was shot through the arm and left for dead at the Siege of Maestricht, 1676. He followed James II to Ireland in 1688, but afterwards retired to Holland. In 1695, by then a Major, he was arrested in London on suspicion of plotting to assassinate William III, and committed to Newgate Gaol, where, scandalously, he was detained for forty years, without ever being tried. During his imprisonment he married for the second time, and had ten children. He published an account of his life in 1729.

BINNS, RICHARD WILLIAM (1819-1900)

Irishman responsible for the Victorian rejuvenation of Worcester porcelain. After studying pottery and art in London, he came to Worcester in 1851, invited by fellow-Irishman William Henry Kerr to become part proprietor of the porcelain works, which was in a sad state, having had a serious fire. Considerable rebuilding went on in the 1850s and the company introduced Parian, which imitated Greek marble, to produce inexpensive statuettes very popular with the growing middle class. When Kerr returned to Ireland in 1862, Binns formed the Royal Worcester Porcelain Company. Over the next twenty-one years the freehold of the works was purchased, the workforce expanded from 80 to 800, and many improvements were made in quality of product, which brought the company plaudits at home and abroad. Binns also found time to research the previous history of his craft and in 1865 published *A Century of Potting in the City of Worcester*. In 1897 he published an autobiographical book, *Worcester China: A Record of the Work of Forty-five Years, 1852-1897*. He retired in 1897 and died at Diglis House, Severn Street, Worcester, now a hotel.

BLOUNT, THOMAS (1618-1679)

Very well-known writer in his day, born at Bordesley Park, Redditch. He qualified as a lawyer, but was prevented from practising because he was a Catholic. However, he didn't need to because he inherited considerable property. His chief studies were on the interpretation of archaic and obscure words in law and sciences. *Glossographia, or a Dictionary Interpreting Hard Words Now Used in Our Refined English Tongue*, was reprinted six times, the last in 1717. His most famous book was *Boscobel, or the History of His Sacred Majesties Most Miraculous Preservation at the Battle of Worcester, 1651*, published 1660, though oddly Blount later denied writing it, even though it contained a preface signed by him. His *Fragmenta Antiquitatis, Ancient Tenures of Land, and Jocular Customs of Some Manors*, first published in 1679, was republished in 1784 and 1815. He died and was buried in Herefordshire.

BONNER, EDMUND (*c.* 1500-1569)

Controversial bishop, hated for persecuting Protestants in the reign of Mary I. Born at Hanley Castle (near Upton), even his birth was controversial. Supposedly the son of a sawyer, another story – doubtless circulated by his many enemies – suggested he was the illegitimate son of a Cheshire clergyman. Certainly he attended Oxford, which was unusual for the son of a sawyer. Ordained about 1519, he became chaplain to Cardinal Wolsey in 1529. From 1532 he was sent on European embassies by Henry VIII, who was fighting opposition to his divorce. Bonner was regarded by many as overbearing, insolent, coarse and unscrupulous, but was an able ambassador, and was rewarded with a number of rectorships, including Ripple, south of Upton. He was apointed Bishop of London in 1539 but he suffered imprisonment and lost his see under Edward. Subsequently reinstated under Mary, he set about restoring Catholicism and persecuting Protestants with an enthusiasm that won him the epithet 'Bloody Bonner'.

Imprisoned under Elizabeth, his knowledge of law made it impossible for his enemies to convict him, and he died at the Marshalsea Prison, London. He had to be buried secretly at midnight at St George's Church, Southwark, to avoid hostile demonstrations, but Catholic sources claim his body was moved soon afterwards to a country church in Essex.

BOSEL (d. *c.* 691)

First Bishop of Worcester, 680-91. Brought up at St Hilda's Monastery, Whitby, he was appointed leader of a monastic mission to Worcester in 680. The monks doubtless built huts, and a timber church, near the Anglo-Saxon settlement clustered around a fort protecting the river crossing. Bosel must have been well respected by his fellow monks, but was said to be 'so pulled down with such extreme infirmity of his body that he could not of himself execute the office', and much of the practical, day-to-day work of the see may have fallen on Ostforus, a younger man and prolific and learned author, nominated by Bosel as his successor.

BOSWELL, JOSEPH (1861-1890) AND SAMUEL (1851-1890)

A couple of rogues, who nevertheless may not have deserved the fate which befell them. The thieving Boswell brothers, of Littleworth Street, Evesham, worked as gardeners. However, on the night of 9 November 1889, they were poaching with workmate Alfred Hill in the grounds of Wood Norton Hall (near Evesham), now a hotel but then the estate of French aristocrat the Duc D'Orleans. Around 2 a.m. they were surprised by patrolling gamekeeper Frank Stephens, 25, who lived with his wife and small son in nearby Lenchwick. All three men began pelting Stephens with stones and Joseph tussled with him on the ground, while the others tried to kick him in the head. Finally Hill coshed him heavily. He was left for dead but recovered consciousness and managed to drag himself to the nearest house. He died thirteen days later, but not before identifying the Boswells as his assailants. Both men denied striking the fatal blow, which had caused horrific damage to Stephens' skull, and the implication was that it was struck by Hill, 23, who had fled to Birmingham but was later apprehended. Tried at Worcester Assizes, they were sentenced to hang, upheld on appeal, despite a petition from 2,000 local people who pointed out that the executions would leave ten children fatherless. But Hill somehow managed to obtain a reprieve. This caused outrage in Worcester, but the information was kept from the Boswells until they were led out for execution on 11 March, and enquired where he was. Stunned by the realisation that the man who may have struck the fatal blow had left them to die for the crime, they both broke down and had to be helped onto the scaffold.

BOTT, THOMAS (1828-1870)

Leading nineteenth-century Worcester porcelain painter. Born near Kidderminster, he gave up his father's trade of making spade handles to study drawing. After a few years in Birmingham as a portrait painter, he joined the Worcester Royal Porcelain Works in 1853, living at 4 Park Hill, St Martins. Queen Victoria and Prince Albert were great patrons of his work, as was their son, the future Edward VII. He died from paralysis in Worcester. His work is still highly valued by collectors.

BOURNE, SIR JOHN (d. 1563)

Of Holt and Battenhall, knighted 1553. One of two Secretaries of State under Mary I (1553-8); MP for Worcester (1553); MP for Worcestershire (1554-8). He received grants of Battenhall, Upton, and other Crown manors, and a lease of Ombersley, but quarrelled with Bishop Edwin Sandys and was committed to the Marshalsea Prison. A prominent Catholic, he was infamous for allegedly having demolished the chapel at St Oswald's Hospital in The Tything, Worcester, and used the materials for work on Holt Castle, reportedly saying he would restore the chapel when the government restored 'the true religion'.

BRADLEY, EDWARD (1827-1889)

Prolific humorous writer and artist, well known in Victorian times under the pen-name Cuthbert Bede. Son of a surgeon, he was born at Swan Street, Kidderminster, and attended the grammar school, contributing his earliest literary efforts to its magazine. Ordained in 1850, he was Rector of Stretton, in Rutland, and elsewhere. His most famous work was *The Adventures of Mr. Verdant Green, an Oxford Freshman* (1853-7), which he illustrated himself. Aside from his books, he also drew for *Punch* magazine, and contributed to many other periodicals. Several of his local sketches were in Kidderminster Museum. He died in Lincolnshire.

BRADLEY, THOMAS (1751-1813)

Distinguished Worcester-born doctor, who ran a school in the city before studying medicine at Edinburgh, 1791. He was physician to Westminster Hospital, London (1794-1811), and for many years edited the *Medical and Physical Journal.* He published a revised edition of *Fox's Medical Dictionary* (1803), and *A Treatise on Worms* (1813). Died in London. His brother Waldron, was a well-known nineteenth-century Worcestershire writer under the pen-name Shelsley Beauchamp.

BRANSFORD, WULSTAN (d. 1349)

Bishop of Worcester, 1339-50. Born at Bransford (near Worcester), where he later built a bridge over the River Teme. He became a monk at Worcester and rose to be prior, being elected bishop by the monks. He built the Guesten Hall at the cathedral, since destroyed by fire. In the time of the Black Death in 1349, he denied burial to victims at the city's only burial ground (at the cathedral) and ordered that they be interred outside the walls, at St Oswald's Hospital, on The Tything, thus perhaps avoiding further spread of the disease – though his decision must have been unpopular at the time. He died at Hartlebury.

BRAY, SIR REGINALD (*c.* 1440-1503)

Leading figure in fifteenth-century national politics. Born second son of Sir Richard Bray in St John's, Worcester, where he attended the grammar school. A loyal administrator to Margaret, mother of Henry VII, he was prominent in the defeat of Richard III and the accession of Henry, for which he was richly rewarded with offices and estates. He built the Bray Chapel at St George's Chapel, Windsor, and is said to have designed Henry VII's Chapel at Westminster, begun in 1503. Bray's portrait is in a window of the priory church of Great Malvern and he is buried at Windsor.

BRIGHT, HENRY (d. 1626)

Distinguished Worcester-born schoolmaster. Master of the King's School for forty years until his death, his teaching in Latin, Greek and Hebrew drew scholars from as far afield as Wales, and was praised by many contemporaries, including the historian Nash. He was buried in Worcester Cathedral with an epitaph composed by the dean.

BRINTON, WILLIAM (1823-1867)

Kidderminster carpet manufacturer's son who became a distinguished doctor. He studied in London and qualified in 1848. By 1854 he was a member of the College of Physicians, and became a lecturer on Forensic Medicine and Physiology at St Thomas's Hospital, London, as well as a physician there. He had a large private practice in Brook Street, Grosvenor Square, and was considered an eminent specialist in diseases of the alimentary canal. He wrote many highly-regarded books and papers. He died and was buried in London.

BRISTOW, RICHARD (1538-1581)

Worcester-born cleric and academic. He studied at Oxford, becoming renowned for oratory, and was chosen with fellow academic Edmund Campion to help entertain Queen Elizabeth I with a public disputation when she visited Oxford. But in 1569 he became a Catholic and went abroad, being appointed the first prefect of studies at Douay College, and afterwards head of the seminary at Rheims, both training grounds for Jesuits. When his health failed he returned to England and died at Harrow-on-the-Hill.

BRITTEN, RICHARD FREDERICK (1843-1910)

Naval officer and Worcestershire landowner. Born in London, the second son of Daniel Britten, of Kenswick, Lower Broadheath (near Worcester) he entered the navy as a midshipman, aged just 13, and saw service in the China War of 1858. As a Lieutenant he served aboard the Royal Yacht, and later as Flag Captain to the *Duke of Edinburgh* in the Mediterranean. He retired as a Captain in 1892, after succeeding to the Kenswick estate, where he died.

BROCK, SIR THOMAS (1847-1922)

Leading sculptor. Born in Worcester, the son of a builder, he attended the city's School of Design and became an apprentice in the modelling department at Royal Worcester Porcelain, later designing for them a figurine, 'Bather Surprised', which was produced for fifty years and is still much sought after. In 1866 he became a pupil of Irish sculptor John Henry Foley, and after his death in 1874 finished several of his commissions, most notably the figure of Prince Albert on the Albert Memorial, London, which made his reputation and brought him many illustrious commissions. In 1901 he undertook the massive equestrian statue of the Black Prince in Leeds City Square, but his most famous work was the impressive Imperial Memorial to Queen Victoria, which stands before Buckingham Palace. Legend has it that George V was so impressed at the unveiling that he called for a sword and immediately knighted Brock! His local work included a monument to Bishop Philpott in Worcester Cathedral, and statues of <u>Richard Baxter</u> and <u>Sir Rowland Hill</u> in Kidderminster. He died in London.

BROMLEY, SIR THOMAS (1530-1587)

Eminent Elizabethan lawyer, of Holt Castle. Recorder of London (1566) and Solicitor General (1569). He was Counsel for the Crown in the trial of the Duke of Norfolk for High Treason (1572). Appointed Lord Chancellor (1579), he presided at the trial of Mary, Queen of Scots in 1586. He was buried in Westminster Abbey. His son, Henry, was MP and High Sheriff for Worcestershire, and purchased Ham Castle, Clifton-upon-Teme.

Judge Sir Thomas Bromley.

BROMLEY, HENRIETTA (1800-1885)

Daughter of Colonel Henry Bromley, of Abberley Lodge, who was MP for Worcester (1806-7), High Sheriff (1809), and notable for raising public subscriptions to release debtors from Worcester Gaol. The old Worcestershire families of Bromley and Walsh ended the male line in this generation, and of the six daughters, only the eldest married. After the sale of Abberley Hall in 1836, the other daughters, including Henrietta, retired to Bewdley, where they spent their lives and fortunes doing good deeds. Henrietta Bromley's life of charitable giving was commemorated on the font at Ribbesford church (near Bewdley).

BROOM, HERBERT (1815-1882)

Lawyer and prolific legal author. Born at Kidderminster, he became a barrister in 1840 and practised on the Home Circuit. Reader of Common Law at the Inner Temple, he was author of many law books. He died in Kent.

BROOM, JOHN (d. 1777)

Shropshire-born entrepreneur who saved the fledgling Kidderminster carpet-making industry from disaster. Carpet weaving began in the town in 1735, but was suffering badly through competition from Wilton carpets, which were regarded as better quality. Having gone to Belgium to study carpet-making, Broom brought back an expert and set up the first loom for piled or 'Brussels' carpets at Mount Skipet, Kidderminster in 1749. It was a great success and other firms followed suit, so that the trade rapidly expanded. In around 1732 Broom built Broomfield Hall in Franche Road, later the Vicarage but since demolished, and was a large contributor to the building of The Old Meeting House (1753). He was buried in Kidderminster churchyard.

BRYAN, STEPHEN (1685-1748)

Printer who published the world's oldest newspaper. A clergyman's son, he was apprenticed in London and became a freeman in 1706. In June 1709 he began weekly publication of *The Worcester Postman*, having presumably purchased the title from a previous management which had produced it irregularly since 1690. He took a house on the south side of the Cross Keys Inn, Sidbury, then outside the city in St Michael's parish, and published a newspaper every Saturday – mostly single-handedly since he only ever had one apprentice

– also selling patent medicines on the side. Three months before his death in 1748, he assigned the paper to Harvey Berrow, a clergyman's son from Bedfordshire, also trained in London, who may already have been working with Bryan. He was buried at St Michael's Church, next to the Lychgate, which was demolished in 1965. Berrow renamed the paper the *Worcester Journal*, later *Berrow's Worcester Journal*, which name it still has today. The present publishers use 1690 as the foundation date and claim it is the world's oldest surviving newspaper.

BUCKNALL, RUPERT THOMAS HAMPDEN (1873-1913)

Distinguished medical specialist. Born at Kidderminster, educated at King Charles I School there, he took first class honours at University College, London, 1896. He became Assistant Professor of Clinical Surgery at University College Hospital and Consulting Surgeon at Victoria Hospital for Children, and was author or joint author of a number of highly praised specialist medical papers. He also had a successful practice in Harley Street, but his career was ended by his early death in a road accident as he returned to London from St Leonards-on-Sea. He was buried at Bexhill.

BULLINGHAM, NICHOLAS (1511?-1576)

Cleric, born at Worcester, son of Thomas Bullingham (one of the Bailiffs of the City, 1528 and 1530). Fellow of All Souls, Oxford, 1536, he became chaplain to Archbishop Cranmer in 1547, and Prebendary and Archdeacon of Lincoln in 1549. But, being married, he was deprived of his positions under Queen Mary and went into exile. Returning in 1558, he rose to become Bishop of Lincoln (1560), and Bishop of Worcester (1571-6), said to be 'much beloved' by the people. He received Queen Elizabeth I on her visit to the city. He was buried in Worcester Cathedral.

BURNET, ELIZABETH (1661-1709)

Philanthropic wife of a Worcestershire landowner. Born near Southampton, she married Robert Berkeley, of Spetchley (near Worcester), in 1678. They lived for a while at The Hague, and became supporters of the Prince of Orange. After his accession as William III they returned to Spetchley, but she was widowed in 1693. In 1700 she became the third wife of Gilbert Burnet, Bishop of Salisbury. Four-fifths of her fortune went to charities. She died in London and was buried at Spetchley.

BURROWS, HERBERT (1904-1926)

Triple murderer – and policeman. On the morning of Saturday, 28 November 1925, probationary Worcester policeman Burrows, 22, asked his colleague, Constable William Devy, if he had heard about the murders at the Garibaldi Inn (Wyld's Lane, Worcester) during the night, and chatted to him about the details of the crimes. Licensees Ernie and Dolly Laight, aged 31 and 30, had both been shot dead in the cellar, and their 2-year-old son was found in a bedroom with his skull caved in. Later that morning, Devy realised that Burrows had told him of these events an hour before the murders were reported to police. Burrows' rented home, opposite the pub, was searched and officers found a gun and a substantial sum of money, tallying with that likely to have been at the pub. They also found evidence that he was in considerable debt to a moneylender. When questioned that afternoon he confessed to the murders. At his trial, which opened in late January 1926, the defence revealed that Burrows, a former sailor, had contracted syphilis, with consequent mental degeneration. Despite this, he was quickly convicted and he refused an appeal. Because of the unusual circumstances he had been held at Gloucester Prison, where he was hanged on 17 February.

BUTLER, SAMUEL (1613-1680)

Satirist Samuel Butler.

Worcestershire-born satirist, chiefly remembered for his Restoration mock-heroic poem, Hudibras. Fifth child of Samuel Butler, farmer and churchwarden of Strensham (near Upton), he is usually thought to have been born there, but John Aubrey (*Brief Lives*) quotes a schoolfellow of Butler's as saying he was born near Barbourne Bridge, Worcester, and it is known that his father owned a house and land there. Educated at King's School under <u>Henry Bright</u>, he became page to the Countess of Kent, then clerk to various Puritans, including Thomas Jeffereys, a Justice of the Peace at Earls Croome; and Sir Samuel Luke, of Caple Hoo, Bedfordshire, one of Cromwell's generals, believed to have been the archetype for 'Sir Hudibras'. Some early prose work may have won him preferment, and after the Restoration he became steward of Ludlow Castle, responsible for overseeing its refurbishment for a year or two until his marriage to a wealthy widow. In 1663, the first part of *Hudibras* appeared, and the clever, stinging satire on the Puritans made him famous overnight. Charles II and his court were particular admirers, and he received a royal gift, probably about £300. A second part appeared in 1664, the third in 1678. Butler's barbed wit won him no friends personally, and he spent his final years in obscurity and relative poverty, much troubled by gout. Buried in London, his funeral was paid for by a friend. Much of the work he produced was not published until 1759. A monument to him was placed in Westminster Abbey in 1721.

BUTLER, WILLIAM JOHN (1818-1894)

Clergyman founder of Worcester's Alice Ottley School. He held a number of parishes, including Wantage (1846-80), before becoming Canon of Worcester in 1880. A great believer in education for girls, he founded the Sisterhood of St Mary's school while vicar at Wantage, and in 1888 took a leading role in founding the Girls' High School, Worcester, later named <u>Alice Ottley</u> School after its first headmistress. He was subsequently appointed Dean of Lincoln.

CALDICOTT, ALFRED JAMES (1842-1897)

Well-known Victorian conductor and light opera composer. Son of a Worcester hop merchant and amateur musician, he became a leading chorister. He studied at Leipzig and became organist of St Stephen's Church, Worcester in 1865. He began to earn a reputation as a composer and conducted his own composition, *The Widow of Nain*, at the Worcester Festival. He settled in London, where he composed operettas and conducted at the Prince of Wales Theatre and in America. Professor at the Royal College of Music and the Guildhall School, then appointed Principal of the London College of Music. He died at Barnwood House Institution (near Gloucester).

CALVERLEY, CHARLES STUART (1831-1884)

Indolent but effortlessly brilliant poet and wit. Born at Martley, son of Revd Henry Blayds, who subsequently resumed the old Yorkshire family name of Calverley. He attended Harrow (1846-50) and won a scholarship to Oxford in 1850 where he was brilliant and charming, but reckless, being removed in 1852 over some escapade. He entered Cambridge and became the only student ever to win the Chancellor's Prize for Latin verse at both universities. Called to the Bar in 1865, he joined the Northern Circuit, but a fall while skating in 1867 ended his career and he spent much of the rest of his life as an invalid. He left only a handful of works but is regarded as the father of 'the university school of humour'. He was buried in Folkestone Cemetery.

CAMERON, LUCY LYTTELTON (1781-1858)

Prolific writer of evangelical tracts and religious allegories for children. Born at Stanford-on-Teme, daughter of vicar Dr George Butt, who was Vicar of Kidderminster from 1787. In 1806 she married Revd Charles Cameron, the eldest son of a Worcester doctor. They spent twenty-five years working in the mining district of Donnington Wood, Shropshire before moving to Louth in 1836, and to Swaby, both Lincolnshire, in 1839. Her evangelical writings were popular in England and America, and were translated into a number of languages. Her sister Mary Martha Sherwood was also a well-known author. She died and was buried at Swaby.

CAMERON, THOMAS (1704-1777)

Well-known Worcester doctor. Born in Edinburgh, he settled in Worcester in 1727, and promoted the establishment of the Infirmary in 1745. He wrote many medical papers.

CAMERON, CHARLES MB (1748-1818)

Born in Worcester, son of Thomas Cameron, he was a physician at Worcester Infirmary (which his father helped found) for forty years. He was eulogised in a *Worcester Herald* obituary.

CANTELUPE, WALTER DE (1195-1266)

Elected Bishop of Worcester in 1236, he was considered one of the greatest bishops of his time. He was enthroned at Worcester in the presence of King Henry III in 1237, and established the White Ladies convent, on a site where the Worcester Royal Grammar School now stands in The

Tything, Worcester. He also began the fortification of Hartlebury Castle, vigorously pursued Church disputes on behalf of his see, and strongly opposed papal interference in English affairs – but also royal interference in Church affairs. In the Barons' War he supported Simon de Montfort, though he attempted in vain to mediate between the two sides before the Battle of Lewes in 1264. De Montfort slept at his manor of Kempsey the night before the fateful Battle of Evesham (1265). After the King's victory he was suspended and summoned to Rome, but died during the journey, and was buried in Worcester Cathedral.

CARPENTER, LANT (1780-1840)

Energetic educator and Unitarian minister. Born at Kidderminster, the third son of carpet manufacturer George Carpenter, he was adopted by his mother Mary's former guardian, Nicholas Pearsall, a benevolent Unitarian who founded a grammar school at Kidderminster. He studied science and theology at Glasgow and became an assistant in a school near Birmingham in 1801, and a preacher at the New Meeting, Birmingham, in 1802; then librarian at Liverpool Athenaeum (1802-5). He married Anna Penn in Worcester in 1806. Co-pastor of St George's Meeting, Exeter (1805-17), he also conducted a boarding school and founded a public library, before moving to Lewin's Mead Chapel in Bristol, 1817, where he took a leading part in politics, public life and scientific education. He also published thirty-eight works on Unitarianism and education. His health broke under the strain in 1839 and he was ordered to travel, but while going by steamer from Livorno to Marseilles he was swept overboard and drowned. His body was buried where it washed ashore, at Porto d'Anzio. His eldest child, Mary (b. 1807), founded the ragged school movement.

CARR, ROBERT JAMES (1774-1841)

Twickenham-born Bishop of Worcester, 1831-41. Son of a schoolmaster, he had become a friend of the Prince Regent while Vicar of Brighton, and had already been Dean of Hereford (1820), and Bishop of Chichester (1824). He attended the Prince, by then George IV, during his last illness in 1830. He died at Hartlebury Castle, and was eventually buried in the churchyard, though there is a story that he owed a substantial sum and the sheriff's officer seized the body and refused to release it until his debts were paid by William Laslett a month later.

CASLON, WILLIAM (1692-1766)

Born at Cradley, son of a Halesowen shoemaker, he became famous as a typefounder. Apprenticed to an ornamental engraver of gunlocks and barrels, he started this business in London in 1716, and was encouraged to add a type foundry by 1720. Dutch Baroque types were then commonly used, but Caslon's attractive types quickly found favour and became renowned throughout Europe and beyond. The first printed version of the US Declaration of Independence was printed in Caslon type. He died at his 'country house' in Bethnal Green and was buried in London. His descendants were involved in type founding until 1937.

Typefounder William Caslon.

George Bernard Shaw insisted that only Caslon must be used in printing his books, and Caslon fonts are still widely used.

CAWOOD, JOHN (1775-1852)

Derbyshire-born evangelical pioneer. Ordained in 1800 to the curacy with sole charge of Ribbesford, Bewdley, and Dowles (near Pershore); he was a zealous pioneer of evangelical work in the district. He founded what was probably the first Sunday school in Worcestershire, held cottage lectures, and started a mission in a remote and lawless part of the Wyre Forest, which subsequently became a parish. He also held the Mastership of Bewdley Grammar School, where his pupils included the future Bishop Edward Feild of Newfoundland, and Bishop Medley of Fredericton, Canada. He completed fifty years ministry at Bewdley, and was buried in Dowles churchyard.

CECIL, JOHN alias SNOWDEN (1558-1626)

A real master spy. Born in Worcester, he joined the Roman Catholic Seminary at Rheims in 1583, was ordained at Rome in 1584, and, in 1591, was sent to England on a secret and perilous mission to minister to British Catholics. Captured at sea and brought to London as a prisoner, it seemed his mission, and his life, would be over. However, he convinced his captors that he had always intended to turn double-agent, and was recruited into the service of Queen Elizabeth's spymaster, Burghley. For the next ten years he combined the roles of English spy, zealous missionary and political agent to the Scottish Roman Catholic earls. Even when sent to Rome or Spain, he maintained his wide correspondence, ever pretending to betray the other side. His espionage career ended abruptly in 1601, when he was denounced as a spy during a trip to Rome, but he evaded potentially fatal consequences, and ended his life in peace and prosperity at Paris, as chaplain to Margaret de Valois.

CHAMBERLAIN, ROBERT (*c*. 1737-1798)

Porcelain manufacturer. Possibly the first apprentice at Dr John Wall's Worcester porcelain manufactory, in 1751. By 1783 he was supervising decoration and gilding of porcelain at the plant, with his son Humphrey. But in that year Joseph Flight bought the company, and the Chamberlains left to set up a rival business on the site in Severn Street which later became home to Royal Worcester Porcelain. Initially they were decorating others' wares, but by 1792 they had begun producing their own products. Chamberlains achieved an enviable reputation for fine quality porcelain. Lord Nelson visited in 1802 and placed substantial orders; a dinner service was produced for the East India Company costing £2,170, and a dinner and breakfast service for £1,047, for the Prince of Wales, who visited in 1807. Chamberlain died at Park Place, St Martin's and was buried at St Oswald's, Worcester. His family firm continued to produce fine quality porcelain until 1840, when Chamberlains merged with Flight, Barr & Barr.

CHAMBERS, JOHN (1780-1839)

Local historian and biographer. Born in London, he was educated as an architect, but devoted himself to literature. He settled at Worcester in 1815, but in 1823 he moved to Norfolk, and died at Norwich. Despite his short stay he wrote *A General History of Malvern*, 1817 (second edition, 1820); *A General History of Worcester*, 1819, and *Biographical Illustrations of Worcestershire*, 1820. Also *History of County of Norfolk*, two volumes, 1829.

CHAMBERS, JOHN CHARLES (1817-1874)

Parish priest, born in The Tything, Worcester, son of <u>John Chambers</u>. While an undergraduate he founded the first Sunday schools in Cambridge. In 1846 he settled at Perth and founded St Ninian's Cathedral (1855). He was appointed Vicar at Harlow, Essex in 1856, before becoming Perpetual Curate of St Mary's, Crown Street, Soho, London.

CHAUCER, GEOFFREY (*c.* 1345-1400)

Iconic early English author. Chaucer wrote *The Canterbury Tales*, the first book ever printed in England. He was employed in 1389 as Clerk of Works and Keeper of the Lodge of the historic Royal Forest of Feckenham, which once covered most of Worcestershire.

CLARE, SIR RALPH (1587-1670)

Zealous Royalist. The eldest son of Sir Francis Clare, of Caldwell, Kidderminster, he descended from the Norman d'Abitot family, and may have been MP for Bewdley before the Civil War. He fought at Worcester in 1642 and 1651, and objected to Parliamentarian churchman <u>Richard Baxter</u>'s retention of Kidderminster. At the Restoration he was appointed a Gentleman Usher of the Privy Chamber in Extraordinary, an honour accorded to only a very few loyal Royalists, which he held until his death. Buried at Kidderminster.

CLARIDGE, RICHARD (1649-1723)

Restless Yorkshire-born churchman, who was Rector of Peopleton (near Pershore), 1673-91. He then became a Baptist preacher, and afterwards joined the Society of Friends in 1700, later becoming a schoolmaster at Barking, Essex. He produced a number of works, including a book, published posthumously and reprinted up to 1836, explaining all these religious changes.

CLARK, JEREMIAH (*c.* 1742-1809)

Organist of Worcester Cathedral, 1806-7. Composer son of a lay-vicar of Worcester Cathedral, he settled in Birmingham as an organist and teacher of music, where he took a leading part in concerts and festivals. He published songs, sonatas, glees, and canzonets. He died at Bromsgrove.

CLAUGHTON, THOMAS LEGH (1808-1892)

Worcestershire cleric, son of an MP in Lancashire, where he was born. He studied at Oxford and maintained links with the university for more than thirty years, being Professor of Poetry there from 1852 to 1857. During the same period he was also Vicar of Kidderminster (1841-67). His work in the parish, which won much praise, was assisted by an enthusiastic band of curates, three of whom went on to become bishops, two deans and two archdeacons. He married Julia Ward, sister of the Earl of Dudley. In 1867 he became Bishop of Rochester, and in 1877 the first bishop of the new see of St Albans. He died in Essex and was buried in St Albans Cathedral.

CLIVE, CAROLINE (1801-1873)

Novelist and poet; London-born daughter of wealthy Worcester MP Edmund Meysey-Wigley, of Shakenhurst (near Cleobury Mortimer). Caroline had an unhappy childhood and suffered from lameness. In 1840 she married Revd Archer Clive, Rector of Solihull (1838-52), and in the same year published her first collection of poetry under the pseudonym 'V'. In 1855 she published her first and best known novel, *Paul Ferroll*, a powerful tale of passion, hatred and murder, which was popular and highly regarded as a pioneering work of psychological fiction. Her husband became Prebendary and Chancellor of the choir of Hereford Cathedral, and the couple moved to Whitfield, Herefordshire. Late in life she was partly paralysed by a stroke, and received fatal burns at her writing desk when her dress accidentally caught fire. *Paul Ferroll* was last reprinted in 1997.

COCKERELL, SIR CHARLES (1755-1837)

Well-travelled Evesham Mayor, 1810 and 1833, and MP, 1818-37. Cockerell served the East India Company (1776-1800), was Postmaster General in India (1804-6), and returned to England as India Agent and Banker.

COCKS, ARTHUR HERBERT (1819-1881)

Worcestershire landowner, grandson of the first Lord Somers, and Justice of the Peace for Worcestershire. He served with distinction in the Bengal Civil Service, 1837-63, and settled at Dunley Hall (near Stourport), now a care home. He died in London.

COLLEY, JOHN (1845-1894)

Manservant turned daring high-wire acrobat. He was born in Fernhill Heath (near Worcester), one of nine children of agricultural labourer Edward and his wife Sarah. In 1861 he was a 'gentleman's servant' in Claines. After marriage to a Bristol woman he moved to London, and by 1871 was servant to daring French acrobat, The Great Blondin, who became famous walking across Niagra Falls on a tightrope in 1859. John took up 'wire walking', perhaps starting by assisting Blondin, and by 1880 was performing in provincial theatres. In 1881 he separated from his wife, with whom he had four children, and was sentenced to three months hard labour for desertion. He subsequently took up with a Worcester woman and had four more children. He died at the County Asylum, Powick, from 'paralysis and general mania', and was buried at Claines. His eldest son may also have become an acrobat, and one of his daughters became an entertainer, with a trick bicycle act.

John Colley – high-wire performer.

COLLIER, GILES (1622-1678)

Clergyman and prolific religious author; born at Norton (near Evesham). In 1654, during the Commonwealth, he assisted commissioners in a religious/political witch-hunt for the ejection of 'scandalous, ignorant, and insufficient schoolmasters and ministers'. In 1648 he acquired the parish of Blockley, Gloucestershire, which he managed to retain after the Restoration despite his Puritan leanings. Author of many tracts, he died at Blockley.

COLLIS, JOHN DAY (1816-1879)

Distinguished Worcestershire educator. Irish-born, he was appointed headmaster of Bromsgrove School in 1842, after a brilliant career at Oxford. Under his direction the school flourished and was accounted one of the best in the country, and he was nominated Honorary Canon of Worcester Cathedral in 1854. His efforts made possible the building of a school chapel in 1856; new schoolrooms were erected and old buildings enlarged and improved. He published nineteen educational books including a history of the school. After twenty-six years he left Bromsgrove to become Vicar of Stratford-on-Avon in 1867, and was founder and first warden of Trinity College School, Stratford, in 1872. He died at Shottery Hall (near Stratford) and was buried in Bromsgrove Cemetery.

COOKES, SIR THOMAS (1648-1701)

Baronet of Bentley Pauncefoot (near Bromsgrove). The eldest son of Sir William Cookes of Norgrove (near Redditch), he succeeded to the baronetcy in 1672. Benefactor of schools at Feckenham and Bromsgrove, though he had no children of his own despite two marriages. His re-endowment of Bromsgrove School in 1693 made possible the first buildings on the school's present site. He left £10,000 to Oxford University, as a result of which Gloucester Hall was converted into Worcester College, which it has remained since. He was buried in Tardebigge.

Sir Thomas Cookes – school benefactor.

COOKSEY, HOLLAND (d. 1792)

Barrister son of Richard Cooksey of Whiteladies (The Tything, Worcester), the farm created on the site of the former White Ladies convent. After completing an MA at Merton College, Oxford (1746), he was called to the Bar at the Inner Temple. He had an estate at Braces Leigh (near Worcester). Chairman of Worcestershire Quarter Sessions, he wrote a number of works on legal matters, including one on the life of John Somers, Lord Chancellor of England, who was born at Whiteladies. He was Justice of the Peace and Deputy Lieutenant of the county, and amongst the first to volunteer for the new Worcestershire Regiment of Militia in 1770, becoming a Major in the part-time force.

COOPER, MARY (*c.* 1750-1814)

A charwoman, transported to Australia on the first convict fleet in 1787. Obviously well known to Worcester law officers, she may have been the Cooper that *Berrow's Worcester Journal* reported on 21 July 1785 was to be whipped in the Cornmarket for an unspecified offence. On Monday, 2 October 1786, she was sentenced to seven years transportation at Worcester Quarter Sessions for stealing a gown, probably from her employer. A <u>Susannah Huffnell</u> was also involved in the crime, and sentence, and on Thursday the *Journal* commented: 'The sentence gives general satisfaction by ridding the country of two very dangerous and abandoned characters.' She never returned and died in Australia twenty-eight years later.

COOTE, RICHARD, LORD COOTE (1636-1701)

MP for Droitwich, 1688-95; Irish baronet; early American administrator; sponsor of the pirate Captain Kidd. Irish-born heir of Richard, first Lord Coote, he succeeded to the title in 1683. In 1676, he wed Catherine, daughter and heiress of Bridges Nanfan, of Birtsmorton Court (near Malvern), who was then apparently only 11 years old. An early supporter of William and Mary, he was rewarded with the title Earl of Bellomont and substantial Irish estates. In 1695 he was made governor of New York, New Hampshire and Massachusetts. Initially a chief sponsor of privateer Captain William Kidd, he subsequently sent him to England, where he was hanged for piracy. Coote died after severe gout and his young widow went on to marry three more times. Both of his titles died out in the next generation.

CORBETT, JOHN (1817-1901)

The 'salt king' of Droitwich. Born in Staffordshire, son of farmer and canal boat owner Joseph Corbett, he left school at 10, and later served an engineering apprenticeship with Leys Ironworks, Stourbridge. However, he was persuaded to join his father's busy canal boat business, with a large fleet of barges plying as far as Liverpool. The business was sold in 1852, and in the same year he acquired the failing salt and alkali works at Stoke Prior (near Bromsgrove). He used his engineering skills to revolutionise production and increase output ten-fold. He purchased other salt works at Droitwich and made similar improvements, making his workings the largest in Europe. He built a massive fortune and used profits to increase wages, build model housing for employees, as well as schools and community buildings, and end cheap female labour. In 1856 the dour Black Countryman married Anna O'Meara, a lively young Irish/French woman brought up in Paris and fourteen years his junior. The couple lived initially at Rigby Hall, Stoke Prior (now a school) and though the marriage lasted about twenty years and they had six children, the difference in their ages and personalities may always have created difficulties. To make her happy, he spent a considerable fortune building a French-style château at Impney, Droitwich, accounted one of the finest houses in Worcestershire and now a hotel. When Anna had a sixth child, which apparently could not have been her husband's, the couple parted. He was Liberal MP for Droitwich from 1874 to 1892. In 1888 he sold his salt interests for the then massive sum of £660,000, and devoted much money to good causes, including developing Droitwich as a health spa, building St Andrews Brine Baths in 1889, and the Worcestershire Hotel, and restoring what became the Raven Hotel. The raven was the Corbett family crest and can be seen on many buildings with which he was associated. He died at Impney. Salt production at Droitwich ended in the 1920s, but continued for some years at Stoke Prior. A road at Stoke Prior is named after him.

COTTON, CHARLES (1630-1687)

Close friend of Izaak Walton. His second wife, Mary, was the eldest daughter of Sir William Russell of Strensham. He shared Walton's passion for angling and his great claim to fame was that he contributed several articles to the most famous fishing book ever written, Walton's *Compleat Angler*, including the sections on fly fishing and making flies. He lived in Staffordshire and was well known in his day for wit and poetry.

COTTON, WILLIAM ALFRED (1852-1889)

Bromsgrove-born coin expert and antiquarian. Son of William, an auctioneer and estate agent, he took over his father's business in 1874. Interested in numismatics and local antiquities, he acquired a valuable collection of old coins and medals, especially rich in Worcestershire tradesmen's tokens. His chief work was *The Coins, Tokens, and Medals of Worcestershire* (1885). He also wrote many books and pamphlets on the church and antiquities of Bromsgrove, and presented some 200 rare old county pamphlets to Worcester Reference Library. His brother, John Cotton, later gave many of his Worcestershire coins to the Victoria Institute Museum, Worcester. He died at Ventnor, Isle of Wight, unmarried, aged only 37 and was buried in Bromsgrove Cemetery. He left £800 towards the erection of an Institute at Bromsgrove.

COVENTRY, THOMAS, LORD COVENTRY (1578-1640)

Leading lawyer, judge, politician and first Baron Coventry. Born at Earls Croome (near Pershore), son of judge Sir Thomas Coventry, by his wife Margaret Jeffreys of Earls Croome, and descendant of John Coventry, Lord Mayor of London in 1426. Entering the Inner Temple, 1594, he was Recorder of London and Solicitor General by 1617. He was appointed Attorney General in 1621, was MP for Droitwich (1621-2) and Lord Keeper of the Great Seal (1625) before becoming Baron Coventry of Aylesborough (near Pershore) in 1628. As Lord Keeper he issued the King's reprimand to Parliament in 1626, but he also advised conciliatory measures to the King in his dispute with Parliament. He remained a Royalist, providing men and

Thomas, Lord Coventry 1578-1640.

money for the King's cause, but had a reputation as a moderate and independent judge. He died in London and was buried at Croome D'Abitot. The title of Baron Coventry continued on through eight descendants, becoming extinct in 1719, but Thomas's grandson, also Thomas (d. 1699), was additionally created Earl of Coventry in 1697, and that title has continued to the present day, with the ancestral seat at Croome Court (near Pershore). The last earl at Croome Court was killed at Dunkirk in 1940, during the Second World War.

COVENTRY, HENRY (1618-1687)

Fourth son of Thomas Coventry. Henry was Groom of the Bedchamber to Charles II, whom he attended in exile. He was also MP for Droitwich (1661-81), Envoy to Sweden (1664-6 and 1671-2), Ambassador to the Congress at Breda (1667), one of the two principal Secretaries of State (1672-80) and a Lord of the Admiralty (1673-7). He was buried in the Church of St Martin in the Fields, London. By his will he left his estate at Hampton Lovett to erect and endow a hospital at Droitwich for twenty-four poor people.

COVENTRY, SIR WILLIAM (1628?-1686)

A younger son of Thomas Coventry, he commanded a company during the Civil War. He went to The Hague in 1660, and was appointed Private Secretary to James, Duke of York. After the Restoration he was MP for Yarmouth (1661), Commissioner of the Navy (1662), Commissioner for Government of Tangier (1662) and Privy Councillor (1665). He was a lively character, accounted the best speaker in the House of Commons, and is frequently referred to in Samuel Pepys' diary. Committed to the Tower of London for sending a challenge to the Duke of Buckingham, but soon released, March 1668. He retired to Minster Lovell, Oxfordshire, died unmarried, and was buried at Penshurst, Kent.

COVENTRY, THOMAS, EARL OF COVENTRY (1629-1699)

First Earl of Coventry. The second son of Thomas (the second Baron Coventry), he succeeded to the barony as fifth Baron Coventry after his elder brother George, and after George's son, John, had died with no heir. He was MP for Droitwich (1660-70) and for Warwick (1681-7), and High Steward of Worcester and of Evesham. He was additionally created Viscount Deerhurst and Earl of Coventry in 1697. He was buried at Croome D'Abitot.

CRANE, JOHN (1750?-1820s?)

A Bromsgrove-born clock-maker, bookseller, and dealer in fancy goods, who became well known for his many racy, topical rhymes. They were first issued in pamphlet form, then in a volume entitled *Poems Dedicated to John Bull, by a Bird of Bromsgrove*, printed by George Nicholson of Stourport. He lived into his 70s but lost his sight later in life.

CREIGHTON, MANDELL (1843-1901)

Noted historian and clergyman, and Canon of Worcester, 1885-91. Born in Carlisle, he combined the role with the post of Professor of Ecclesiastical History at Cambridge (1884-91). Best known of his many works was a five-volume history of the papacy. Worcester was then primarily an industrial centre, and he was said to be shocked by the urban poverty and damage to the environment caused by industry. During his time in Worcester he worked hard for the religious and social life of the city, inaugurating the Worcester Charity Organisation Society and lecturing on historical subjects and local history. Bishop of Peterborough (1891-7) and London (1897-1901), he died in London and was buried at St Paul's Cathedral.

Mandell Creighton – cleric and historian.

CROWTHER, SAMUEL (1817-1888)

Elderly, infirm murderer. Crowther was a lame, elderly shoemaker convicted of killing gardener John Willis at Dodderhill (near Droitwich) on 1 August 1888. Willis saw the 71-year-old stealing fruit from trees on his property, and challenged him. Perhaps there had been bad feeling between the men and this was the final straw. Whatever the reason, amazingly the old man, who was frail and walked with a stick, suddenly pulled out a knife and fatally stabbed Willis. Crowther was convicted at Worcester Assizes in November and hanged in the city on 11 December. He had no visitors in his final weeks; his only relative, a daughter, had given evidence against him at his trial.

CURTLER, THOMAS GALE (1797-1885)

Purchased Bevere Estate, Claines (near Worcester), in 1837 and devoted himself to public service in city and county. He was Vice Chairman of Worcestershire Quarter Sessions from 1845 to 1866. A keen agriculturist, he raised a noted herd of Shorthorns.

CYNEWEARD OF LAUGHERN (d. 1079-1086)

Last Anglo-Saxon Sheriff of Worcestershire. Born into a wealthy Mercian family, one of two sons of Aethelric, a relative of Wulfstan I, Bishop of Worcester, he became a thegn, and seems to have had his seat at Laughern, Worcester. He was clearly a member of the county's land-owning elite, holding land also at Wyre Piddle, Elmley Castle and Hanley, and in Gloucestershire and Warwickshire. It is not clear when he became sheriff, but he held the position until 1069, when Urse d'Abitot became the first Norman sheriff, though Cyneweard continued to hold lands in the county and was a leading citizen until his death.

DANCOX, FREDERICK GEORGE (1879-1917)

Victoria Cross winner. Worcester-born Fred, a hay-baler from Deansway, served with 4th Battalion, The Worcestershire Regiment, during the Second World War. On 9 October 1917, his unit came under machine gun fire from an enemy blockhouse, near the village of Langemark, Belgium. Braving a British barrage, Private Dancox surprised the enemy position from behind, single-handedly capturing the machine gun and about forty German soldiers. Sadly, before he received his VC he was killed in action. It is now in the Worcestershire Regimental Museum. A memorial was placed in Bull Entry, Crowngate Shopping Centre, in May 2010.

DARBY, ABRAHAM (1678-1717)

Founder of the Coalbrookdale industrial dynasty. He was probably born at Wren's Nest, Dudley (then in Worcestershire). After an industrial apprenticeship in Birmingham, he brought some Dutch brass-founders to a plant near Bristol where, in 1708, he patented a new, much cheaper way of making pots and pans, which formerly had to be imported. In the following year he leased the Coalbrookdale Works, Shropshire, and in that same year became the first person to successfully use coke instead of charcoal in the smelting of iron, facilitating large-scale production and greatly increasing the quality of the iron. His wife, Mary, was buried at the Friends' Meeting House at Bewdley in 1718. His grandson built the first iron bridge in Great Britain, still in use as a footbridge.

DAVIES, SARAH (*c.* 1761-1794)

Illiterate glove-maker, transported to Australia in the first convict fleet in 1787. She appeared in court at Worcester in August 1783, aged about 22, and was sentenced to death for shoplifting silk handkerchiefs valued at sixteen shillings; her sentence was subsequently commuted to seven years transportation. The fleet arrived in Australia in late January 1788, and in June she married convict Thomas Crowder, transported for life for burglary. She may already have been married in England, since she was also known to use the surname Ashley, but it was not uncommon for convicts to conveniently forget about previous spouses they might never see again. Crowder quickly became an overseer, and in 1792 was pardoned and given a grant of land. But in January 1794, while he was imprisoned awaiting trial for assault, Sarah died, aged only about 33 years old.

DAVIS, EDWARD THOMPSON (1833-1867)

Victorian painter. Born at Worcester, son of a tradesman, he was a contemporary of Edward Burne Jones at Birmingham School of Art and also studied at Worcester School of Design. He lived for much of his life in Foregate Street and at Northwick, Worcester, and specialised in rural and childhood scenes. He exhibited in Worcester and Birmingham, and achieved great success when he exhibited at the Royal Academy in 1854. His early death followed a short illness while visiting Rome, and he was buried in the English cemetery there. His paintings are still much in demand and fetch good prices when they come on the market.

DEACLE, JOHN (1660-1709)

Born at Bengeworth, Evesham, he made a fortune as a wool-stapler or dealer, and was made an alderman of London. He endowed a charity school in his birthplace for the education and clothing of thirty poor boys. He was buried in old St Peter's, Bengeworth, which was pulled down in 1872; his monument was replaced in the new church.

DEE, JOHN (1527-1609)

Worcestershire clergyman and perhaps the first 'celebrity guru'. London-born, of an old Welsh family, he studied astronomy, astrology, and chemistry, attended Cambridge University when only 15, and was regarded as the foremost mathematician of his age. He was Rector of Upton from 1553, but his main interest was in magic and the supernatural. Not surprisingly, the Church often took him for a Devil-worshipper, though he managed to avoid harm because of his powerful clients, including Elizabeth I, who asked him to choose a favourable day for her Coronation. Many courtiers visited him, often seeking lost or missing personal possessions, though what they may chiefly have desired was the elixir of eternal youth, or perhaps the much-dreamt-of philosopher's stone to

John Dee – clergyman and 'celebrity guru'.

turn base metal into gold. He built the greatest private library in the land and advised on navigation for Elizabethan voyages of discovery; credited with coining the term, 'British Empire'. He could be naïve and in 1582 hired as assistant Worcester-born Edward Kelley, who claimed to interpret the wishes of spirits using a crystal from the angel Gabriel. He married twice and wrote seventy-nine works, but many remained in manuscript. One, said to be longer than the Bible, was 'so dreadful to the printers' that they refused to publish it. He spent his final years in poverty at Mortlake, London. He has appeared in many fictional works, and was thought to be the inspiration for Prospero in Shakespeare's *The Tempest*.

DERHAM, WILLIAM (1657-1735)

Clergyman and polymath, born at Stoulton, between Worcester and Pershore. Ordained in 1682, he became Vicar of Wargrave, Berkshire, then Upminister, Essex, and was appointed Canon of Windsor in 1716. In 1711 and 1712 he delivered the Boyle lecture, an annual Christian lecture revived in 2004, and published many books and papers on theology, natural history, astronomy, clock-making, and other subjects. His scientific knowledge enabled him to act as medical as well as spiritual adviser to his parishioners. He died in Essex.

DODD, CHARLES (1672-1743)

Author of Church History of England, *in three volumes, 1737/1739/1742, which, like his sixty-three other works, was written under his real name, Hugh Tootel.* He was Catholic priest in charge of Harvington, Chaddesley Corbett (1726-43). He died at Harvington.

DOOLITTLE, THOMAS (1633-1717)

Clergyman, born at Kidderminster. He initially entered an attorney's office but left to train for the ministry. He became Pastor of St Alphage, London Wall in 1653, but, being a dissenter, he was ejected in 1662, and opened a boarding school at Moorfields. He proposed the first meeting house in Bunhill Fields; was licensed, in 1672, to a meeting house in Mugwell Street, and also educated young men for the Nonconformist ministry. His name was associated with that of his friend, Richard Baxter, on an old chair in Kidderminster parish church.

DOUGHARTY, JOHN (1677-1755)

Educator and map-maker. An Irish surveyor and mathematician who kept a school, first at Bewdley then for many years in Worcester; in the High Street from 1711 and in Edgar Tower from 1720. His mathematical works were highly popular. His *General Gauger*, published in London, 1750, went through six editions in a year. He also wrote *Mathematical Digests, Containing the Elements and Application of Geometry and Plane Trigonometry, with Tables for Finding the Mean Times of the Moon's Phases and Eclipses.* He made a plan of Worcester (1742), a drawing of the Guildhall, and a plan of Kidderminster (1753). He was buried in the cloister of Worcester Cathedral. His son, Joseph, published a plan of the cathedral in 1736.

DOUGLAS, ARTHUR JEFFREYS (1871-1911)

African missionary, born at Salwarpe Rectory, son of Canon William Douglas, and nephew of the Bishop of Wakefield. He became Rector of Salwarpe in 1898, but resigned to join the Universities' Mission to Central Africa in 1901. He settled first at Kota Kota, on Lake Nyasa, Malawi, and then at Likoma, where he helped build the cathedral in 1905. He was invalided home in 1907, but returned in 1908 as head of St Michael's College, in which post he was very successful. He was shot dead by a Portuguese official, allegedly while trying to protect some African girls from molestation.

DUDLEY, DUD (1600-1684)

Ironmaster. Fourth natural son of Edward Sutton, fifth Baron Dudley, by his mistress Elizabeth Tomlinson of Dudley (then in Worcestershire). His boyhood interest in metallurgy was encouraged by his father, and in 1619, after attending Oxford, he superintended his father's ironworks at Pensnet (near Dudley). He invented a method of smelting using plentiful pit coal, instead of scarce charcoal, and his father obtained a thirty-one-year patent, but he was never to realise its full potential. Iron-making went ahead at Pensnet, and Cradley, Staffordshire, but the massive May Day flood of 1620 swept Cradley away and threatened to drown many at Stourbridge. He quickly restored production, but other iron producers, fearing competition, harassed him with underhand tactics. By 1625 the Pensnet works had been let to Richard Foley, who later got Cradley too. In 1626 he married Eleanor Heaton of Friar Street, Worcester, at St Helen's Church. In 1639 he obtained a new patent, but probably was not able to exploit it before the Civil War, in which he served as a Royalist Colonel. Captured in 1648, he escaped to Bristol where he lived in hiding, posing as a doctor. After the Restoration he successfully appealed for the reversion of his lands and patents. He probably spent his last years at Friar Street, Worcester; buried in St Helen's Church.

DUDLEY, EARL OF *see* Ward, William, first earl, 1817-1885

DUGARD, WILLIAM (1606-1662)
Controversial educator and printer. Born at The Hodges, Bromsgrove, son of a clergyman and schoolmaster. Educated at King's School, Worcester, under <u>Henry Bright</u>, and at Cambridge, he became master of Stamford School, Lincolnshire, about 1633, where he caused controversy by suing the corporate officers over alleged misappropriation of school lands. During 1637-43 he was master of the Free School, Colchester, now the Royal Grammar School, where a house is named after him. He greatly increased the numbers on roll, but cited some local disagreement when resigning. During 1644-50 he was master of Merchant Taylors' School, London. It must have been around this time that he purchased a printing business and became an official printer to the Commonwealth, but he was deprived of his teaching job and imprisoned in Newgate Gaol for printing work favourable to King Charles I. He was quickly released though, perhaps thanks to the influence of his friend, the poet Milton. He was restored to Merchant Taylors', but again dismissed in 1661, after falling out with the school. He set up a very successful private school, but died before he could properly build it up. He printed works of all kinds at his press, many of them intended as school textbooks.

DUNSTAN, SAINT (*c.* 909-988)
Bishop of Worcester, 957-60. Born near Glastonbury, son of an Anglo-Saxon nobleman, he entered the monastery there, and became abbot in 904. He proved to be a skilled silversmith, artist, musician and illuminator, and subsequently served as minister to several kings. He was appointed by King Edgar to the Bishopric of Worcester, and to London also from 958. He became Archbishop of Canterbury in 960, and was leader of the monastic reform movement in the English Church. There were many stories of him defeating the Devil; one, which is claimed as the origin of the 'lucky horseshoe' superstition, had him nailing a horseshoe on the Devil's hoof, and refusing to remove it until the Devil swore never to enter any house with a horseshoe over the door.

DYSON-PERRINS, CHARLES WILLIAM (1864-1958)
Businessman and philanthropist who saved Royal Worcester Porcelain. Born in Lansdowne Crescent, Worcester, grandson of sauce-maker <u>William Henry Perrins</u>, he attended Charterhouse School and Oxford, and joined the Highland Light Infantry. He took over Lea & Perrins after his father's death in 1892, using his considerable financial resources to support a wide range of local and national causes. At Oxford he funded the Dyson Perrins Laboratory as a major centre for organic chemistry research, 1916-2003. He was a major benefactor, and Chairman of Governors, of Worcester Royal Grammar, his father's old school, where he endowed Perrins Hall as a memorial. He also endowed what is now called Dyson Perrins C of E Sports College, in Malvern, where he lived for many years, and supported projects at the library and Malvern Hospital. He was elected Mayor of Worcester in 1897 and High Sheriff of Worcestershire in 1899. Like his father before him, in 1891 he became a director, and subsequently chairman, of Royal Worcester Porcelain,

of whose products he was an expert collector. When orders were slow in the 1920s he paid workmen's wages out of his own pocket, and in 1927 purchased the museum collection – which remained at the factory – for well above market value. He saved the company from receivership by purchasing it in 1934. He also built one of the world's finest private collections of medieval illuminated manuscripts and early printed books, but sold much of it after the Second World War to re-establish the factory. In 1946 he set up the Perrins Trust to support the factory museum, where he placed his own substantial collection, thus founding what, for many years after his death, was known as Dyson Perrins Museum. He died at Malvern, leaving generous bequests to many national museums. His widow bequeathed their home, Davenham in Graham Road, Malvern, to the charity Friends of the Elderly, and it is now a residential home. Royal Worcester closed in 2009, but the museum is still open.

Philanthropist Charles Dyson-Perrins.

EDES, RICHARD (1555-1604)

A noted preacher, he was Prebendary of Hereford (1590) and Treasurer (1596). Dean of Worcester from 1597 to 1604, and Rector of Upton, he later became chaplain to James I and was selected as one of the translators of the King James Bible, though he died before it was begun.

EEDES, RICHARD (1610-1686)

Born at Feckenham (near Redditch), he changed sides in the Civil War, though to little ultimate effect. Curate of Bishop's Cleeve, Gloucestershire (1634), he supported Parliament and was made Vicar of Beckford (near Evesham) in 1647. After eleven years he returned to his original parish and claimed to be a Royalist, but his efforts were in vain and he lost Bishop's Cleeve in 1662, though he still attended services, and was buried there.

EGINTON, FRANCIS (1737-1805)

Gifted artist, possibly born at Eckington (near Pershore). Beginning as an enameller at Bilston, he subsequently joined Matthew Boulton at Handsworth, Birmingham, and invented a mechanical process for reproducing oil paintings in colour, for the homes of the growing middle class. At the time it was not a success, though it was afterwards revived and improved. In 1784, he had workshops at Soho, Handsworth, where, during the next twenty years, he produced a large number of windows in 'stained glass' – though his work was really painted on glass. His first work was the Arms of Knights in St George's Chapel, Windsor, followed by commissions for many cathedrals and mansions. His window at St Chad's, Shrewsbury, has been called 'a national treasure, its colours aglow even on a dull day'. He was buried at Handsworth. His son continued the glass works for many years.

EGWINE, SAINT (d. 717)
Third Bishop of Worcester, 693-717, and founder and first Abbot of Evesham Abbey in the early 700s. Worcestershire-born, probably of the Mercian royal house, he was an eloquent preacher and his elevation to bishop had widespread support from the King, clergy and people, but his strict discipline afterwards alienated many in his see, and he had to go to Rome to clear himself of their accusations. According to a mythical tale, the bishop fastened shackles on his ankles before setting off, as a sign of penitence, and threw the key into the River Avon, but in Rome the key was miraculously found in a fish caught in the Tiber, and he was freed from his bonds, and quickly cleared of wrongdoing by the Pope. He supposedly founded Evesham Abbey after a swineherd named <u>Eof</u> had a vision of the Virgin Mary there. His position as a friend of the Mercian King meant he obtained special privileges and immunities for Evesham, and after its re-foundation around 975 it was one of the great Benedictine abbeys of England. Only the bell tower now remains.

ELGAR, SIR EDWARD WILLIAM
(1857-1934)
Probably Worcestershire's most famous son, and certainly one of the world's great composers. Born in Lower Broadheath (near Worcester), fourth of seven children of music dealer William and his wife Anne, the family soon moved into the city and lived above their music shop at 10 High Street. Mr Elgar was organist at St George's Roman Catholic Church, and the two great influences of the young Elgar's life were music and a love of nature from bicycle jaunts into the surrounding countryside. Later in life he wrote: 'The trees are singing my music. Or have I sung theirs?' As a boy he had lessons in piano at a school in Britannia Square, and later in violin, his favourite, but was self-taught in music theory and

Composer Edward Elgar.

composition. At 15 he had completed his first compositions, and also gave his first public performances – on organ and violin – but had to leave school to work in a local solicitor's office. After a few months he gave up law for a precarious musical career, helping out at times in the family shop, teaching privately and in local schools. He was an enthusiastic member, with his father, of the Worcester Glee Club, and aged 22 became bandmaster at the County Asylum, Powick, succeeding his father in 1885 as organist of St George's

Church, constantly arranging and composing. In the 1880s he began visiting London in fruitless attempts to interest music publishers. His fortunes changed in 1886 when, through his teaching, he met published poet and author Alice Roberts, daughter of a Major General. Three years later they married, very much against the wishes of her family, and she did everything she could to further his career. Throughout the 1890s he was building a reputation as a gifted composer, and in 1899 finally achieved fame with the first performance of *Enigma Variations*. A year later came *The Dream of Gerontius*, and in 1902 the first of the Pomp and Circumstance marches, to which words were later added, making it *Land of Hope and Glory*. Elgar was knighted in 1904, became Master of the King's Musick in 1924, and a baronet in 1931. He lived in London, Sussex and Hereford, but mainly in Worcestershire, especially at Worcester, Malvern, and during 1923-7 at Kempsey (near Worcester). He spent his final years at Marl Bank, Rainbow Hill, Worcester, where he re-erected some of the balustrades removed from his much-loved Worcester bridge during widening in 1932. Golf was amongst his sporting passions, but the last was horse racing. The great violinist Yehudi Menuhin recalled running through the great man's Violin Concerto. Elgar listened to the first page, then said everything seemed fine so he was off to the races at Pitchcroft! He liked an occasional flutter, and with no legal local bookmakers, Sir Edward had to telegraph his bets from Worcester post office, then in Foregate Street. An inoperable cancer was discovered in late 1933. He died the following year, and was buried beside his wife at St Wulstan's Church, Little Malvern. The family music shop closed in 1928, and the building was demolished in the 1960s, though a plaque marks the site. Elgar's final home was also demolished in the 1960s and replaced with flats, but his birthplace is preserved as a museum. Amongst his many memorials are statues in Worcester and Malvern.

ELLIS, SIR HENRY WALTON (1783-1815)
Gallant soldier, born at Kempsey, son of a Major General, he had a distinguished military career, seeing action in Europe, the Caribbean, and the Mediterranean. A Lieutenant Colonel by 1810, he went to The Peninsula opposing Napoleon's armies, and was engaged in almost every battle and siege. Often wounded, he returned home a Colonel in 1814, when the Napoleonic wars seemed over, and received a presentation from Worcestershire. Returning for the final battle with Napoleon at Waterloo in 1815, he received a fatal wound whilst charging with his regiment, and was buried on the field, aged just 32. A monument by Bacon was erected by his regiment in the nave of Worcester Cathedral. He was not married, but left two illegitimate sons whom Wellington commissioned.

ELSTOB, ELIZABETH (1683-1756)
Evesham resident and possibly schoolteacher, she was a noted scholar and has been called one of the first feminists. Born in Newcastle at a time when there was no higher education for young women, she nevertheless learnt eight languages and became a distinguished Anglo-Saxon scholar, producing the first Anglo-Saxon grammar ever published. She was only able to pursue this work because of her brother, William, an Oxford scholar with whom she lived in London, so his early death in 1715 was disastrous for her. She afterwards lived at Evesham, probably for some twenty years. Some sources say she ran a school, but she endured great hardship

from poverty, until aided by Queen Caroline, who gained her the support of the Duchess of Portland for the last seventeen years of her life. She was buried at St Margaret's, Westminster.

EOF (fl. 700)

Swineherd whose vision supposedly led to the foundation of Evesham Abbey and town. The story told by later monastic historians was that Eof kept pigs on the bishop's lands beside the Avon, and was searching for some stray animals in the forest margin, when he had a vision of the Virgin Mary. He hurried to Worcester and told Bishop Egwine, who returned with him and had the same vision, convincing him to build an abbey at the spot. The town which grew up around the abbey took its name from the swineherd, as Eof's ham or homestead. A statue of Eof's vision was unveiled in Market Place, Evesham, in 2008.

EVESHAM, HUGH DE (d. 1287)

Born at Evesham, where he was also a monk, he was accounted the finest physician of his age. He studied at Oxford, Cambridge, France, and Italy. He became Archdeacon of Worcester in 1275 and was created a cardinal and physician to Pope Martin IV in 1280. He was buried at Rome.

FABER, ARTHUR HENRY (1831-1910)

First headmaster of Malvern College, 1865-80. At its opening there were twenty-four pupils and six teachers, but by 1877 there were 290 on roll. The loss of his wife was a great blow to him, and in 1880 he accepted the Rectory of Sprotborough (near Doncaster). He became Prebendary of York in 1887.

FACCIO, NICHOLAS (1664-1753)

Eminent Swiss mathematician who retired to Worcestershire after a colourful life. He invented a method of using a ship's motion for grinding corn; made known a conspiracy to kidnap William of Orange, 1686; and became connected with an odd religious movement known as 'the French prophets'. As a result of the latter, he stood in the pillory at Charing Cross, London, as an impostor in 1707. He travelled in Asia and retired to Worcester about 1720, where he died more than thirty years later at the age of 90. His burial was recorded in the register of St Nicholas Church, now a bar.

FALKNER, THOMAS (1707-1784)

South American missionary who retired to Worcestershire. Son of a Manchester surgeon, he studied at St Thomas's Hospital, London, and went as a surgeon on a slave ship. He was said to be so touched by the kindness of Jesuits who nursed him when he fell ill at Buenos Ayres, that he afterwards joined their order, and became a missionary amongst the inhabitants of Paraguay and the Straits of Magellan, where his surgical skill was of great assistance. He also surveyed the coast for the Spanish Government. After thirty-eight years the society was dissolved, and he retired to Spetchley as chaplain to Robert Berkeley. There he wrote an account of Patagonia with a map corrected by his own observations. He died and was buried in Shropshire.

FECKENHAM, JOHN DE
(*c.* 1518-1584)

Poor Worcestershire boy who rose by his own efforts and ability. Born in Feckenham Forest (near Redditch), son of a yeoman family named Howman, his parish priest gained him admission to Evesham Abbey, from where he entered Gloucester Hall, Oxford in 1539, and returned to Evesham as a teacher. When the monastery was dissolved in 1540, he returned to Oxford, but soon became chaplain to John Bell, Bishop of Worcester; then, 1543-9, to Catholic <u>Edmund Bonner</u>, Bishop of London. He also became Rector of Solihull in 1544, but when Bonner fell in 1549 he was sent to the Tower of London. On the accession of Mary (1553), he was released and became her chaplain and confessor; also Prebendary and then Dean of St Paul's; Rector of Finchley, London, and Greenford Magna, Middlesex

Abbot Feckenham with Lady Jane Grey.

(1554) with a growing reputation as a preacher; also last Abbot of Westminster Abbey. He ministered to pretender Lady Jane Grey before her execution, and pleaded for the life of the future Queen Elizabeth I when she was sent to the Tower. Nevertheless Elizabeth's accession (1558) ended his career. The abbey was dissolved in 1560, and he was sent back to the Tower. He spent most of the rest of his life in confinement, though still much admired for his many good deeds. He died in prison at Wisbech Castle, Cambridgeshire and was buried in an unmarked grave there.

Edward Feild – hard-working bishop.

FEILD, EDWARD (1801-1876)

Stern, but gifted and hard-working bishop, born in Worcester. Educated first at Bewdley under <u>John Cawood</u>, then at Rugby and Oxford (1819) where he took mathematics. Ordained in 1827, he was curate in Oxfordshire (1827-34), then Gloucestershire (1834). Showing the energy that would be a hallmark of his career, he was involved in rebuilding, starting schools, encouraging allotments on Church land, and raising money. He became an expert on village schools, and was the first Inspector of Schools under the National Society, 1840. In 1844 he was consecrated Bishop of Newfoundland, eastern Canada, where he remained the rest of his working life. His High Church views were not always popular, either there or in England, but his energy was much admired. He reinvigorated a theological college, recruited and trained clergy, built a school, a cathedral and twenty-seven parish churches. He bought a boat to travel the length of his diocese, and despite the hardships of his life he outlasted many younger men. In 1875, however, his workload finally took its toll and he went to Bermuda – also part of his see – to recuperate, but died and was buried there.

FELL, JOHN (1625-1686)

Master of St Oswald's Hospital, The Tything, Worcester; son of Margaret, daughter of Thomas Wylde of the Commandery, Worcester. A Royalist and student of Christ Church, Oxford, he became dean after the Restoration, and also received the mastership of St Oswald's, which had formerly been held by his father, Samuel. When he visited Worcester he found that the chapel had been demolished. He had it rebuilt, paying the £450 cost himself. His chapel was replaced in 1873. He also did much building at his college and in Oxford (becoming Bishop of Oxford in 1676) and founded the Oxford University Press. But it is his sad fate to be remembered chiefly as the subject of the undergraduate jingle:

John Fell.

> I do not love thee, Dr Fell;
> The reason why I cannot tell;
> But this I know and know full well,
> I do not love thee, Dr Fell.

FLAVEL, JOHN (1630?-1691)

Clergyman and popular religious author, the son of Revd Richard Flavel, of Bromsgrove. He did well at University College, Oxford, and in 1650 was sent to the parish of Diptford, Devon. In 1656 he removed to Dartmouth, but as a Puritan was ejected in 1662, though he continued to minister there secretly. In 1671 he was granted an indulgence to return, which was afterwards withdrawn. When the law was liberalised in 1687, he became minister of a Nonconformist church. He married four times. He was a popular writer, whose works included *Husbandry Spiritualised* (1669), *Navigation Spiritualised* (1671), and *The Seaman's Companion* (1676). Selections from his writings were published in 1823. Bromsgrove's Charford Estate has a Flavel Road. Died in Exeter.

FLEETWOOD, JAMES (1603-1683)

Bishop of Worcester, 1675-83, after a lively career. He was chaplain to a Royalist regiment in the Civil War, and was present at the Battle of Edge Hill where he took the young princes to safety off the field. He became chaplain to the future Charles II and Rector of Sutton Coldfield, but was ejected from there after the war. At the Restoration he became Provost of King's College, Cambridge, where he had studied. He was buried in Worcester Cathedral.

FLIGHT, THOMAS (d. 1792)

London agent of the Worcester Porcelain Company, he and his brother bought the business for £3,000 in 1783, for his sons Joseph and John. They faced considerable technical problems, especially following the departure of finishing expert <u>Robert Chamberlain</u>, but after Flight studied manufacture in France they began to progress. In 1788 the company received a royal visit. George III and the royal family inspected the company's new premises, clambering up and down ladders, heedless of dirt and sawdust, so that they might see the new works being built. The King gave the company enthusiastic support and a royal warrant, making them the Royal Porcelain Company, and advised the opening of a London shop. The prestigious premises which were set up

Porcelain manufacturer John Flight.

at Coventry Street, off Piccadilly Circus, received royal patronage. When Flight died in London the business passed to his sons, who entered a partnership with technical expert <u>Martin Barr</u>, and the firm became Flight & Barr.

FLORENCE (d. 1118)

Monk at the monastery of Worcester; once supposed to have written a very valuable book on early English history, though credit is now given to another monk. The *Chronicon ex Chronicis*, written in the early twelfth century, was a world history from the Creation, though chiefly chronicling events in Celtic and Anglo-Saxon history, based on earlier annals and histories. It is important today because it contains information that can be found nowhere else, from works since lost. It was originally supposed that it had been written down to 1118 by Florence, and continued after his death to 1141 by another monk, John of Worcester. Copies were circulated amongst monasteries, and it was first printed in 1592, appearing in 1853 under the title *The Chronicle of Florence of Worcester* – reprints of which are still readily available. In the twentieth century, however, scholars have decided that the whole work was actually written by John, with help from Florence, and the latest Oxford University Press edition (1995, 1998) is entitled *The Chronicle of John of Worcester.* An account by another early eleventh-century historian, Orderic Vitalis, said John entered the monastery at Worcester as a boy, and was working on his chronicle at the request of Bishop Wulfstan II.

FOLEY, RICHARD (1580-1657)

Ironmaster of Stourbridge (then in Worcestershire) who founded the family fortune. The son of a nailer at Dudley (also then in Worcestershire) he may have traded in nails rather than made them, and his partnership in a number of south Staffordshire ironworks in the 1620s was the basis of the Foley fortune. He is sometimes called 'Fiddler Foley' because of a colourful tale, told by Victorian writer Samuel Smiles, which had him travelling to Sweden, disguised as a fiddler, to steal the secret of the slitting mill, which was enabling Swedes to undercut English nails. It has been proved that this never happened, or at least not with Richard Foley. He married twice and had five sons and a daughter.

FOLEY, THOMAS (1617-1677)

Thomas Foley 1617-1677.

Eldest son of the second marriage of Richard Foley of Stourbridge (then in Worcestershire), he amassed a large fortune in the iron industry by supplying the warring armies with armaments during the Civil War. He used it to acquire much landed property at Kidderminster and Stourbridge. He married Anne, daughter of John Browne of Kent, the largest gun manufacturer in the country, and in 1652 inherited a half-share in his father-in-law's business, giving him a fabulous reputed annual income of £5,000. In 1655 he purchased the Great Witley estate and considerably expanded a Jacobean manor house on the site, which would become the vast stately home of Witley Court. First of eight Thomas Foleys at Witley, he was friend of Richard Baxter of Kidderminster, and High Sheriff of Worcestershire (1655). He was MP for Worcestershire (1659) and Bewdley (1660-1 and 1673-7). In 1677 he endowed Old Swinford Hospital, Stourbridge, a school for sixty boys from 'poor but honest' families. A century ago it was said to be feeding, clothing, educating, and finding apprenticeships for 160 boys. It is now a state maintained boarding school for around 600 pupils, with descendants of its founder amongst the trustees. He had four sons and two daughters, and was buried in Witley church.

FOLEY, PAUL (*c.* 1644-1699)

The second son of Thomas Foley of Witley Court. He purchased the Stoke Edith estate in Herefordshire in 1670 and built a new house there. He was Tory MP for Hereford (1679-85 and 1689-99), and was elected Speaker of the House of Commons (1695-8). He collected a valuable library at Stoke Edith, where he died. His great-grandson, Thomas, was made Baron Foley in 1776, when the title was revived. Stoke Edith House was destroyed by fire in 1926, but the estate remained in the hands of the Foley family.

FOLEY, THOMAS, LORD FOLEY (1673-1733)

First Baron Foley, son of Thomas Foley of Witley Court and Kidderminster. MP for Stafford (1694-1711) and for Droitwich (1698-9), he was created Baron Foley of Kidderminster in 1712. He enlarged Witley Court considerably, and began the process of selling off industrial holdings as the Foleys reinvented themselves as landed gentry. Buried at Witley. He had seven children but five died before their parents and only one son, Thomas, remained to inherit the title and estates. When he died without heir the barony became extinct, and the estates passed to Thomas Foley, of the Stoke Edith branch of the family, for whom the title of Baron Foley was newly created, 1776.

FOLLIOTT, HENRY, BARON FOLLIOTT (1568-1622)

The second son of Thomas Folliott, of Pirton (near Kempsey, Worcester), by his second wife, Katherine (daughter of William Lygon, of Madresfield, near Malvern). He served in the wars in Ireland from about 1594, and was knighted by the Lord Lieutenant in 1599. In 1603 he was commissioned to develop a township near Ballyshannon Castle, which was incorporated in 1613. He fought at the victory of Kingsale in 1620, and was created Baron Folliott of Ballyshannon in that year. He lived at Wardtown Castle and owned substantial lands in County Donegal. He had four sons and three daughters. His title became extinct in 1716, leaving five sisters as co-heiresses to the estate.

FORSYTH, WILLIAM (1834-1915)

Leading Worcester sculptor and carver. Scottish-born son of an architect, he trained and worked at Edinburgh and London, and came to Worcestershire, with older brother James, to work on Eastnor Castle and church, before setting up a workshop beside the Saracen's Head in The Tything, where he lived and worked for some forty years. James also worked in Worcester, and became better known as a sculptor for his work in cathedrals nationwide, but William's fine work can still be seen throughout his home city and surrounding areas. It included fine interior and exterior carving at Worcester City and County Bank (now Lloyd's), near the Cross; marble altars at St George's Roman Catholic Church; Pitchcroft entrance gates, and the tableau of hop pickers in Sansome Street. Both brothers were probably involved with the superb figures of Perseus, Andromeda and Triton, on the magnificent fountains at Witley Court, Great Witley. William was also president of Worcester City Bowling Club, and a long-time member of Worcester Glee Club, having apparently had a fine voice. Buried at Astwood Cemetery. *Berrow's Worcester Journal* said in its obituary that he was a man 'whose sociability and geniality made him one of Worcester's most popular citizens'.

His firm was also known for its connection with apprentice, <u>Herbert Henry Martyn</u>, who founded a very successful architectural decorating business.

FOSTER, REGINALD ERSKINE 'TIP' (1878-1914)

Worcestershire sporting legend who set two world records and was the only man ever to captain England at both cricket and football. Born at Malvern, the third of seven legendary cricketing sons of Revd H. Foster, housemaster of Malvern College, which he attended before Oxford. At school and university he excelled at football, cricket and racquets. His obituary in *Berrow's Worcester Journal* called him 'the most brilliant cricketer that Worcestershire ever produced', but all the Foster brothers played for the county at one time or another, causing it to be nicknamed Fostershire. On three occasions he scored two separate centuries in one match, and in 1899, with his brother W.L., shared a world record partnership, each scoring two centuries during a match at New Road for Worcestershire during the county's inaugural first-class season. In 1900 he scored a record double-century in a varsity match at Lord's. 'Tip', as he was known to friends, played cricket only seven times for England, but made a considerable impact. In 1903-4, he went with the MCC team to Australia and beat all Test match records, scoring 287 in his first test innings. In 1907 he captained the three-match series in which England beat South Africa. His England football career was equally successful, though also short, because in the days of amateur sport, he had to give time to his career as a stockbroker. He appeared only five times, but England never lost a match he played in. In three internationals in 1901 he scored three of England's eleven

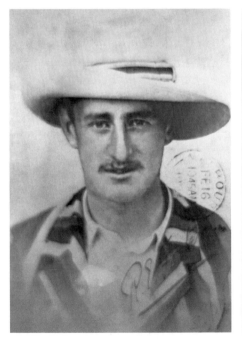

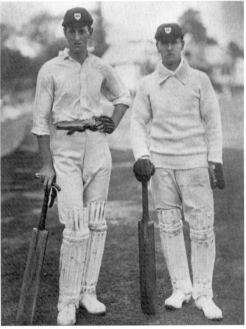

Record-breaking sportsman 'Tip' Foster on an old postcard.

'Tip' Foster and his brother W.L. Foster.

goals. In 1902 he captained an England no-score draw against Wales. He was also national singles champion of racquets, for seven consecutive years. By 1913 it was clear he was suffering severely from diabetes and he died in London the following year. On the day of his funeral, the flags at Lord's were flown at half-mast. The service was at Malvern Priory and burial in Malvern Cemetery.

FREAKE, EDMUND (*c.* 1516-1591)

Bishop of Worcester, 1584-91, and former chaplain to Elizabeth I, though it was as Bishop of Rochester (1572) that he attended the Queen on her visit to Worcester in 1575. He also served as Bishop of Norwich from 1575 to 1584. He reformed the lax administration of church services, and reformed revenues. His memorial in Worcester Cathedral, by Anthony Tolly of Worcester, was one of the earliest signed tombs.

FREWEN, JOHN (1558-1628)

Clergyman of an old Worcestershire family which owned property near Earls Croome. He was ordained in 1582 and was presented by his father to the living of Northiam, Sussex. His Puritan views brought conflict with his parishioners, who in 1611 vainly preferred a Bill of Nonconformity against him. One, named Cresswell, was excommunicated for openly calling him 'old fool, old ass, old cockscombe'. He married three times, naming his eldest son 'Accepted' and the second 'Thankfull'. He published several religious works. Died in Northiam. Some of his sermons were re-preached in his church 250 years later by Octavius Lord, the rector, who was Frewen's descendant in the female line.

GAINSBOROUGH, WILLIAM (1260-1307)

Bishop of Worcester, 1302-7. As a young man he was a Franciscan friar and lectured on divinity at Oxford. In 1302 he was selected for Worcester by Edward I, sparking a tussle between King and Pope. Edward withheld the see until Gainsborough renounced the Pope's authority over it, and afterwards an oath of renunciation was required by all new bishops appointed under papal provision. On his arrival in Worcester he was met by the Grey Friars at the door of St Wulfstan's Hospital, from where he walked barefoot to the cathedral to be enthroned. Sent on an embassy to France in 1307, to arrange the marriage of Prince Edward with Isabella of France, he died at Beauvais on the return journey, and there were dark rumours that he had been poisoned.

GALTON, SIR DOUGLAS STRUTT (1822-1899)

Distinguished engineer, architect and sanitation expert, who helped secure many improvements from which we benefit. Son of John Howard Galton, of Hadzor House (near Droitwich), he became Captain in the Royal Engineers in 1855. He advised, to great effect, on the main drainage of London (1857), was the chairman of commission on submarine cables (1857) and was appointed to a royal commission to improve sanitary conditions in barracks and hospitals. He also held the positions of Assistant Inspector General of Fortifications (1859), Assistant Under-Secretary of State for War (1862-70), Director of Public Works and Buildings (1870-5), President of British Association (1895), and judge at Philadelphia

Exhibition (1876) and at Paris Exhibition (1878). This is only a brief selection of the many activities in which he was involved. He was knighted in 1887, and published books on sanitation and education. He was also county councillor for Worcestershire (Hanbury) and Justice of the Peace. He lived at Himbleton Manor, Droitwich, but died in London of blood poisoning and was buried at Hadzor. His cousin, Sir Francis Galton from Birmingham, was an eminent, if eccentric, Victorian scientist.

GASCOIGNE, OLIVE / OLIVIA (1761-1830)

Transported to Australia in the first convict fleet in 1787, though she may have been of an aristocratic family. A good deal of mystery surrounds her life and crimes. Born either at Severn Stoke (near Worcester) or at Droitwich, she is said to be the daughter of John Gascoigne Gaskin of Wentworth Castle (High Sheriff of Yorkshire) and Sarah Vernon Wentworth, of Hanbury Hall, Droitwich, and christened Olivia. *Berrow's Worcester Journal* of 10 March 1785 reported that an Olive Gascoigne had been sentenced to death at Worcester Assizes on 8 March 'for stealing thirteen guineas out of a box in Severn Stoke', though other accounts suggest that the householder was robbed at pistol point; the sentence was subsequently commuted to seven years transportation. At court she gave her occupation as servant, which may suggest either that she was not a legitimate child, or that she hid her true origins to avoid a scandal. In Australia she married convict carpenter Nathaniel Lucas, Australia's first millwright, possibly related to the Earl of Kent. The couple thrived and had thirteen children in all, though twin 2-year-old girls were tragically killed when Lucas accidentally felled a tree onto their house in 1792, destroying it and almost killing his wife. He increasingly took to drink, perhaps to ease the pain of a throat cancer, but his death in 1818 was another mystery. It appeared to be suicide but his wife believed it to be murder by a business rival. She never returned to England and was buried in Australia. Several of her sons became substantial landowners there.

GAUDEN, JOHN (1600-1662)

Bishop of Worcester, 1662. Son of an Essex vicar, he initially sided with Parliament in the Civil War, but protested against Charles I's execution in 1649. At the Restoration he became Bishop of Exeter, 1660-2, but demanded a richer see, claiming to be the author of *Eikon Basilike* (Greek for 'royal portrait'), a very popular book supposedly written by the late king, which appeared within days of his execution. The bishop's claim has never been proved, though it is widely regarded as true. He wanted Winchester but got Worcester, and died later that year, probably without ever coming here, except for his burial in the cathedral.

GHINUCCI, JEROME DE

Bishop of Worcester, 1522-34, the last foreigner to hold the see. An Italian cardinal and Archbishop of Florence, who served Henry VIII and Cardinal Wolsey as a diplomat. He was deprived of Worcester for non-residence by Act of Parliament, 1534.

GIBBONS, BENJAMIN (1824-1912)

Church and school builder. Staffordshire-born, obviously of a wealthy family, he was educated at Eton and was Curate of Kidderminster (1850-61) and Vicar of Lower Mitton, Stourport (1861-94). He erected schools at Kidderminster and Stourport, chiefly at his own expense. He wrote a short *History of Kidderminster* (1859) and edited the *Stourport Church Chronicle*. In 1881 he laid the foundations of a new St Michael's Church at Stourport, a replacement for a 1792 building. Much of it was again constructed at his expense, but the substantial building was never finished to the original plan, and what was built was not consecrated until 1910, when Revd Gibbons was present, though very elderly. In his later years he lived at Waresley House or Court, Hartlebury, demolished in the late 1920s. The site

Benjamin Gibbons.

was redeveloped, though the Court is remembered in a road name. His church was badly damaged in a storm in 1976, and the present building opened in 1980.

GIFFARD, GODFREY (1235-1302)

Bishop of Worcester, 1268-1302. Son of a Wiltshire Royal Justice, and brother of Walter, Archbishop of York, he held a string of positions in the Church before becoming Chancellor of England (1266-70). Enemies said his progress was due to his brother, claiming he was only in minor orders and 'deficient in learning'. There may have been some truth to this, but he was strong-willed and a determined supporter of royal and episcopal authority. He was said to travel with a hundred knights to enforce his authority. He was elected to Worcester by the monks, but was often in dispute with them, mostly over rights to appoint priests. He fortified Hartlebury Castle, built mansions at Wick and Worcester, and made improvements in the cathedral. His armorial bearings became the arms of the see. He gave nuns at White Ladies, The Tything, land at Aston and tithes in Claines. Buried in Worcester Cathedral. His Register, the earliest remaining, was edited with a comprehensive introduction in 1902. A controversial 1960s hotel opposite the cathedral was named after him.

GIGLIS, SYLVESTER DE (1463-1521)

Italian bishop accused of involvement in murder. He was Bishop of Worcester from 1499 to 1521, though it's doubtful if he came to Worcester much. He was Ambassador at Rome for Henry VII and VIII, and agent of Cardinal Wolsey. He was accused of complicity when Cardinal Bainbridge, no friend to Wolsey, was poisoned by his chaplain in 1514, and though nothing came of the accusations, his hopes of further progression in the Church ended.

GILES, NATHANIEL (1558-1634)

Organist and composer, born at Worcester. He may have been organist of Worcester Cathedral, and was at St George's, Windsor, from 1595, as organist and choirmaster. He worked with Shakespeare's dramatist friend, Ben Jonson, at Blackfriars Theatre, London, and also composed hymns, services, and anthems.

GORDON, ADAM LINDSAY (1833-1870)

Worcester schoolboy widely regarded as Australia's leading nineteenth-century poet. Born in the Azores, he lived at Worcester with an uncle (1852-3), and was a pupil at Worcester Royal Grammar School. He already had a reputation for wild living; *Worthies of Worcestershire* noted disapprovingly: 'His company was mostly that of sporting men and ostlers, and the chief exploit of his Worcester life was the stealing of a horse from the stable of the Plough Inn to ride in the Crowle steeplechases.' More positively, he fell in love with Jane Bridges, a 17-year-old farmer's daughter from Broughton Hackett (near Worcester), though he was too shy to propose until he was, perhaps reluctantly, leaving Worcestershire. He spent the rest of his life in Australia and committed suicide in his 30s.

GOSSE, PHILIP HENRY (1810-1888)

Naturalist Philip Henry Gosse.

Influential Worcester-born Victorian naturalist. Born in High Street, son of an itinerant painter of portrait miniatures and a former lady's maid, he sailed to Newfoundland in 1827 to work as a clerk in a whaler's office, and began his lifelong interest in the natural world by recording the entomology of the island. He also experienced a religious awakening, which would be the other major theme of his life. Returning to England, he briefly ran a school in London, and wrote his first two books, *The Canadian Naturalist*, and *Introduction to Zoology*. The public warmed to his writing style and enthusiasm and in 1844 he went to Jamaica, having been recommended by the British Museum, and subsequently wrote *Birds of Jamaica* (1847) and *A Naturalist's Sojourn in Jamaica* (1851). He later settled in Devon, continuing his naturalist researches and writing, as well as lay preaching. He was married twice and had a son, Edmund, in 1849, but the two did not agree over religion or much else. Edmund's story of their troubled relationship, *Father and Son*, was published in 1907, and has never been out of print. The story was dramatised for television by Dennis Potter as *Where Adam Stood* (1976).

GRAINGER, THOMAS (1783-1839)

Porcelain manufacturer. The nephew of <u>Robert Chamberlain</u>, of the Chamberlain Porcelain Works, he was an apprentice in his factory. In 1801, with partner John Wood, he founded his own works in Lowesmoor, Worcester, which moved to St Martin's Gate after a fire in 1809. They also had a shop in the high street from 1806, and developed a reputation for high quality wares. On Thomas's death his son George took over and developed chemical porcelain and semi-porcelain, for industrial and commercial uses which are now mostly supplied by plastics, as well as embossed tiles and china figures. After George's death in 1888 his son Frank carried on the business until 1889, when it was acquired by Worcester Porcelain, and in 1902 all work was transferred to the Severn Street works. Grainger's former premises at St Martin's Gate were demolished in 2009.

Porcelain manufacturer George Grainger.

GRAZEBROOK, HENRY SYDNEY (1836-1896)

Genealogist from Pedmore, Dudley (then in Worcestershire). Educated at Bromsgrove and the Inner Temple, and called to the Bar in 1869, he held a clerkship at the Treasury from 1887 until his death. He is best known for *The Heraldry of Worcestershire*, a valuable two-volume survey of the landowners and residents of the county, published in 1873. In 1879 he was appointed one of the original trustees of the William Salt Library, Stafford, and as one of the Editorial Committee contributed many valuable papers. He died at Chiswick and was buried at Old Swinford, Stourbridge.

GREEN, VALENTINE (1739-1813)

Leading eighteenth-century engraver and Worcestershire historian. Born at Salford Priors (near Evesham), son of a dancing-master, he was articled to attorney William Phillips, Town Clerk of Evesham, for two years. In 1760 he became the pupil of <u>Robert Hancock</u>, a painter and engraver for Worcester Porcelain Company. In 1765 he went to London, having apparently taught himself mezzotint engraving, which enabled much higher quality reproduction, and soon achieved success with his fine work. His prints were exhibited at the Royal Academy in 1774, and in 1775 he was appointed mezzo-engraver to George III. Granted exclusive right of engraving and printing from pictures in the Dusseldorf Gallery in 1789, its destruction by the French in 1792 caused him very

Engraver Valentine Green.

serious loss. Reduced to poverty, in 1805 he became, and remained for the rest of his life, keeper at the British Institution (a private art gallery in Pall Mall, London), which closed in 1867. During his career he engraved about 400 plates, including many of old masters, which fetch high prices when they come on to the market. Best known in Worcestershire as a local historian, his books included *A Survey of the City of Worcester* (1764), *The History and Antiquities of the City and Suburbs of Worcester* (1796), and *An Account of the Discovery of the Body of King John in the Cathedral Church of Worcester* (1797).

GREY, WALTER DE (d. 1255)
Bishop of Worcester, 1214-16. A favourite of King John, he was previously Chancellor of England (1205-14), and supported the King at Runnymede (1215) when John was forced to sign the Magna Carta. John afterwards made him Archbishop of York (1215-55) despite considerable opposition.

GRIFFITH, GEORGE (*c.* 1811-1883)
Birmingham-born corn merchant at Bewdley from 1837. His ruling passions were verse and prose writing and the reformation of grammar schools. His best known work was *The Free Schools of Worcestershire* (1852). He died at the County Asylum, Powick and was buried at Ribbesford.

GRONNIOSAW, JAMES ALBERT UKAWSAW (*c.* 1705-1775)
African prince and former slave who wrote a pioneering book in Worcestershire. Born the grandson of a tribal king, probably in Nigeria, he was taken and sold into slavery, becoming the servant of a Calvinist minister in New York, who taught him to read. He later enlisted as a cook on a privateer, and subsequently as a soldier in the British Army, eventually making his way to England. In London he married Betty, a young widow, and after hard times looking for work, they pawned all they had to come to Kidderminster in the late 1760s, where Betty worked as a weaver. He chose the town because of its connection with Richard Baxter, a churchman he much admired. With the help of 'the elegant pen' of a young lady from Leominster, probably a church member, he set about writing his autobiography, published in 1772, giving a graphic account of all his adventures. His book was believed to be the first published by an African in Britain, and the first book written by a former slave. He died and was buried in Chester.

GROSVENOR, GEORGE HERBERT (1880-1912)
Brilliant academic. Eldest son of a Kidderminster Justice of the Peace, he gained first class honours at Oxford in Natural Science, 1903. In the following year, aged just 24, he read a paper before the Royal Society, and in 1908 was appointed Lecturer in Economic Entomology at Oxford. He was also a respected researcher in marine biology. His career was cut tragically short when he drowned at Polzeath, Cornwall, while trying to assist a companion in difficulty.

GUEST, EDWIN (1800-1880)
Historian and antiquarian; of an old family settled at Row Heath, Kings Norton (then in Worcestershire). He attended King Edward's School, Birmingham, and Caius College (1824). He was called to the Bar in 1828, but after some years of practice, he turned to historical

and literary research. In 1842 he was a founder member of the Philological Society, which studied language, was Master of Caius (1852-80) and then Vice Chancellor of Cambridge University (1854-5). Much of his work on Romano-British history and the formation of the English language was published posthumously, such as *Origines Celticae* (1883). He died at his Oxfordshire estate.

GULLY, JAMES MANBY (1808-1883)

Largely responsible for making Malvern a stylish spa town, he also became one of Victorian society's most despised villains. Son of a West Indian plantation owner, he practised medicine in London without great success, but his fortunes changed when, with friend Dr James Wilson, he set up in Belle Vue Terrace, Malvern, offering 'water cures'. Short and balding but charismatic, he soon built up a 'celebrity' clientele which included Florence Nightingale, Charles Darwin, George Eliot, John Ruskin, Lords Tennyson and Macaulay, and Mrs Charles Dickens amongst others. By 1845 more space was needed for the many patients, and they built a handsome property, now Park View, on Priory Road. Other doctors moved into the area and a building boom saw other premises and accommodation created. Wilson died in 1867, and Gully moved back to London in 1872, supposedly in retirement. In fact the elderly doctor had begun a torrid affair with a 25-year-old married patient, Mrs Florence Riccardo, and had moved to live near her. With the death of her husband, the couple toured Europe together, but never married, and after a few years Florence married young barrister Charles Bravo. Four months later Bravo was dead of horrendously painful antimony poisoning. Gully had been in attendance, and both he and Florence were suspected of murder, but nothing could be proved, and the crime remains unsolved. At least six books and several television dramas have been written on the case. Agatha Christie believed Gully was guilty, but others have blamed Florence, her companion, and even the victim. Victorians were appalled by Gully's behaviour, and the disgraced doctor was no longer welcome in polite society. He spent his last years dabbling in spiritualism. Fearing desecration of his grave, Gully left instructions to keep his interment secret, and it is not known where he is buried. One of his sons was an MP and Speaker of the House of Commons, and was created Viscount Selby in 1905.

HABINGTON, THOMAS (1560-1647)

Worcestershire historian, born in Surrey. The younger son of John Habington (cofferer to Queen Elizabeth I) of Hindlip Hall (near Worcester). He became a Catholic, and with his older brother Edward, was implicated in plotting for Mary Queen of Scots. His brother was hung, drawn and quartered, but he did not share that fate, perhaps because he was Queen Elizabeth's godson. After six years in the Tower of London, where he busied himself with a classical translation and a history of Edward IV, he was allowed to retire to Hindlip, where he gave himself up to antiquarian research and made his collections for the history of Worcestershire. At Hindlip he constructed

Local historian Thomas Habington.

eleven secret chambers to conceal priests, which were so cunningly disguised that after the Gunpowder Plot it took searchers twelve days to find the Jesuits hidden there. He was arrested, but again released, possibly through the influence of his brother-in-law Lord Monteagle, to whom Habington's wife Mary, Monteagle's sister, may have written the famous warning letter. He was, however, confined to the county for life. He continued his antiquarian research until his death at Hindlip, aged 87 years. His valuable manuscript collections for the history of Worcestershire have been published by the Worcestershire Historical Society.

HABINGTON, WILLIAM (1605-1654)
Minor poet. Born at Hindlip Hall, son of Thomas Habington. Educated as a Catholic at St Omer and Paris, he refused to become a Jesuit and returned to England where he married Lucy, daughter of William Herbert, first Baron Powis. In her praise he printed anonymously a collection of poems, *Castara*, in 1634. In 1640 he wrote a play, *Queen of Aragon*. He also published his father's *History of Edward IV*, the same year. He was buried in the family vault at Hindlip Hall, now West Mercia Police Headquarters.

HADLEY, JAMES (1837-1903)
Probably the finest ceramic modelling designer of the nineteenth century, whose work created what was known as the 'Worcester school' in ceramic art. Born in London, he moved to Worcester when very young, and in 1852 was apprenticed to Kerr & Binns, the new management of the factory of Robert Chamberlain, at Severn Street, Worcester. He would have been enrolled by the company at the newly-opened Worcester Government School of Design, where he was a contemporary of artist Benjamin Williams Leader. By 1870 he was principal modeller for what was then called Royal Worcester, and in 1875 he went freelance – a common arrangement with artists – with a studio at 95 High Street. Also an enthusiastic amateur musician, he came to know Sir Edward Elgar, who, it was said, regularly frequented his studio. Almost the entire output of ornamental figures and vases from the studio went to Royal Worcester until 1895, when due to dwindling demand for luxury goods the contract was cancelled. With three of his sons, he began his own porcelain business, first in temporary premises at Shrub Hill, then from 1897 in purpose-built premises at Diglis Road, concentrating on what became known as Hadley ware – distinctive, high quality, decorative 'art pottery'. His company was acquired by the Royal Worcester Porcelain Company in 1905. His work is still much sought after by connoisseurs.

HALL, JOHN VINE (1774-1860)
Norfolk-born Worcester bookseller, writer and alcoholic. After a drunken youth, he underwent a religious conversion and settled in Worcester (1804-14) as a bookseller, marrying a local girl and struggling with intemperance, which he finally vanquished through total abstinence. His later years were spent in Maidstone, Kent, devoted to philanthropic and religious work, and writing a religious book, *The Sinner's Friend*, in 1821, which went through numerous editions throughout the nineteenth century. His son was a London clergyman.

HALL, EDMUND (*c.* 1620-1687)

Son of a Worcester clothier, born in St John's, educated at King's School. He attended Oxford, but left without a degree at the start of the Civil War to take up arms for Parliament. He returned in 1647, and graduated MA, but his political views had changed, and for writing in favour of monarchy he was imprisoned in 1651. Later he was chaplain to Sir Edmund Bray, of Great Rissington (near Cheltenham), and after the Restoration received the parish of Chipping Norton. In 1680 he returned to Great Rissington as rector, and 'took to him in elderly years a fair and comely wife'.

HALL, JOHN (1633-1710)

Academic and cleric, born into a Puritan family at Bromsgrove, the son of the vicar, who was <u>Edmund Hall's</u> brother. He attended Oxford under his uncle Edmund, and graduated MA in 1653, becoming a Fellow of Pembroke and Master of the College in 1664. He also received the parish of St Aldate's, Oxford, which he held to his death, and where he drew large congregations with his preaching. Chaplain to Charles II, and Bishop of Bristol (1691), he continued to hold the mastership of Pembroke and live chiefly in Oxford, where he died in the master's lodgings, which he had built. Buried at Bromsgrove, he left £800 for the poor of the town.

HALL, RADCLYFFE (1880-1943)

Banned lesbian author. Born also Marguerite Antonia, names she later dropped, in Hampshire, her parents separated when she was young and she had an unhappy childhood. In 1907 she formed an attachment with Mabel Batten, a 51-year-old grandmother and popular amateur singer, nicknamed Ladye. After the death of Batten's husband they moved in together, and lived for a time in Malvern, first at Highfield in Wells Road, where Hall kept five horses because of her love of hunting, and afterwards at The White Cottage, Malvern Wells. They scandalised local people by walking arm-in-arm in Great Malvern, Hall dressed as a man. Batten died in 1917. Hall had other affairs and lived in London and on the coast. Her first novel appeared in 1924, but she is best known for her 1928 book, *The Well of Loneliness*, the only one of her novels to deal with lesbianism. Though not sexually explicit, it was judged obscene and banned. She died and was buried in London.

Controversial writer Radclyffe Hall.

HALLEN, ARTHUR WASHINGTON CORNELIUS (1834-1899)

Clergyman, author and antiquary. He was the nephew and ward of Revd William Hallen (Vicar of Wribbenhall, near Bewdley, 1836-50), descended from the family of Van Halen of Malines, Belgium, who settled at Stourbridge in the time of Charles I. He was Curate of Redmarley D'Abitot in 1858. Although by 1862 he had received the parish of St John's, Alloa, his book of Christmas sketches, *The Queen of the Holly Bush*, published in that year, was warmly dedicated to the rector and inhabitants of his former parish. His wife, Catherine, was a keen student of genealogy, and he edited the registers of a number of London parishes, as well as researching the history of his family name and editing the *Scottish Antiquary*.

HAMMOND, HENRY (1605-1660)

Surrey-born Royalist cleric. Chaplain to Charles I at Oxford, he was imprisoned in 1649. After release he spent the rest of his life at Westwood, Droitwich, as a guest of Royalist Sir John Pakington. He wrote several theological books. At the Restoration he was to be appointed Bishop of Worcester, but died as he prepared to go to London. He was buried at Hampton Lovett, Droitwich.

HANBURY, JOHN (1664-1734)

Ironmaster; son of Capel Hanbury, of a family at Hanbury, Droitwich. He gave up law studies to manage the family's Pontypool iron works. He improved the machinery and introduced, possibly by 1697, a method of rolling iron plates through revolving cylinders, superseding the hammering process, and producing more even iron sheets. This facilitated higher quality tin-plating, though the claim that he introduced tin-plating into this country in 1720 has not been proved. His descendants lived at Pontypool Park House, now partly a local museum, and continued to develop the business. A descendant was created Baron Sudeley in 1838. In 2006 a pub in Pontypool was named the John Capel Hanbury.

HANCOCK, ROBERT (1731-1817)

Worcester porcelain engraver and painter. Born in Badsey, Evesham, he was apprenticed to Birmingham engraver George Anderton in 1745, and in the early 1750s worked in London. In 1756 he came to Worcester as chief engraver to the Porcelain Company. He executed the design for the famous King of Prussia mug, and the delicate Worcester transfer ware, which contributed largely to the success of the company at that time. His pupils included Valentine Green. In 1772 he became a partner, but fell out with his co-proprietors and left the firm around 1775, working as a portraitist in the Midlands and West. One story was that he lost all his savings in a bank failure. He finally settled near Bristol, where he died. He drew a number of portraits, including poets Coleridge, Southey and Wordsworth, 1798, copies of which are in the National Portrait Gallery.

HARPER, THOMAS (1786-1853)

Leading trumpet player. Born in Worcester, he went to London aged just 10 to study trumpet, and joined the East India Volunteer Band; appointed inspector of musical instruments to the company. In 1806 he was engaged as principal trumpet at the Drury Lane and Lyceum opera houses. He distinguished himself at the Birmingham Festival, 1820, and in the following year became principal trumpet in many of London's leading orchestras. The instrument he played was the slide trumpet, considered inferior to the more modern instrument, though not in his hands. He taught trumpet at the Royal Academy of Music (1829-45) and was first trumpet at the Philharmonic Concerts until 1851. He was taken ill at a London rehearsal in 1853, and died within a few hours.

HASTINGS, SIR THOMAS (1790-1870)

Innovative naval officer and skilled artist. Elder brother of <u>Sir Charles Hastings</u>, fourth son of Revd James Hastings, he entered the navy in 1803 and was First Lieutenant on the *Undaunted* which took Napoleon to Elba, 1814. When at leisure he painted sea scenes, and when in action he was regarded as an excellent naval gunner. In 1832 he was made superintendent of the Royal Naval College and captain of the school of gunnery, Portsmouth, where he introduced new training methods and scientific concepts which greatly improved naval gunnery. Knighted in 1839, he was appointed store-keeper of Ordnance in 1843, Rear Admiral in 1855, and Admiral of the Fleet in 1866. He died in London. His son, Francis, also became an Admiral.

HASTINGS, SIR CHARLES (1794-1866)

Distinguished Worcester doctor and founder of the British Medical Association. Sixth son of Revd James Hastings (Rector of Bitterley, near Ludlow, who became Rector of Martley, near Worcester in 1795). Charles grew up at the Old Hall, attending the Worcester Royal Grammar School. As a boy he was always interested in the natural world, but his choice of a medical career may have been influenced by a serious accident his father had in 1806, which left him permanently incapacitated. He studied under two surgeons at Stourport, and after a few months in London was elected, aged just 18, as house surgeon to Worcester Infirmary. He made experiments on the nervous system there, and in 1815 continued his studies at Edinburgh. Amazingly he was the only student there at that time to use a microscope in medical research. Qualifying in 1818, he declined a lectureship

BMA founder Sir Charles Hastings.

and returned to Worcester Infirmary, where he spent the rest of his working life. He soon became a recognised authority on infectious diseases, caring for the sick selflessly during cholera outbreaks in 1832, 1849 and 1853. In 1828 he founded the *Midland Medical and Surgical Reporter*, to which he sent many reports. Four years later, in the board room at the Infirmary in Castle Street, he formed the Provincial Medical and Surgical Association, which became the British Medical Association in 1856, of which he was permanent President of the Council and Treasurer. He was knighted in 1850. He argued strongly for improvements in public health, studying the health and working conditions of local glovers, porcelain and salt workers. In 1854 he put a good deal of his own money into a scheme of better housing for working people at Copenhagen Street, since demolished, which was said to have dramatically improved death rates amongst residents. He also pioneered health statistics for the county. His boyhood interest in the natural world led to his book, *Illustrations of the Natural History of Worcestershire* (1834), and the foundation of the Worcestershire Natural History Society and its museum, which later became part of the city museum. He spent his last years in the Malverns and was buried at Astwood Cemetery, Worcester. The BMA honoured his memory by the foundation of an annual Hastings Medal and Prize. A marble bust of Sir Charles, presented to the city in 1892, is still on display at the city art gallery, and a plaque on a house opposite in Foregate Street marks the location of one of his homes.

HASTINGS, FRANCIS DECIMUS (1795-1869)

Heroic naval officer, brother of Sir Charles Hastings and Sir Thomas Hastings. Seventh son of Revd James Hastings, he entered the navy in 1807, and by 1840 had risen to Captain. It was in that year that he became the hero of the storming of Acre. The port city on the Mediterranean was held by the Pasha of Egypt, who sought to conquer Syria. The attack on the port, held by the expansionist Pasha, was a complete success, and on the following day Hastings, who had been wounded in the action, was honoured for his part in the victory. Victorian commentators likened his exploits to those of medieval crusader, King Richard 'the Lionheart'. He retired as Rear Admiral in 1859, and lived at Thorneloe House (Barbourne, Worcester), then at Barbourne House, since demolished, where the access track, now Lavender Road, was christened 'Admiral's Walk' by locals who regularly saw the old sailor pacing up and down it for exercise.

HASTINGS, WARREN (1732-1818)

Empire builder who retired to his ancestral home in Worcestershire. Born in Oxfordshire, son of a clergyman, he joined the East India Company in 1750. He rose to be the first Governor General of Bengal by 1772, and first Governor General of India in 1773. Over the next decade he greatly extended British rule in India. He had not risen this far without making enemies however; he hanged one opponent and wounded another in a duel. When he retired to England in 1784 he was charged with corruption and cruelty. His trial began in 1788, and dragged on at intervals for seven years, ending in acquittal. He claimed to have spent most of his fortune

Empire builder Warren Hastings.

on his defence, but managed to purchase the ancestral family estate at Daylesford, near Stow-on-the-Wold (then a detached part of Worcestershire, transferred to Gloucestershire in 1931), where he rebuilt Daylesford House and lived out his remaining years embellishing his grounds, riding fine Arab horses, fattening prize cattle, and trying to rear Indian animals and Indian vegetables. Aged 82 he was made a Privy Councillor, treated with honour by the Prince Regent, and applauded by the people. He was buried in Daylesford churchyard.

HAVERGAL, WILLIAM HENRY (1793-1870)

Clergyman father of writers <u>Francis Tebbs Havergal</u> and <u>Frances Ridley Havergal</u>. Born in Buckinghamshire, he was curate at Bristol (1816), Gloucestershire (1820), and Astley (near Stourport) in 1822, becoming rector in 1825. In 1829 he was thrown from his carriage, and incapacitated for some years, which gave him the leisure to indulge his love of music. He composed services, hymn tunes, chants, and anthems, as well as sacred songs and carols, which were well received. His children clearly inherited his musical and literary talents. Later the family moved to Henwick House, Hallow (near Worcester), and in 1845 he became Rector of St Nicholas, Worcester. Vicar of Shareshill, Wolverhampton, 1860. Died at Leamington; buried at Astley.

HAVERGAL, FRANCES RIDLEY (1836-1879)

Religious poet and hymn writer. She was born at Astley Rectory, the youngest child of <u>William Henry Havergal</u>. The family moved about six years later to Henwick House, Hallow (near Worcester). She was said to have learnt to read aged 3 and at 7 was writing verses. She was partly educated in Germany, where she studied music – a love she inherited from her father. She never married and did not enjoy good health, sometimes travelling, especially to Switzerland, for that reason. She wrote hymns and produced almost twenty books of her poems or devotional content. She died at the Mumbles (near Swansea) and was buried in Astley churchyard. Much of her work was only published posthumously by her sisters, and was very popular in Britain, and especially in North America, where a Toronto girls' school is named after her.

Poet Frances Ridley Havergal.

HAVERGAL, FRANCIS TEBBS (1829-1890)

Church historian. The elder brother of <u>Frances Ridley Havergal</u>, he was born at Astley Rectory. He held various positions, including Vicar-Choral in Hereford Cathedral (1853-74), Vicar of Pipe with Lyde, Herefordshire (1861-74), Upton Bishop, Herefordshire

(1874-90), and Prebendary of Hereford (1877-90). He died at Upton. He wrote a visitors' guide to Hereford Cathedral, 1869; *Monumental Inscriptions in Hereford Cathedral*, 1881; *Records of Upton Bishop*, 1883, amongst other works.

HAYES, WILLIAM (1708-1777)

Composer and organist. Born at Hanbury (near Droitwich), he studied as a chorister and organ pupil at Gloucester. He was organist at St Mary's, Shrewsbury, and in 1731 at Worcester Cathedral, before moving to Magdalen College, Oxford. He became a member of the Royal Society of Musicians, and Professor of Music to the University of Oxford (1742). He composed a great deal, and was especially successful in vocal part-writing.

HEATH, NICHOLAS (1501-1578)

Bishop of Worcester, 1543-51 and 1553-5. Previously Bishop of Rochester (1539); it was claimed that much Church property was plundered in his time by the greedy counsellors of Edward VI. He opposed a new ordination rite in 1551, and was deprived of his see, but restored in 1553, by Mary I. Mary also made him President of Wales and, due to his zealous promotion of Catholicism, promoted him to Archbishop of York in 1555, and Lord Chancellor (1556-8). In 1559 he was deprived of his position by Elizabeth I and imprisoned, but after three years was allowed to retire to Surrey, where he died.

HEMINGES, JOHN (*c.* 1566-1630)

Without him many of Shakespeare's greatest plays would have been lost. Born in Droitwich, he was sent to London as an apprentice, aged 12, and became a freeman of the Grocers' Company (1587), beginning an acting career by 1593. In 1594 he joined Shakespeare's company, becoming a fellow actor and friend of the great dramatist. He acted with him in several of Ben Jonson's plays, and is said to have been the first actor to play Shakespeare's great comic character, Falstaff. Business skills he learnt in the grocery trade were put to good use in his handling of the company's financial affairs. In 1623, seven years after Shakespeare's death, Heminges and Henry Condell, a fellow member of the King's Men, published the famous First Folio edition of Shakespeare's plays. Without this we would have no copies of seventeen of Shakespeare's plays, including some of his most famous, and only very incomplete copies of most of the others. Since the plays belonged to the theatre company, the involvement of Heminges, as business manager, was essential to their publication, and the intention seems to have been to preserve his friend's work for posterity. He continued his involvement with the theatre right up until his death.

HEMMING

Eleventh-century monk and sub-prior of Worcester, whose Cartulary, *or collection of monastic charters – essential records of land tenures and rights held – is regarded as among the earliest surviving from medieval England.* Little is known of him personally. He had a Danish name, but that was not uncommon in Anglo-Saxon England. He included a preface in which he said that Bishop <u>Wulfstan II</u> had asked him to compile the cartulary of the church of Worcester, though it may not have been completed until after the bishop's death. Twentieth-century scholars determined that the *Cartulary* was in two parts, the earliest of which dated from the early eleventh century and was not written by Hemming. His contribution, dating from the late eleventh or early twelfth century, also included details of lands of which the church at Worcester had been deprived by monarchs or others, as well as information on the lives of Wulfstan and Ealdred, Archbishop of York. Hemming's *Cartulary* is in the British Library. An edition was published in 1723, and a new edition is in preparation.

HEMMING, RICHARD (d. 1806)

A rogue who achieved the unfortunate distinction of being both perpetrator and victim of the dramatic events known as 'The Oddingley Murders'. A Droitwich carpenter and wheelwright with a reputation for violence, he was seen lurking suspiciously in the lanes of Oddingley (near Droitwich), on the afternoon of 24 June 1806. Suddenly a shot rang out. Hemming had killed George Parker, the unpopular rector. A villager saw him fleeing in panic and recognised the killer, but he disappeared without trace. Some twenty-four years later, in 1830, workmen digging the floor in a barn at nearby Netherwood Farm for the new farmer, found his body. The previous farmer, Thomas Clewes, was arrested, and at an inquest at The Talbot in Barbourne, Worcester, he confessed that, along with several other local farmers and a farrier named James Taylor, he had paid Hemming to kill the rector, then, when Hemming sought refuge with them, they clubbed him to death and buried his body. Clewes took to drink and lost his farm. The inquest accepted that Taylor, by then dead, was chiefly to blame, and the other conspirators were cleared, to be given a hero's welcome back to the village. Clewes became the landlord of the Fir Tree Inn at Oddingley, where The Murderers Bar remembers these events.

HERBERT, SIR HENRY (1594-1673)

Welsh-born Master of the Revels from 1623. He bought Ribbesford Manor (near Bewdley), from Sir Henry Mildmay in 1627, and presented to the church there a chalice and flagons still in use in recent times. He was MP for Bewdley in 1640, but he lost his seat in 1642, for supporting the King, and was heavily fined, 1646. Restored as Master of the Revels at the Restoration, he was again MP for Bewdley from 1661 until his death in London. He introduced Richard Baxter at court, and was a friend of diarist John Evelyn.

HICKMAN, HENRY HILL (1800-1830)

Anaesthetic pioneer. The Shropshire-born son of a tenant farmer, he qualified as a doctor aged 20 and in the following year married Eliza Hannah Gardner of Leigh Court (near Worcester). He set up a practice in Ludlow, but spent years fruitlessly seeking support in both England and France for painless surgery through anaesthesia. Sir Humphrey Davy withdrew his initial support because Hickman had proved his system with experiments on animals. In 1829 he set up a medical practice in Teme Street, Tenbury Wells, but died there nine months later of tuberculosis and was buried in Shropshire. It was almost two decades later before anaesthesia was first used in Britain. His house still exists and was recently a restaurant.

HILL, JAMES (d. 1817)

Actor and singer, born at Kidderminster; educated by an uncle and apprenticed to a painter. In 1796 he appeared successfully at the Bath Theatre in a comic opera. Further study led to his engagement in comic operas at Covent Garden, London. He went to perform in Jamaica in 1816, and died there.

HILL, MARY, BARONESS SANDYS (1764-1836)

Formidable lady who owned considerable estates in Worcestershire and other parts of England and Ireland. Born Mary Sandys, after the early deaths of her parents she was brought up by her uncle, Edwin, Baron Sandys. Aged 21 she married Arthur Hill, future Marquess of Downshire, a minor figure in London politics. Her father-in-law described her as 'a genteel, agreeable little girl … of a cheerful, sweet disposition'. She was also very wealthy. The couple had five sons and two daughters, but Hill was dead by 1801. His wife angrily attributed this to the strain of a political struggle with Viscount Castlereagh, another County Down landowner. In 1802 she cleverly made a political deal to allow Castlereagh an unopposed election in return for her inheritance of her uncle's estate and the title Baroness Sandys of Ombersley, with a seat at the 1740s Ombersley Court (near Droitwich). But when Castlereagh was forced to seek re-election in 1805, on being appointed Secretary of State for War, she openly opposed him and ensured her candidate won. She was horrified, in 1812, when her son, who had taken charge of the Irish estates, made a permanent deal with Castlereagh's family to help pay his father's debts. She retired to England and occupied herself renovating Ombersley parish church. She died in Surrey after a long illness. The title Baron Sandys had twice become extinct, in 1683 and 1797, but she had ensured that it would pass to her sons, and it is still in existence.

HILL, THOMAS WRIGHT (1763-1851)

Father of Sir Rowland Hill. Born at Kidderminster, he was apprenticed to a brassfounder in Birmingham, and had a business in Kidderminster which failed due to war with France, leading him to open a school. He was a remarkable man with many interests, friendly with reformers such as Joseph Priestley. Many of the advanced educational ideas which made Rowland famous probably first came from his father. He encouraged the boys to govern themselves, making their school, Hill Top, 'a small republic', and had a school magazine printed and illustrated by the boys themselves. He also invented a system of shorthand, and is credited with inventing, at Hill Top, the proportional representation system of Single Transferable Vote, which Rowland used for the first time in a public election in Adelaide. He died in Tottenham. He had six sons and two daughters. His eldest son, Matthew, became a criminal law reformer; his second son, Edwin, was an inventor and writer on currency; and another, Frederick, was an inspector of prisons.

HILL, SIR ROWLAND (1795-1879)

Inventor of the modern postal system and an important educational innovator and social reformer. Born in Blackwell Street, Kidderminster, in a house belonging to at least three generations of his family. His father, Thomas Wright Hill, was a remarkable man, and his mother, Sarah,

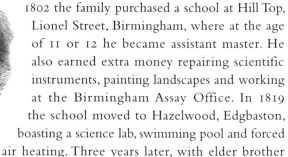

Postal reformer Sir Rowland Hill.

belonged to the Lea family, which was said to have taken a leading role in the intellectual, municipal, and business life of the town for generations past. The French war ruined his father's business when he was 5, and in 1802 the family purchased a school at Hill Top, Lionel Street, Birmingham, where at the age of 11 or 12 he became assistant master. He also earned extra money repairing scientific instruments, painting landscapes and working at the Birmingham Assay Office. In 1819 the school moved to Hazelwood, Edgbaston, boasting a science lab, swimming pool and forced air heating. Three years later, with elder brother Matthew, he wrote a book on education which attracted much attention, drawing many admiring national figures to the school. As a result it transferred to London in 1826 as Bruce Castle School, Tottenham. In 1835 he became Secretary of the South Australian Colonization Commission, which established the city of Adelaide, where he organised the world's first Single Transferable Vote public election. He was already thinking about the problems caused to commerce and individuals by the inefficient, expensive postal regime, and in 1837 he published his famous pamphlet, 'Post Office Reform'. In 1839 the government employed him to carry out his plans, and in 1840 the new postal system began. In 1842, after a change of government, he was dismissed and became director and subsequently chairman of the London & Brighton Railway, where he almost doubled the share price. In 1846 he returned to the Post Office and was knighted in 1860. He died in London and was buried in Westminster Abbey. Bruce Castle School continued until 1891, when Tottenham Council purchased the house and grounds for use as a park. Statues of him were placed in London and Birmingham (not there now), but the earliest, by Sir Thomas Brock, was unveiled in 1881 in Kidderminster, appropriately financed by 200,000 people who contributed stamps. We still use the postal system he invented.

HILL, THOMAS FORD (d. 1795)

Antiquary son of a Quaker Worcester glove-maker. He left his father's business for literature and archaeology, and from 1780 onwards made antiquarian tours in Scotland, Switzerland, Savoy, Italy, and Germany. He collected ancient Erse (Irish Gaelic) songs (1784) and was a Fellow of the Royal Society (1792). He died at Ariano on his second visit to Italy.

HILL, THOMAS ROWLEY (1816-1896)

Worcester MP and philanthropist, born at Stourport of a Worcester family. He was Sheriff of Worcester (1858), Mayor (1859), High Sheriff of Worcestershire (1870), and MP for Worcester (1874-85). He married Esther, only child of Richard Evans, Justice of the Peace, of Worcester in 1838, and later Mary Hilditch, the daughter of leading Worcester businessman Edward Evans. He was well known for his philanthropy, and founded and endowed almshouses in Worcester. His son, Edward Henry (1849-1911), followed in the family tradition, leaving substantial bequests to a string of good causes, including the Royal Albert Orphan Asylum, St John's, Worcester, now the YMCA.

HOLBECH or HOLBEACH, HENRY (c. 1477-1551)
Last Prior and first Dean of Worcester. Born Henry Rands, he took the name of his Lincolnshire birthplace on entering Crowland Abbey. He became prior in 1536, and Bishop of Bristol two years later. After the Dissolution he became the first Dean of Worcester (1541-4) and much of the priory property passed to the Dean and Chapter. He became Bishop of Rochester (1544), London (1547), and Lincoln (1548). He was believed to have been the first of the post-Reformation bishops to marry, and left a son.

HOLL, HARVEY BUCHANAN (1821-1886)
Worcestershire doctor and active amateur geologist. Son of William Holl, proprietor of the weekly *Worcester Herald*, and grandson of its founder, he qualified in 1840, and was an army doctor during the Crimean War. Afterwards he lived at St George's Square, Worcester, and later at Malvern, and devoted himself to studying geology. An enthusiastic member of the Worcestershire Naturalists' Field Club, of which he became secretary, and Herefordshire's Woolhope Club, he often gave addresses at their meetings, frequently using geological samples collected around Worcester and Malvern, and regularly contributed to scientific periodicals. After his father's death he became joint proprietor of the *Herald* until 1882. He died, unmarried, at Cheltenham. The *Worcester Herald*, once the county's biggest selling newspaper, ceased publication in the 1930s.

HOLLAND, SETH (d. 1561)
Fourth Dean of Worcester, 1557-9. Previously Fellow of All Souls, Oxford, and warden in 1555. He was chaplain to Cardinal Pole, whose dying message to Queen Mary I was: 'Give credit to whatever he shall say on my behalf.' He was also Rector of Fladbury (near Pershore), and Hanbury (near Droitwich), and Canon of Worcester, then dean. He lost all his positions under Elizabeth I, died in the Marshalsea Prison, London, and was buried in St George's, Southwark, 'some three-score gentlemen of the Inns of Court attending'.

HOLLICK, ROBERT (1798-1820)
Highway robber. He stopped two men, Thomas Gittins and Thomas Hawker, at Claines (near Worcester), and robbed them, 'besides ill-treating the latter in a most cruel manner', reported the *Worcester Herald*. Convicted at Worcester Assizes, he was publicly hanged before the County Gaol, since demolished, at Castle Street, Worcester. As he was being led out from his cell, his elderly mother, with his wife, child and sister, arrived at the gaol, and the execution had to be delayed for their last meeting. Press reports said he was penitent and met his death with resignation. Public hangings ended in 1868.

HOUGH, JOHN (1651-1743)

Bishop of Worcester; courageous academic and churchman. Born in Middlesex, he graduated MA at Magdalen College, Oxford (1676) and became a Fellow, but his election as president of the college in 1687 began a bitter struggle with the King. James II claimed to stand for toleration, but wanted Catholic sympathisers in key positions, and substituted his own man, James Parker, Bishop of Oxford, as president. Hough stood firm, and it took a troop of cavalry to remove him. All twenty-six of the Fellows who supported him were deprived of their positions. Appointed Canon of Worcester in 1685, he was restored as president in 1688, when James was ousted. He later became Bishop of Oxford (1690-9), Bishop of Lichfield and Coventry (1699-1717), and Bishop of Worcester (1717-43). He rebuilt the front of the Bishop's Palace at Worcester, and contributed £1,000 in 1741 towards building All Saints' Church. He has a fine monument by Roubiliac in Worcester Cathedral.

HOUSEMAN, ALFRED EDWARD (1859-1936)

Poet A.E. Houseman.

World-famous poet, usually associated with Shropshire rather than his home county. He was born at Valley House, Fockbury (near Bromsgrove), eldest of seven children of a solicitor. The family moved into the town for a time, then Fockbury House, later known as The Clock House, in 1873. He was educated mainly at Bromsgrove School and, clearly a brilliant boy, won a scholarship to Oxford, but concentrated only on the work which interested him, and to his great shame, failed his degree. He took a job as a clerk at the Patent Office, London, continuing to study and publish scholarly articles on a range of classical authors, especially poets. He gained such a reputation that in 1892 he was made Professor of Latin at University College, London, removing in 1911 to a similar post at Cambridge, where he remained for the rest of his life. Whilst in London he wrote sixty-three poems published as *A Shropshire Lad*, 1896. He visited Shropshire and included local references in the poems, but it is possible that many of the memories evoked may have been from his Worcestershire childhood. The book has never been out of print since, and Houseman's reputation as a poet was made. His words have often been used in literature or media; the last Inspector Morse television episode, *The Remorseful Day*, took its title from Houseman, as did the 2002 James Bond movie, *Die Another Day*. Other poetry was published in his lifetime and after his death, though none which had the impact of that first collection. He died in Cambridge but his ashes were buried at St Laurence's Church, Ludlow, where there is a memorial to him. A statue of him stands in Bromsgrove.

HOUSEMAN, LAURENCE (1865-1959)

Author and playwright; brother of <u>Alfred Edward Houseman</u>. Born at Bromsgrove, after Bromsgrove School he studied art in London, and first worked as an illustrator, producing intricate *art nouveau* covers for books, including his sister Clemence's 1896 novel, *The Werewolf*. As he began to lose his eyesight he turned to writing, producing about 100 published works, including plays, poetry and novels. His first, and perhaps best known, novel was *An Englishwoman's Love-letters*, published 1900, and his best known play was probably *Victoria Regina*, which premiered in London in 1937 and was also staged in New York. He spent the last thirty-five years of his life with his sister in Street, Somerset. He was a socialist and pacifist, and a radical bookshop in London is named after him.

Author Laurence Houseman.

HUFFNELL, SUSANNAH (*c.* 1765-?)

Servant transported to Australia for seven years on the first convict fleet in 1787. She was convicted at Worcester Quarter Sessions on Monday, 2 October 1786, for stealing shoes, probably from her employer. A <u>Mary Cooper</u> was also involved in the crime and sentence. The association between the two women is something of a mystery; Huffnell was only about 21 at the time while Cooper was almost 40, and it is not impossible that they could have been mother and daughter. Cooper never returned from Australia, but there is no Australian record of the date of Susannah Huffnell's death, suggesting she may have eventually got back to England.

HULLAH, JOHN PYKE (1812-1884)

Composer and important teacher of music, born at Worcester, son of a Yorkshireman. After attending the Royal Academy of Music, he produced an opera to words by Dickens in 1836, followed by two more operas (1837-8), both produced at Covent Garden, London. In 1839 he studied music in France and from 1840 began teaching in England. So highly regarded was he that a public subscription raised the money to build St Martin's Hall, Long Acre, London, inaugurated in 1850, which was presented for his use. It was a considerable blow to him when it burnt down ten years later. He took to lecturing and conducting classical concerts, and from the mid-1870s held many remunerative musical appointments. He was attacked by paralysis in the early 1880s. His compositions, mostly ballads, were popular for some years after his death, but his opposition to the tonic sol-fa system, since universally adopted, limited his influence on modern music, though his popularisation of musical education is still regarded as important.

HURD, RICHARD (1720-1808)

Bishop of Worcester, 1781-1808. Son of a Staffordshire farmer, he was Preacher of Lincoln's Inn, London (1765), Archdeacon of Gloucester (1767), and Bishop of Lichfield and Coventry (1774-81). He was also tutor to George III's two sons and the royal family visited him at the Bishop's Palace, Hartlebury, in 1788. He repaired Hartlebury Castle and built the library there, which is named after him. Dr Johnson said of him: 'Hurd, sir, is a man whose acquaintance is a valuable acquisition.' He was buried in Hartlebury churchyard.

HUSKISSON, WILLIAM (1770-1830)

Politician who has the misfortune to be remembered chiefly as one of the world's first railway casualties. Born at Birtsmorton Court (near Malvern), he was MP for several constituencies, none local. He was also President of the Board of Trade (1823-7), Secretary of State for War and the Colonies, and Leader of the House of Commons (1827-8). He was accidentally killed in Lancashire by George Stephenson's *Rocket*, at the opening of the Liverpool & Manchester Railway and was buried in Liverpool, the constituency he then represented. He is often regarded as the world's first railway casualty, but there were two previous deaths on the lines, in 1821 and 1827, though his was the first widely reported.

Railway casualty William Huskisson.

HUXTER BROTHERS – CECIL, TED, PERCY & SYDNEY

Comedy acrobatic stars of circus and music hall. Their father, Edward, was a clown who liked Worcester so much during a circus engagement that he settled here, and the brothers, mostly born in the 1880s, also made it their home, though they followed their dad into show business, forming a comedy acrobatic act, topping music hall bills and performing in more than twenty countries worldwide. A highlight of their career was appearing in the 1927 Royal Command Performance, at the Victoria Palace Theatre, London. Percy appeared at the first Bertram Mills circus at Olympia, London, in

Three of the Huxter Brothers (left-right) Ted, Cecil and Percy.

the 1920s, and spent forty years with it, becoming famous as one of the world's greatest 'white face' clowns. He last appeared as guest celebrity at the Odeon Cinema, Worcester in 1956, before the screening of a Danny Kaye film. Sydney moved to Devon and was killed in his 60s, while cycling; Percy lived in Henwick Road, Worcester, and died in 1960, aged 70; Cecil, of Victoria Avenue, died in 1969, and Ted, of Comer Road, in 1973, both aged 85.

INETT, ANN (1754-1825?)

Dressmaker from Grimley (near Worcester), perhaps with her own business, transported to Australia in the first convict fleet in 1787 – though she made good there. Born at Abberley (near Great Witley), youngest of four children of Samuel and Mary Inett, she presumably moved to Grimley to live with a man, since she had two illegitimate children in her 20s. On 14 July 1785, *Berrow's Worcester Journal* reported that the house of Susannah Brookes at Grimley had been broken into 'and several items of her wearing apparel taken', value twenty shillings (later revised to twelve). The following week Ann Inett was reported apprehended for the crime. At Worcester Assizes on Monday, 13 March 1786, she was sentenced to death for burglary, subsequently commuted to seven years transportation. Described by a contemporary as an attractive woman, small-framed and dark haired, with a neat and clean appearance, in Australia she became mistress to naval lieutenant Philip Gidley King, and bore him two sons. He became governor of New South Wales, 1792, and his sons were then brought up in his household. In that same year Ann married convict Richard John Robinson, from Hull, a man of some education and ability, transported for stealing a horse. They received grants of land and became wealthy, opening a hotel and eating house, which they sold in 1820 to return to England, after which there is no trace of them. Some descendants suggest Ann may have lived in St John's, Worcester, and died in 1825. One of her sons by Lieutenant King married at St John's Church in 1825, and gave his middle name as Inett.

INGRAM, ARTHUR HENRY WINNINGTON (1818-1887)

Clergyman, traveller, antiquary, astronomer, geologist, and poet. Born at Ribbesford (near Bewdley), grandson of Sir Edward Winnington (second baronet, of Stanford Court, Stanford-on-Teme). He was Rector of Clifton-upon-Teme, and Harvington (near Evesham) from 1845 to 1887, and was appointed Honorary Canon of Worcester in 1854. A man of many interests, he was an inspector of schools for some years, and chairman of Evesham magistrates. In 1879 he founded and endowed a charity to send poor invalids to sanatoria. He wrote two volumes of poetry, published by his widow in 1888, and left three almost complete ichthyosaur skeletons to Worcester Museum, one of which was found at Bickmarsh on the Warwickshire border, and is described on the museum's website as 'one of the most popular and finest specimens in Worcester Museum's large geological collection'.

JEFFREYS, JOYCE (d. 1649?)

She left a valuable personal account of the Civil War period. Daughter of Henry Jeffries (of Ham Castle, Clifton-upon-Teme) and Anne (widow of John Coningsby, of Neen Sollers, on the Shropshire border), she never married, but inherited property and carried on various businesses, including farming and money lending. For ten years from 1638 she lived in Widemarsh Street, Hereford, and her household account books, which contain much valuable information on prices, became also a journal of the times, and the hardships she suffered. A Royalist sympathiser, she left Hereford before the Parliamentary Army arrived, but her house was burnt. She fled to Ham Castle, but that too was besieged by Parliamentarians and her account books include entries for having valuables buried and dug up, according to the movements of the enemy. On one occasion this activity led to the discovery of gold and silver buried in some bygone age. Ham Castle was left ruined by the war and was replaced by a mansion, which burnt down in 1887, after which another house was built on the site. Joyce's journal has recently been published as *The Business and Household Accounts of Joyce Jeffreys, Spinster of Hereford, 1638-1648* (OUP).

JEFFRIES, EDWARD (d. 1725)

Distinguished barrister and judge, the third son of MP Sir Francis Winnington (of Stanford Court, Clifton-upon-Teme), he was at Middle Temple in 1687. He married Jane Bloome, of Yorkshire, niece of Henry Jeffries (of Ham Castle, Clifton-upon-Teme), who left his estates to her provided the marriage went ahead, and Edward took the name of Jeffries. He became a QC (1710), Honorary Freeman of Worcester (1719), MP for Droitwich (1708-25), Justice of Carmarthen, Cardigan, and Pembroke (1711-12) and Justice of Chester (1714-25). He had no children, and left his estates to his eldest brother Salwey Winnington.

JELF, SIR JAMES (1763-1849)

Eldest son of Michael Jelf, a substantial farmer in Bushley (near the Gloucestershire border). He became a banker at Gloucester, was elected Mayor of the city, and was knighted by George III. One of his sons, Richard William, was Principal of King's College, London.

JENKS, SYLVESTER (1656?-1714)

A village lad, born at Chaddesley Corbett. Lady Mary Yate of Harvington (near Evesham) sent him to the Catholic English college at Douay, where he afterwards became Professor of Philosophy. In 1686 he returned to Harvington as missionary priest, and was made chaplain to James II. A Protestant mob from Kidderminster attacked the Hall in 1688, after James was ousted, but was kept back by the moat. He was elected Vicar Apostolic of the Northern District in 1713.

JOHN, KING OF ENGLAND (1167-1216)

The king who became infamous for trying to succeed to the throne while his brother Richard 'The Lionheart' was away fighting a crusade — thus becoming the villain of the Robin Hood stories — and for being forced by the barons to sign Magna Carta in 1215. He was buried in Worcester Cathedral. He had visited at Christmas, to pray at Wulfstan's tomb, and requested that his tomb be placed between the shrines of former prelates Oswald and Wulfstan II. Cynics suggested that his only hope of entering heaven was to slip in unnoticed between the two saints.

JOHN OF WORCESTER (d. *c.* 1141) *see* Florence.

JOHNSON, JAMES (1705-1774)
Wealthy Bishop of Worcester 1759-74. Son of a Suffolk clergyman, he was previously chaplain to George II on two trips to Hanover, Canon of St Paul's, London, and Bishop of Gloucester (1752-9). He was wealthy enough to spend considerable sums on embellishing his palaces at Worcester and Hartlebury. He died at Bath after falling off his horse and was buried at Laycock, Wiltshire. His sister erected a monument to him in Worcester Cathedral.

JOHNSON, SIR CHARLES COOPER (1827-1905)
Old soldier who retired to Worcestershire. Sixth son of a Bath baronet, he joined the Indian Army in 1844 and served with distinction in a number of campaigns, including the Indian Mutiny. In 1860 he married Jemima, a Devon clergyman's daughter. He retired as a Colonel and in 1880 moved into The Hill, Upton. He was knighted in 1881, and later promoted to General on the inactive list. He sat as magistrate in Upton, was active in many community organisations, and was elected County Alderman for Worcestershire. Lady Johnson also supported many organisations, including the home for waifs and strays at Hanley Swan. One of their sons became a Brigadier General in the British Army.

JOHNSTONE, JAMES (1730-1802)
Scottish physician who settled at Kidderminster in 1751. He published a dissertation on the malignant epidemic fever of 1756, and wrote on the uses of the ganglions of the nerves, angina, scarlet fever, hydrophobia, and many other subjects, for which he received the honorary medal of the Medical Society. He attended George, the 'good' Lord Lyttelton in his last illness. He was buried at Kidderminster and has a monument in Worcester Cathedral. Three of his sons became doctors.

JOHNSTONE, JAMES (1754-1783)
Older brother of Edward Johnstone, he became physician to Worcester Infirmary in 1774 and wrote on a variety of medical issues. A volume of his essays, published posthumously in 1795, is in the Worcester Cathedral medical library. He was zealous in visiting the poor and prisoners, but this proved to be his downfall, since he contracted the fatal gaol fever, now known as typhus. His premature and heroic death is said to have inspired social reformer John Howard in his work for prison reform. Buried in Worcester Cathedral.

JOHNSTONE, EDWARD (1757-1851)
Born at Kidderminster, third son of Dr James Johnstone (1730-1802). He became a leading physician in Birmingham, and was one of the original doctors at the General Hospital, where he worked for twenty-two years. He was the first president of the Provincial Medical and Surgical Association, founded by Sir Charles Hastings in Worcester in 1832, and later renamed the British Medical Association. He was also the first principal of Queen's College, Birmingham. He wrote on puerperal fever and hydrophobia. He died at Edgbaston Hall, now the clubhouse of Edgbaston Golf Club. There is a classical bust

of him by Chantrey in Birmingham Museum and Art Gallery. His son James was also a doctor at the General Hospital.

JONES, WILLIAM (1839-1913)

William Jones VC.

Soldier hero. Born at Evesham, he was aged about 39, a private in the 2nd Battalion, 24th Regiment of Foot (later South Wales Borderers), when he won the Victoria Cross during the 1879 Zulu war action at Rorke's Drift, which was immortalised in the 1964 film *Zulu*. His heroic defence of the field hospital there made possible the evacuation of six patients in imminent danger from Zulu attack. He blamed the southern African climate for the chronic rheumatism he contracted, and left the army in 1880, but could find little work in Birmingham, and in 1887 joined Buffalo Bill's Wild West Show, which featured a re-enactment of the Zulu attack. Later he moved to Manchester, but had to pawn his medal in 1910, and subsequently entered the workhouse, being buried in a pauper's grave. A new headstone for his grave was unveiled in 2007. His VC was acquired by his regimental museum.

JORDEN, GEORGE (1783-1871)

Manservant who gained a considerable reputation as a botanist. Born on the Clee Hills, in the parish of Farlow (near Kidderminster), where his father was a labourer and his mother was a herb-doctress. He went to Bewdley as an errand boy, taught himself to read and write, and became servant to local physician, James Fryer, with whom he stayed for fifty years. Thanks to his employer's sympathetic attitude, he was able to follow his interests, and became known as 'the curator of the Wyre Forest', and an expert on the extremely rare Sorb Tree found there, said to be the only tree of the species then growing wild in Britain. He regularly rose in darkness, and spent hours in the forest before his day's work began. He invariably came back loaded with specimens for his herbarium. His book, *Flora Bellus Locus*, was lodged in the Worcester Museum. His aid was acknowledged by the authors of *Flora of Shropshire*, and *Botany of Worcestershire*. He bequeathed a mass of local antiquarian lore, including old ballads and electioneering songs, to the Worcester Museum.

JUDGE, JACK (1872-1938)

Composer of the great First World War song, It's a Long Way to Tipperary. Born in Oldbury (part of Worcestershire 1844-1966), of an Irish family with its roots in Tipperary, he was a fishmonger, but turned music hall entertainer after winning a talent contest. There are differing stories of how he came to pen the song, but the most popular is that it was written for a five-shilling bet in the Newmarket Tavern, Stalybridge, Cheshire, and sung by him the next night, 31 January 1912, at the Grand Theatre, where he was then performing. It was purchased by a music publisher for £5, popularised in the music halls by the great Florrie

Forde, and achieved world-wide popularity after famous Irish tenor John McCormack recorded it in 1914. It was sung by both sides in the First World War. Jack became a music hall star, and many of his other songs were popular at the time, though none as much as *Tipperary*. He also wrote songs for his beloved West Bromwich Albion. He died in West Bromwich. Stalybridge has a statue of him, and a plaque is on the Newmarket Tavern.

JUKES, FRANCIS (1745-1812)

Accomplished and popular engraver. Born at Martley, he set up in business at Hosier Lane, London, where he produced his first known engraving in 1779. Originally a line engraver, he subsequently developed the use of aquatint, a variant of etching, on copper or zinc plates, initially in partnership with Valentine Green. He produced a large volume of wide-ranging, high-quality work, especially topographical prints for books. He collaborated with many of the leading artists of his day, including the caricaturist Thomas Rowlandson. His work was highly regarded, but in later years his health suffered from 'the fumes of aquafortis' (nitric acid) used to treat the plates and he died in London. His prints are still much in demand and a complete set can cost thousands of pounds.

JUXON, WILLIAM (1582-1663)

A famous Archbishop of Canterbury and Dean of Worcester (1627-33), having previously been president of St John's College, Oxford, where he had studied. He was Bishop of London (1633-49) and attended King Charles I on the scaffold, but afterwards retired to Gloucestershire, where his pack of hunting hounds was said to be one of the finest in the country. At the Restoration he became Archbishop of Canterbury (1660-3) and crowned Charles II. He was buried at St John's College, Oxford. In a troubled age it was said that 'his reverence was the only thing all factions agreed on'.

KECK, ANTHONY (1727-1797)

Architect. He designed St Martin's Church, Worcester; Worcester Infirmary; the cupola of Upton old church; Dr Nash's house at Bevere, and many other buildings of note in and around Worcestershire. He was buried in St George's churchyard, Kings Stanley, Gloucestershire.

KELLEY, EDWARD (1555-1597)

Colourful conman, medium, occultist and assistant to John Dee. Born at Worcester and educated at the King's School, he became an apothecary's assistant, though later claimed to have studied at Oxford under an alias, and also sometimes claimed to be 'Sir Edward'. He apparently had his ears cropped in the Lancaster pillory in 1580, for forgery or counterfeiting. Another story had him digging up a corpse to question the dead. In 1582 he became assistant to Dr Dee, claiming to interpret the wishes of spirits with a crystal from the angel Gabriel. He also wrote several books in a strange, apparently self-invented language, which he claimed had been dictated to him by angels. In a later episode, confirmed by

Edward Kelley and John Dee conjuring spirits.

Dee, Kelley told the doctor that spirits had said they should have everything in common – including Dee's new, attractive, young second wife. Though she was reluctant, the doctor didn't question Kelley's claim, and the liaison went ahead. In 1583 Kelley accompanied Dee to central Europe, where he became increasingly wealthy through the patronage of Emperor Rudolf II, thanks to his alchemical claim that he could turn base metal into gold, using a magic book and red powder to which he had been led by a spirit on Northwick Hill, Worcester. Dee broke with Kelley in 1588, probably over his wife, and returned to England, but Kelley was imprisoned in 1591 by Rudolph, impatient to see some results from his patronage. He died in 1597, possibly from injuries sustained in an escape attempt. He left a suitably colourful biography.

KENELM, SAINT, 'KING', AND MARTYR (d. *c.* 819)

Prince of the Anglo-Saxon kingdom of Mercia, traditionally believed to have been murdered in the woods at Clent. Son of King Coenwulf, he was supposedly murdered at the instigation of his sister, Quendreda, by her lover, Ascobert. In an old legend, retold in an 1890 history of Clent, Kenelm was murdered after becoming King as a child, but it's likely he died before his father, probably in battle as a teenager. St Kenelm's Way is a sixty-mile walk following the route from St Kenelm's Church, Romsley (near Halesowen), where his body was supposedly found, to the Abbey of Winchcombe (Gloucestershire), where he was buried. A church at Clifton-upon-Teme is also dedicated to him.

KENNEDY, GEOFFREY ANKETELL STUDDERT (1883-1929)

Famous as 'Woodbine Willie'. Leeds-born son of a vicar, he became curate at Rugby, and in 1914, Vicar of St Paul's, the populous Worcester parish covering the poverty-stricken Blockhouse district, since demolished. When the First World War broke out he immediately volunteered,

Revd Kennedy – legendary hero of the First World War.

and was a chaplain on the Western Front, winning the Military Cross at Messines Ridge in 1917, for selflessly running into no-man's-land under fire to care for wounded soldiers. His care and compassion for the fighting men, handing out Bibles and cigarettes, made him a household name as 'Woodbine Willie'. His poems of wartime experiences were published in two volumes after the war. He returned to St Paul's a convinced pacifist and Christian socialist, and began writing lively and forceful books expressing his disgust for society's acceptance of the grinding poverty he saw every day in his parish. In 1922 he took over a London parish and embarked on national lecture tours at which he spoke with such emotion, said one newspaper, that 'women wept and men broke down'. It was while at Liverpool on one of these crusades that he fell ill and died. His burial in St John's Cemetery brought Worcester to a standstill. An anthology of his work was published in 2008.

KNIGHT, RICHARD (1658-1745)

Ironmaster, second son of ironmaster Richard Knight, of Madeley, Shropshire. He developed the iron trade in Shropshire and at Wolverley (near Kidderminster), where he bought a large estate about 1721. His second son, Thomas, was Rector of Ribbesford (near Bewdley) from 1730 to 1765, and rebuilt the tower of Bewdley Church in 1745.

KNIGHT, RICHARD PAYNE (1751-1824)

Son of Revd Thomas Knight (Rector of Ribbesford) and grandson of <u>Richard Knight</u>. He inherited the Downton estate (near Ludlow, Shropshire), and in 1776 built Downton Castle and laid out the famous grounds. His distaste for the Capability Brown school of landscaping was enthusiastically expressed in his work, *The Landscape: A Didactic Poem, in Three Books* (1794). A man of many interests, he was regarded as the best Greek scholar of his time, and was renowned as a coinage expert. He travelled in Italy when young, developing a taste for ancient art. He became MP for Leominster (1780) then Ludlow (1784-1806) and a Trustee of the British Museum, to which he left a superb collection of antiquities. He died in London and was buried in Herefordshire.

KNIGHT, THOMAS ANDREW (1759-1838)

Brother of <u>Richard Payne Knight</u>; friend of scientists Sir Joseph Banks and Sir Humphrey Davy, his experiments and publications helped make Herefordshire pre-eminent for cider. His daughter Charlotte married Sir William Rouse-Boughton (Baronet of Downton Hall, Shropshire, and Rous Lench, near Evesham), by which the Boughton family came into possession of the Downton Castle estate. He died in London and was buried in Herefordshire.

KNIGHT, SIR FREDERICK WINN (1812-1897)

MP and eldest son of John Knight, of Wolverley House, a descendant of ironmaster <u>Richard Knight</u>. MP for West Worcestershire (1841-85) and Parliamentary Secretary to the Poor Law Board in the 1850s. He was an energetic supporter of the Volunteer movement, and first member enrolled in the county. He was Lieutenant Colonel 1st Worcestershire Rifle Volunteers (1860-91), Lieutenant Colonel, Queen's Own Worcestershire Hussars (Yeomanry) from 1866 to 1878, and was knighted in 1886. Family Trustee of the British Museum. He also had an estate in Exmoor, Devon, where he improved the breed of Exmoor ponies.

KYDERMINSTRE, RICHARD (*c.* 1461-1533)

Born at Kidderminster, he was admitted at 15 into the Benedictine monastery of Winchcombe. He was sent to Oxford University at 19, and in 1487 was elected abbot. In 1500 he journeyed to Rome, and afterwards had much influence at the English court. He was buried at Winchcombe Abbey.

LAMBE, JOHN (1545-1628)

Astrologer and rogue, probably born in Worcestershire, having been a children's writing tutor here. He apparently practised astrology at Tardebigge (near Redditch). In 1607 he was convicted of 'execrable acts' against Lord Windsor. Reportedly many of those present in court at

Worcester died soon afterwards, probably from 'gaol fever', but he was quickly transferred to a London prison. He began styling himself 'Dr Lambe', claiming to read fortunes, identify diseases, combat witchcraft and find missing or stolen items with his crystal ball – and charging up to £50. Regarded by some as a fraud, his activities gave rise to many accusations from ordinary Londoners that he possessed demonic powers. By 1625 he gained the support and protection of George Villiers, Duke of Buckingham, favourite of Charles I, but the populace detested the duke's influence on the King, and Lambe became known as 'the duke's devil', regarded as a malign influence over both nobleman and monarch. In 1627 he was convicted of raping a girl aged 11, but was pardoned when the charge was found to be false. Hated by the London mob, he was brutally attacked after leaving a theatre, and died the next day.

LANDOR, ROBERT EYRES (1781-1869)

Author and clergyman. Warwick-born younger brother of prolific writer Walter Savage Landor, he was Rector of Birlingham (near Pershore), from 1829, and was famous for never missing a single Sunday service in forty years. He wrote several tragedies (of which the then popular *Count Arezzi*, 1824, was wrongly attributed to Byron) and also prose and verse, a collection of which was published in 1927. Birlingham Church was rebuilt in 1871 with £4,000 he left.

LANE, SIR RICHARD (1667-1756)

Son of a Worcester sugar-baker, he was Mayor (1709), later sheriff of the city, knighted (1714) and MP for Worcester (1727-34). He is chiefly remembered for revolutionising salt production at Droitwich (1725) by sinking pits to lower, more pressurised brine deposits. When this was first done the brine broke out with such violence that two workmen were thrown to the surface and killed. Massive deposits were accessed and the older, shallower pits, in which many individuals and charities invested, became worthless overnight. He does not seem to have benefited much from this, and died one of the Poor Knights of Windsor.

LANGLAND, WILLIAM (1325?-1390?)

Early English poet. He was perhaps born at Cleobury Mortimer, just across the Shropshire border, and educated at the priory of Great Malvern; he later lived in London where he may have been in lower clerical orders. The famous poem attributed to Langland, *The Vision of Piers the Ploughman*, narrated a vision experienced by the ploughman as he slept on the Malvern Hills. Three versions are known, the earliest from 1362. He is believed to have died in Oxfordshire.

LASLETT, WILLIAM (1801-1884)

Worcester-born lawyer, MP and philanthropist. He practised as a solicitor at Foregate Street, Worcester, until 1846, and gave much to good causes, but he could also be parsimonious and eccentric. He married Maria, daughter of <u>Robert James Carr</u>, Bishop of Worcester, after paying off the bishop's substantial debts – though the marriage was apparently not a happy one. He became a barrister in 1856 and was MP for Worcester (1852-60 and

1868-74). He founded the Laslett Hospital almshouses in Friar Street, Worcester, for thirty-three married couples, with a chapel and resident chaplain. He also generously endowed a charity for educational and benevolent uses, donated to the city cemetery and many other city and county charities. He lived at Abberton Hall (near Bishampton), still a private house. His presentation portrait still hangs in Worcester Guildhall.

Lawyer William Laslett.

LAWRENCE, BRIAN TURNER TOM (1873-1949)

Victoria Cross winner. Born at Bewdley, the eldest of five sons of timber merchant John Lawrence, of Park Lane, Kidderminster, he attended grammar school at Kidderminster, and joined the army in the ranks. He had risen to Sergeant in the 17th Lancers by 1900, during the second Boer War, when he won the Victoria Cross. On patrol with a Private Hayman, they encountered a dozen Boers and Hayman's horse was shot from under him. Lawrence put Hayman on his own horse and sent him back to their lines; then firing two carbines, he fought on foot for two miles until help arrived. He served in both world wars, rising to Lieutenant Colonel, and competed, though unsuccessfully, in the eventing team in the 1912 Olympics. He died and was buried in Kenya.

LAYAMON (fl. 1200)

Important historian. First known priest of St Bartholomew's parish church, Areley Kings (near Stourport) around 1200; confirmed by discovery of an old font base bearing his name, during church restoration work in 1885. He was author of a work regarded as the first survey of British history in English, sometime between 1189 and 1207, usually known as the *Brut*, from Britain's mythical founder, Brutus of Troy. Though partly

Lieutenant Colonel Lawrence VC.

fabulous, it influenced many later medieval historians. The *Brut* is the first English source for the stories of Cymbeline and King Lear, both dealt with in plays by Shakespeare, and the stories of King Arthur and the Knights of the Round Table; it influenced Malory's *Le Morte d'Arthur*, on which the modern Arthurian legend is based. The *Brut* was published in 1847, and several times since. A memorial tablet and window in his church recall Layamon.

LEA, JOHN WHEELEY (1791-1874)

Chemist and sauce manufacturer. One of eight children of a Feckenham farmer, he joined the pharmacy of George Guise at 68 Broad Street, Worcester, and in 1823 went into partnership with chemist William Henry Perrins. They built up a chain of four pharmacies by the 1850s, including shops in Kidderminster and Cheltenham, but are best known as makers of Worcestershire Sauce, the origins of which are somewhat mysterious. Labels on early bottles said it was '… from the recipe of a nobleman of the county', though that person has never been definitely identified. The recipe may have been Indian originally, and it was probably true that they found it very unpalatable when first made, but after it lay forgotten for several years in the cellar, it had fermented and was very tasty. They began to sell it in 1837 and launched in America in 1839. Clever marketing and quality of product led to world-wide sales. By 1865 they had given up the pharmacies to concentrate on sauce production. Lea died at Stanfield House, Upper Wick (now a nursing home) and was buried at Powick. Lea family ownership ended in 1892, though they still sat on the board. In 1897 the firm moved to Midland Road, and in 1930 it was taken over by HP.

LEA, SIR THOMAS (1841-1902)

Son of George Butcher Lea, of The Larches, Kidderminster, now a residential care home. Chairman of carpet manufacturers Lea Ltd, of Kidderminster, and of the Metropolitan Bank. MP for Kidderminster (1868-74) and South Londonderry (1886). He was created a baronet in 1892. His brother, George Harris Lea, was County Court Judge of Herefordshire and Shropshire.

LEA, WILLIAM (1819-1889)

Clergyman and expert fruit grower, born at Stone House (near Kidderminster). He was Vicar of St Peter's, Droitwich (1849-87), Archdeacon of Worcester (1881) and an enthusiastic Secretary of the Worcester Board of Education. He was considered a great authority on, and promoter of, fruit-growing, personally testing the suitability of nearly every variety of apple, pear, and plum to the Worcestershire soil and climate. He wrote several religious works.

LEADER, BENJAMIN WILLIAMS (1831-1923)

Leading Victorian artist. He was born in Worcester, the son of Quaker Edward Leader Williams, ironmonger at 94 High Street. When his father became a civil engineer the family moved to the Severn-side Diglis House, now a hotel, and the young artist's first paintings were of river scenes. His father was also a keen amateur artist and Constable was amongst the visitors to their home. He attended the grammar school and tried engineering and banking before becoming a painter, changing his surname to Leader since there were already several painters named Williams. He submitted his first painting to the Royal Academy in 1853, and quickly achieved success, exhibiting in every summer exhibition thereafter until his death. His naturalistic paintings of countryside scenes, including several of Claines, brought him world-wide success. He lived at Whittington Lodge (near Worcester), until 1889, when he moved to Surrey, where he lived for the rest of his life. He was Director of Royal Worcester Porcelain for many years. He received the Freedom of the City of Worcester in 1914. Several of his paintings are in Worcester's art gallery and others are in major national and regional collections. Any sold fetch substantial sums.

LECHMERE, SIR NICHOLAS (1613-1701)

Lawyer, MP and landowner. He was born at the fifteenth-century Severn End, Hanley Castle (near Upton), of a family ceded land at Hanley by William the Conqueror. He was called to the Bar in 1641, sided with Parliament in the Civil War, and was present at the Siege of Worcester in 1646. He became MP for Bewdley in 1648, was a Member of Special Commission for trial of Welsh insurgents (1651), MP for Worcestershire (1654, 1656, 1658-9), and walked in Oliver Cromwell's funeral procession. Despite this, he obtained a full pardon from Charles II for the very modest sum of £200. He was one of the founders of Greenwich Hospital, London. He died at Hanley Castle.

LECHMERE, NICHOLAS, BARON LECHMERE (1675-1727)

Lawyer, MP and landowner, born at Hanley Castle, son of Edmund Lechmere. He was called to the Bar in 1698 and became QC in 1708. Variously MP for Appleby, Cockermouth, and Tewkesbury (1708-50), he helped writer and MP Richard Steele with a pamphlet on the Hanoverian succession (1714) which got Steele barred from the House. He was appointed Solicitor General (1714-18), Attorney General, Privy Councillor, and Chancellor of the Duchy of Lancaster (1718). He appeared in several high-profile trials of the period, and was created Baron Lechmere of Evesham, 1721. He married but had no heir and the title became extinct on his death. He died at Kensington and was buried at Hanley Castle.

LECHMERE, SIR EDMUND ANTHONY HARLEY (1826-1894)

Born at Rhydd Court, Hanley Castle, built by his family about 1805. Senior partner in the Worcester Old Bank, he was MP for West Worcestershire (1876-92) and South Worcestershire (1892-4). He zealously took up the cause of the Christians in the Balkan wars, and was made Commander of the Servian Order of the Takova, Knight of the Holy Sepulchre, Knight Commander of the Order of St John of Jerusalem, and Knight of Malta. He gave the site for the Church of St Gabriel, at Hanley Green, built at the cost of Samuel Martin, 1874; and also erected a beautiful chapel adjoining Rhydd Court. The Court was later a school, sold privately in 2004, at a price estimated as over £2m.

LEES, EDWIN (1800-1887)

Writer and skilled amateur botanist; son of a Worcester woollen draper. A printer at 87 High Street, in 1828 he published his first known publication, *Strangers' Guide to Worcester*, under a pseudonym. In 1829 he started *The Worcestershire Miscellany*, and in 1831 founded the Worcestershire Literary and Scientific Society, of which he became the chief authority on botanical research. Later he gave up business and devoted himself to study. He wrote many papers and addresses, but his chief work was *The Botany of Worcestershire* (1867). He died at Green Hill, London Road, Worcester and was buried in Herefordshire.

LEIGHTON, SIR THOMAS (d. 1611)

MP and landowner. Shropshire-born MP for Worcestershire (1601-4) and distinguished soldier, he received Feckenham Park (near Redditch) from Queen Elizabeth I. He was one of the general officers consulted to repel the Spanish Armada in 1588. His wife, Elizabeth, was a relative of Anne Boleyn.

LICHFIELD, CLEMENT (d. 1546)

Abbot of Evesham. He built St Clement's Chapel in St Laurence's Church, 1500-7, and the beautiful clock tower and gateway, which is all that now remains of Evesham Abbey. It was later purchased by the townspeople, when Sir Philip Hoby was about to pull it down for the sake of the materials. He was buried in the Lichfield Chapel of All Saints.

LIND, JENNY (1820-1887)

World-famous singer who retired to Malvern. A Swedish soprano, regarded as perhaps the finest singer of the nineteenth century, she started life as the illegitimate daughter of a schoolmistress, but won world-wide acclaim as 'the Swedish Nightingale'. She moved to Wynds Point, Malvern, near the Malvern Hills Hotel in 1883, after her daughter moved nearby. She came out of retirement for one last performance, in aid of the Railway Servants' Benevolent Fund, at the since demolished 2,600 seat Royal Malvern Wells Spa Hall, West Malvern Road, 23 July 1883. When she died of cancer four years later, twenty-seven carriages followed her hearse to Great Malvern Cemetery, and she was buried to the strains of Chopin's *Funeral March.* Her husband lived in Malvern for another twenty years. Wynds Point was subsequently purchased by the Cadbury Trust.

Jenny Lind – the Swedish Nightingale.

LINES, HENRY HARRIS (1800-1899)

Gifted Worcester-based painter, eldest son of Samuel Lines, who helped found the Birmingham School of Art in 1821. His mother, Elizabeth Ashcroft, was from Rock (near Bewdley). He came to Worcester in 1832, and was living in London Road in the 1840s. Around 1855 he moved to Albany Terrace, off Britannia Square, where he lived for the rest of his life, but after some thirty-five years at No. 7 (now 27), he spent the last decade of his life with his daughter at No. 22 (now 14). He exhibited landscapes at the Royal Academy, and major regional art galleries. Some of his watercolour and line and wash paintings, carried out over half a century, include the only known visual representations of the now-vanished old St Peter's Church, the old deanery kitchens, and the Guesten Hall beside Worcester Cathedral, destroyed by fire the year after he painted it. Many of these paintings were presented to the city after his death. He also became a keen amateur archaeologist, making studies of the old camps of Worcestershire and the border counties, some of which were published after his death by the Shropshire Archaeological Society.

Landscape artist H.H. Lines.

LITTLETON, HUMPHREY (1576?-1606)

Executed for his part in the Gunpowder Plot of 1605. One of the eight sons of Sir John Lyttelton, the founder of the family estates. It was doubtful whether he was actually one of the conspirators, but when the plot failed he hid two of them – his nephew, Stephen Littleton, and Robert Wintour – at the half-timbered forerunner of the present eighteenth-century Hagley Hall. His cook informed, and a search revealed the plotters and Catholic priest Edward Oldcorne. All were hanged, drawn and quartered – Oldcorne at Red Hill, Worcester.

LITTLETON, SIR THOMAS (*c.* 1407-1481)

Lawyer, judge and pioneering legal author. Born at the manor house at Frankley, eldest son of Thomas Westcote of Oxfordshire, he had the name Littleton as heir of his mother Elizabeth, sole heir of Thomas de Littleton, Lord of Frankley. In 1445 he was appointed Escheator of Worcestershire, dealing with land tenure. By 1466 he was Justice of the Common Pleas and was knighted in 1475. He died at Frankley and was buried in Worcester Cathedral.

Through his eldest son he was ancestor of the Lyttelton family of Hagley. He has a unique place in legal history as author of the very first English law book, his *Treatise on Tenures*, published posthumously. It was the standard authority on property law for centuries, going through more than 100 editions, the last published in Washington, DC in 1903. His rigorous scientific method also influenced many later legal writers.

Judge Littleton 1407-1481.

LLOYD, WILLIAM (1627-1717)

Bishop of Worcester, 1699-1717. Son of a Reading clergyman, he was a devoted Royalist, and after the Restoration held many preferments, including Bishop of St Asaph (1680). He was one of seven bishops sent to the Tower of London by James II in 1688, but was subsequently cleared. Translated to Lichfield and Coventry in 1692, then Worcester. Much interested in education, he founded Bishop Lloyd's School for poor boys and girls in the city, from the estate of a Mrs Palmer of Upton Snodsbury (near Worcester), who had been murdered by her own son. He influenced Sir Thomas Cookes in founding Worcester College, Oxford. He died and was buried at Fladbury, where his son was rector. His school continued until 1896 and is remembered by a plaque just off The Trinity.

LOVETT, RICHARD (1692-1780)

Lay Clerk of Worcester Cathedral, born in Buckinghamshire. He experimented with electrotherapy, applying electricity as a remedy for sore throats (1758) and other ailments. He wrote works on philosophy and physics. He was buried at St Swithin's Church, Worcester.

LYGON, WILLIAM, EARL BEAUCHAMP (1747-1816)

The first of eight earls of the family who made their home at Madresfield Court (near Malvern). A twelfth-century hall house remodelled in the fifteenth, it was intended as the Second World War refuge of Princess (later Queen) Elizabeth, and is thought to have been the inspiration for Evelyn Waugh's *Brideshead Revisited.* The only son of Reginald Pyndar, he took the name of Lygon on becoming heir to the Court through his mother, Margaret Lygon. MP for Worcestershire (1775-1806), he was created Baron Beauchamp of Powyk in 1806, and later Viscount Elmley and Earl Beauchamp (1815). His eldest son, William, succeeded.

LYGON, HENRY BEAUCHAMP, EARL BEAUCHAMP (1784-1863)

Fourth earl, and third son of the first earl to succeed to the title. He joined the army and served in the Peninsular War (1809-10), fighting at Talavera, and was severely wounded at Busaco. He became Lieutenant Colonel in the 1st Life Guards (1821-37), then Major General (1837), and finally General (1854). He was also MP for Worcestershire (1816-31) and West Worcestershire (1832-53), and a Member of the Court of Inquiry into the Administration of the British Array in the Crimea (1856). He succeeded his brother John as fourth Earl Beauchamp in 1858.

LYGON, FREDERICK, EARL BEAUCHAMP (1830-1891)

Younger son of fourth earl. He was MP for Tewkesbury (1857-63) and West Worcestershire (1863-6), and was one of the founders and council of Keble College (1871-82). He was Civil Lord of the Admiralty (1859), Lord Lieutenant of Worcestershire (1876-91), Lord Steward of the Household (1874-80) under Benjamin Disraeli, and Paymaster General (1885-7) under Lord Salisbury. He was also a Captain, Worcestershire Yeomanry (1854-9), and Official Trustee of the British Museum. He succeeded his brother Henry as sixth earl in 1866. He was succeeded by his eldest son, William, when Evelyn Waugh was a frequent guest. William was succeeded by his eldest son, also William, but on his death in 1979 the title died out, though Madresfield Court is still held by a descendant.

LYTTELTON, SIR JOHN (1520-1590)

Founder of the estates of the Lyttelton family of Hagley Park. Son of Sir John Lyttelton of Frankley, he became constable of Dudley Castle and park in Staffordshire in 1553. He was knighted by Queen Elizabeth I in 1566, and purchased the manors of Halesowen (formerly Halesowen Abbey) from Elizabeth's favourite Lord Robert Dudley (1558) and Hagley (1565). Together with Frankley and Upper Arley (near Kidderminster), which he inherited, these formed the basis of the family estates.

LYTTELTON, JOHN (1561-1601)

Son of Gilbert Lyttelton, MP for Frankley, he lost the family lands – but his wife regained them. MP for Worcestershire, 1584-7 and 1597-8. As a Catholic he was implicated in the Essex rebellion against Queen Elizabeth I, and convicted of high treason in 1601. Sir Walter Raleigh saved him from execution, but he died in prison within a few months, and the family estates were forfeit. However, his wife Muriel, daughter of a Lord Chancellor, was a formidable lady. On the accession of James I in 1603, she threw herself at his feet at Doncaster, and pleaded her children's cause so ably that the estates were returned to the family.

LYTTELTON, SIR THOMAS (1596-1650)

Eldest son of John Lyttelton. Created a baronet in 1618, he was MP for Worcestershire (1620-2, 1624-6, 1640) and Colonel of the Worcestershire Horse and Foot for the King (1642) but was taken prisoner at Bewdley in 1644, imprisoned in the Tower of London, and heavily fined. He was buried in Worcester Cathedral.

LYTTELTON, SIR CHARLES (1629-1716)

Second son of Sir Thomas Lyttelton, he defended Colchester for the King in 1648. Sent to the Tower of London by Cromwell, he escaped to France, and served the future Charles II in 1650. He took part in a Royalist rising (1659) and was knighted after the Restoration. Lieutenant Governor and Governor of Jamaica (1662-4), he founded the city of Port Royal and summoned the first Legislative Assembly. He was appointed Colonel of the 'Maritime Regiment' (afterwards the Marines) in 1684, and was MP for Bewdley (1685-9). He died at Hagley and was buried at Upper Arley (near Kidderminster).

LYTTELTON, GEORGE, BARON LYTTELTON (1709-1773)

The 'good' Lord Lyttelton. He was the first Baron Lyttelton, politician and patron of the arts, and eldest son of Sir Thomas Lyttelton. He was MP for Okehampton (1735-56), Secretary to the Prince of Wales (1737), a Lord of the Treasury (1744-54), Cofferer to the Royal Household (1754), and Chancellor of the Exchequer (1755). He was appointed High Steward of Bewdley (1753-73) and created Lord Lyttelton, Baron of Frankley in 1757. In

George Lyttelton 1709-1773.

1751 he had begun to lay out the grounds at Hagley in the new Picturesque style, and between 1754 and 1760 he oversaw the building of the present Hagley Hall, designed by Sanderson Miller, and said to be the last of the great Palladian houses built in England. He was a distinguished poet and author, friend of Alexander Pope and Henry Fielding – who dedicated *Tom Jones* to him – and a generous patron of literature. He was included in Dr Johnson's *Lives of the English Poets*. He was highly regarded, being called the 'good' Lord Lyttelton. He was buried at Oxford.

LYTTELTON, THOMAS, BARON LYTTELTON (1744-1779)

The only son of <u>George Lyttelton</u>, the first baron, he was brilliant but profligate, and thus often called the 'bad' Lord Lyttelton. He attended Eton and Oxford, and was briefly MP for Bewdley (1768-9). Regarded as accomplished, witty, clever, a brilliant orator and a good debater, profligacy doubtless led to his early death, aged just 35. According to family legend, a bird flew into his room, changed into the apparition of a woman in white, and bade him prepare to die within three days. His widow, Apphia, lived in Malvern until her death in 1840, and founded several Church institutions. The Lyttelton Rooms, in Church Street, rebuilt in 1887, were named for her. They had no children and the title became extinct after the baron's death. It was revived 1794-1889, when the fifth baron succeeded as Viscount Cobham, and all descendants since have held that title.

LYTTELTON, ALFRED (1857-1913)

High-flying lawyer, politician and gifted cricketer; eighth son of the fourth Baron Lyttelton. He qualified as a barrister in 1881 and became a QC in 1891. He was Recorder of Hereford (1893) and Oxford (1894), and was MP for Warwick (1895-1906). His services were often in demand in important arbitration matters overseas. He entered the Cabinet as Colonial Secretary in 1902, and initiated the idea of forming a permanent Imperial Council with representatives from all the self-governing overseas dominions, similar to the present Commonwealth. He was also a fine cricketer, an excellent batsman, and said to be the best amateur wicket-keeper in England. He was captain of the Eton and Cambridge Elevens; and wicket-keeper for England against the Australians four times. He was buried at Hagley.

MADDOX, ISAAC (1697-1757)

Bishop of Worcester 1743-59. Said to have been destined for a pastry cook's apprentice after his father's early death, he was sent to university instead, and rose by his merit. He was Clerk to Queen Caroline, Dean of Wells (1734), and Bishop of St Asaph, Wales (1736). A kindly, hospitable man, he was a founder of the Worcester Infirmary (1746) at a building still standing in Silver Street, and restored the chapel at Hartlebury Castle. He died at Hartlebury and was buried at Worcester Cathedral.

MALVERNE, JOHN DE

Born at Malvern; Sacrist and Prior of Worcester in 1395. He was credited with writing the continuation, from 1344 to 1357, of Chester monk Ranulf Higden's long history chronicle, *Polychronicon*, which was very popular throughout the country in the fifteenth century, and was printed in the late nineteenth century. The date of his death is uncertain, but he was certainly alive in 1410, when he was present at the trial of Lollard <u>John Badby</u> in Worcester.

MARLEBERGE, THOMAS DE (d. 1236)

Prior of Evesham, 1218; abbot, 1229. Educated at Paris, he taught at Oxford, before coming as a monk to Evesham in 1199, bringing with him many books on law and medicine. He rebuilt the Tower at Evesham, added stained-glass windows, dedicated a new infirmary chapel, and wrote several historical works.

MARSH (DE MARISCO), ADAM (*c.* 1200-1259)

Probably the most famous English friar of his time, he joined the order of the Grey Friars at Worcester shortly before 1230. Born at Bath, he had already received a parish from his uncle, the Bishop of Durham before 1226, but decided to forsake it to become a Franciscan. An expert lawyer and theologian, he achieved fame as spiritual director of some of the greatest in the land, including the Queen and <u>Simon de Montfort</u>, thus having a great influence on public policy.

MARTYN, HERBERT HENRY (1842-1937)

Poor Worcester boy who made a rags-to-riches progression to become head of a large business. Born in the slums of the former Lich Street, his health was so poor as a child that a doctor told his mother to take him home to die. He survived, taking on a string of menial jobs as a youngster, including china gilding, errand boy, leather button polisher and railway clerk. At 12 he attended the Worcester School of Design, where older student <u>Benjamin Williams Leader</u> disparaged him as a 'ragamuffin'. His design experience may have assisted him, aged 19, in becoming an apprentice with Worcester sculptor James Forsyth. In 1867 he moved to Cheltenham with another sculptor, and in 1888 started his own architectural decorating business there – which eventually employed 400 craftsmen – and carried out work at Buckingham Palace, earning him the title Architectural Decorator to the King. His firm worked on 'palaces, cathedrals, ocean liners, trains, stately homes, churches and public buildings'. Locally he provided the splendid

H.H. Martyn and wife Fanny in 1913.

altar piece in the Jesus Chapel at Worcester Cathedral, and worked at Stanbrook Abbey Church, Callow End, and Battenhall Mount. His motto was always to produce 'The Best'. During the First World War the company began making aircraft parts, and by the end of the war was making complete aircraft, having formed in 1917 what became the Gloster Aircraft Company, taken over by Hawker Aircraft in 1934.

MASON, GEORGE (1629-1686)

Great-grandfather of one of the founding fathers of the United States. Born at Pershore, third of seven children of a yeoman farmer, he became an MP and took the Royalist side in the Civil War, leading a troop of horse at the Battle of Worcester in 1651, after which he fled to Virginia with a number of neighbours and relatives from Worcestershire and Staffordshire. He held several important positions there and founded a political dynasty. His great-grandson, also George Mason, wrote the first ten amendments to the US Constitution, collectively known as the Bill of Rights.

MASON, SIR JOSIAH (1795-1881)

Nineteenth-century industrialist, born in Mill Street, Kidderminster, son of a poor carpet-weaver. He had little education and was in turn a street hawker, shoemaker's apprentice, baker, carpenter, blacksmith, house-painter and carpet-weaver, before moving to Birmingham in 1816, aged 21, as a factory supervisor. His employer, Samuel Harrison, made the first recorded steel pens, crafted by hand. Josiah bought the business for £500 in 1824, convinced he could turn pens out cheaply using machinery. It was a great success and he became the largest pen producer in the world. About 1840 he also joined his cousin, George Elkington, in an innovative electro-plate works and other ventures. He and his wife, Annie, were childless and he dedicated his wealth to helping young people and the poor. He established an almshouse for women at Station Road, Erdington in 1858, and Mason's Orphanage in Bell Lane, now Orphanage Road, which by 1874 accommodated 300 girls, 150 boys, and 50 infants. He was knighted in 1872 and opened Mason Science College, Edmund Street, Birmingham in 1880. When he died he was buried in the orphanage grounds. In 1900 his college became the nucleus of Birmingham University, but the original building was demolished in 1962, and the Central Library was built on the site. His orphanage was demolished in 1964, and the almshouse ten years later. A bronze bust of him was erected in 1951 at the junction of Chester Road and Orphanage Road.

MAUGER (d. 1212)

Bishop of Worcester 1200-12. Previously physician to Richard I and the Dean of York, he was elected to Worcester in 1199. His election was annulled because of his illegitimate birth, but the Pope relented after a personal appeal. During his episcopate frequent miracles were reported at <u>Wulfstan</u>'s tomb, and canonisation was obtained. Income generated from pilgrims repaired the damage from a recent fire. In 1208 he incurred King John's wrath and fled to France, where he died.

MAUND, BENJAMIN (1790-1863)

Tenbury-born pharmacist, bookseller and printer at Bromsgrove. A keen amateur botanist, on the committee of the Worcestershire Local History Society, in 1825 he started a monthly publication, *The Botanic Garden*, printing thirteen volumes over twenty-five years, illustrated by the finest botanical artists of the day. The series showed ornamental flowering plants in royal gardens, and also featured supplements on subjects including fruit growing and botanical terms. In 1852 he retired to Folkestone and Sandown, Isle of Wight, where he died. Almost as soon as his publication finished in 1850, special editions of material from it began to be published. The original drawings of *The Botanic Garden* are in the British Museum, but there is still a thriving trade in prints. A memorial tablet was unveiled in St John's Church, Bromsgrove in 1928.

MAY, GEORGE (1803-1871)

Bristol-born Evesham printer and bookseller from 1828. He studied the historical records of the town and published his *History of Evesham* in 1834, followed by a fuller better-produced volume in 1845. In 1850 he disposed of his business and went with his family to America, but returned in 1854. A London street accident in 1862 left him permanently incapacitated, though he managed the occasional summer visits to cathedral towns, and a last to Evesham in 1870.

MEUNIER, AMIE HOLMAN (1868-1893)

Frenchman hanged at Worcester for the brutal murder of an elderly woman. A smartly dressed former valet, he visited Worcestershire towns selling stationery from a case, showing potential customers a card falsely claiming he was deaf and dumb. On 9 January 1893, the young man visited a small, isolated shop at Long Eye (near Lickey End, Bromsgrove), run by Joseph Pearcey, 69, and his wife, Charlotte, 71, in the front room of their small cottage. On 13 January he returned, and as Mrs Pearcey served him he hacked the old woman to death with an axe, presumably to steal the small amount of money believed to be in the shop. He fled abroad, but was caught in Belgium and extradited back to Britain. En route, and after arrival in Worcestershire, he confessed to the crime, claiming initially that the killing was part of an anarchist plot – though no evidence of this was ever found. Later he changed his mind and the defence entered a plea of insanity at Worcester Assizes in late June, but this was rejected after a report from Dr Cooke, Medical Superintendent of Powick Hospital (near Worcester). Meunier was convicted and executed on 19 July.

MIDDLETON, SAMUEL (1857-1902)

Labourer who murdered his wife at Foxlydiate, Redditch. Middleton, 45, was said to be a pleasant man when sober, but 'a very terror' during frequent drinking bouts, and neighbours often heard violent quarrels with his wife Hannah, aged about 50. On 10 May 1902, a row had gone on for much of the day. It seemed to have stopped by late evening, but broke out again about midnight and continued until a scream was heard. Some time later neighbours awoke to find the Middletons' cottage on fire, and when firemen finally doused the fierce flames they found the charred remains of Hannah. The search began for her husband

and he was subsequently found wandering near Worcester, in a state of shock. He denied murder at Worcester Assizes, and though evidence suggested he had attacked his wife with a poker and a machete, her body was so badly burned that no injuries could be discerned. He may have set their home alight to cover his crime, but it was also possible a lamp had been knocked over accidentally during a tussle. Nevertheless he was convicted, and was said in some accounts to have confessed in the death cell. He was executed on 15 July.

MILLET, FRANCIS DAVIS (1846-1912)

American artist and writer, who lived in Worcestershire for many years. Born in Massachusetts, he began an adventurous life enlisting in the Union Army during the US Civil War, aged just 16. Afterwards he went to Harvard and became a journalist, serving as war correspondent for US and British newspapers, while also studying art and painting in Europe, and befriending many leading artistic and literary figures of the time, including Mark Twain, who was best man at his wedding in Paris in 1879. By 1885 he was living at Farnham House, Broadway, moving to Russell House in 1886, and attracting many artistic and literary visitors to the area, including Edward Elgar, *Peter Pan* author J.M. Barrie, composer Vaughan Williams and American writer Henry James. Frank, as he was known to everyone, produced meticulously

American artist Francis (Frank) Millet.

detailed classical scenes, including many murals for European and American locations, inventing the first form of spray paint in Chicago in 1893. He translated Tolstoy and was a gifted writer himself. His many appointments in the art world involved much travel, and in 1912 he booked passage to New York aboard the ill-fated *Titanic*. He was last seen helping women and children into lifeboats. His body was recovered and buried in Massachusetts. His many friends erected a graveyard lychgate in Broadway, with a Latin memorial inscription.

MILWARD, EDWARD (*c.* 1712-1757)

Doctor and student of medical history, probably born at Lindridge (near Tenbury Wells). He left Cambridge without a degree, and obtained one abroad in 1733, but later qualified MD at Cambridge and became a Fellow of the College of Physicians in 1741. A keen student of classical medical literature, he was best known for an essay, written at the age of 21, on Alexander Trallianus, a sixth-century Greek physician. He died at Worcester and was buried at Lindridge.

MONTFORT, SIMON DE (1208-1265)

The 'father of parliamentary democracy' died and was buried in Worcestershire. A French nobleman, he came to England to claim the earldom of Leicester, but in 1238 married Eleanor, sister of Henry III, and became a powerful man in England. In the 1260s the King and barons fell out, and in 1264 De Montfort defeated Henry and made him a puppet king. In the following year he summoned Parliament, insisting all representatives must be elected, thus creating Europe's first democratic parliament, but Royalist forces were massing against him, and later that year he was killed, and his army and cause destroyed, at the Battle of Evesham. He was buried at Evesham Abbey and in 1965 a memorial stone was laid on the abbey site.

MOORE, FRANCIS (1708-1756?)

Worcester-born explorer. He entered the service of the Royal African Company as a writer at James Fort, River Gambia in 1730. After promotion two years later, he travelled 500 miles inland, making careful calculations and drawings, and subsequently wrote accounts of his travels. He helped to establish the colony of Georgia (1735-42) and then returned to Worcester and married at Feckenham in January 1756, but there is no further trace of him.

MOORE, JOSEPH (1766-1851)

Manufacturer and musical enthusiast, born at Shelsley Walsh or Shelsley Beauchamp (near Clifton-upon-Teme). Sent to Birmingham in 1781, to learn die-sinking, he became wealthy in the button trade and devoted himself to charity and music. He planned and virtually took charge of the Birmingham triennial festival, begun in 1784, and in 1808 established Birmingham Oratorio Choral Society. He greatly increased the festival's popularity and played a major role in persuading the city to build Birmingham Town Hall, as a venue worthy of an international festival of growing renown. He commissioned Mendelssohn's *St Paul* and *Elijah* for the festivals of 1837 and 1846. He died and was buried in Birmingham. The festivals continued until the First World War, and from 1900 regularly commissioned works by <u>Edward Elgar</u>.

MORE, WILLIAM (1472-1559?)

One of the last priors at Worcester, and apparently not one of the best. He entered Worcester Priory in 1488, becoming prior in 1518. His journal suggests he spent most of his time visiting his manors at Battenhall and elsewhere, lavishly entertaining distinguished visitors and using his position for the benefit of friends and relatives. His behaviour caused much dissension in the priory. Foreseeing the Dissolution he resigned in 1535, obtaining a good pension, exemption from a debt of £100, and the repair of his house at Crowle (near Worcester), where he died. The last prior was <u>Henry Holbech</u>, appointed 1536, who became first Dean of Worcester after the Dissolution.

MORGAN, HENRY FREDERICK STANLEY (1881-1959)

Car manufacturer. Son of a Herefordshire clergyman, he studied engineering in London and served an apprenticeship at the GWR Railway Works in Swindon. In 1905 he and a friend opened a garage and motor works in Malvern Link, and he also ran bus services to Malvern Wells and later Gloucester. In 1909 he built his first three-wheeler car, with the help of family friend W. Stephenson-Peach, engineering master at Malvern College, where he was allowed use of the well-equipped workshop. There was no intention of marketing the car – in fact he had initially intended to make a motorbike – but after favourable comments, three single-seaters were displayed at the Olympia Motor Show in 1910, though greater success came in the following year, with a proposed two-seater version, and the Morgan became the only car ever to appear in the shop window at Harrods. In 1912 a limited company was formed, with 'Harry' as managing director, and his father, Revd H.G. Morgan, as chairman. Its first base was on the Worcester Road leading into Great Malvern, and car production began at its present site in Pickersleigh Road after the

Malvern car-maker 'Harry' Morgan.

First World War. The reputation of the company's models was established through frequent sporting and reliability trial successes, in which both he and his sister, Dorothy, drove. The first four-seater prototype was made in 1912 and produced from 1919. The firm is now run by the founder's grandson and employs more than 160 people who hand-build almost 700 cars each year, for which there is always a waiting list.

MORLEY, GEORGE (*c.* 1598-1684)
Bishop of Worcester, 1660-2 – the first bishop after the Restoration. As a Royalist, he was ejected from an earlier position in 1648, and ministered to the Royalists abroad. In 1660 he was received at Worcester with great joy, and escorted into the city by troops of Royalist volunteers under Sir John Pakington and Lord Windsor. He preached the sermon at the Coronation of Charles II in 1661. The difficult times led him to refuse a licence to <u>Richard Baxter</u> as Vicar of Kidderminster. He was translated to Winchester in 1662.

MORRIS, THOMAS (1660-1748)
Disappointed Stuart supporter, whose epitaph inspired poets. Born at Upton, he was a Minor Canon of Worcester and Vicar of Claines in 1688, but in that year James II, last of the Stuart kings, was replaced by William III. Thomas refused the oath of allegiance to the new king, and in 1689 lost his parish. Further disappointment at the failure of the last attempt at Stuart restoration by Bonnie Prince Charlie in 1745, led him to direct that he be buried

in Worcester Cathedral under a flat stone bearing only a single word, *Miserrimus* (most miserable). The pathos of this epitaph inspired several poets, most notably Wordsworth. His sonnet appeared in a publication edited by Frederic Mansel Reynolds, who wrote a novel of that name in 1833. Neither man knew whose gravestone it was, since Thomas had insisted his name must not be on it.

MORRIS, WILLIAM, LORD NUFFIELD (1877-1963)

Industrialist Lord Nuffield.

Father of the British motor industry, and leading philanthropist. Born at 47 Spring Hill Cottages, St John's, Worcester (now 47 Comer Gardens), he was the son of drapery traveller Frederick Morris and wife Emily, who had moved from Oxford. When he was 2 they returned there and at 15 he began work repairing bicycles, starting his own business at the family home nine months later when he was refused a pay rise. He progressed to manufacturing bicycles, then motorbikes, and by 1912 was producing the first Morris Oxford cars at a site at Cowley, Oxford. He pioneered mass-production of cheap, efficient cars, and by 1939 his company had produced a million vehicles. He took over a string of other companies, including Wolseley, Riley and Autovia, and in 1952 Morris merged with Austin to form British Motor Corporation. He married in 1904, but had no children and donated £40 million to good causes. He often returned to Worcester, being one of the guests at the opening of the widened Worcester Bridge in 1932, and was a generous supporter of Worcester Infirmary. He was made Freeman of Worcester (1937) and Droitwich (1951), baronet (1929), Baron Nuffield (1934), and finally Viscount (1938). All of these titles became extinct on his death. BMC became British Leyland in 1968, but the company closed in 2005.

MORTON, RICHARD (1637-1698)

Clergyman who became a notable doctor. Son of Robert Morton (Minister of St Anne's, Bewdley), he became vicar of a Staffordshire parish, and friend of <u>Richard Baxter</u>, but was ejected in 1662 for religious reasons, and studied medicine, becoming physician to William III. An innovative doctor, he wrote pioneering books on consumption (tuberculosis) and fevers, widely read throughout Europe. He died and was buried in London.

Cleric and doctor Richard Morton.

MORTON, SIR WILLIAM (1605-1672)

Lawyer and judge; son of James Morton, of Clifton, south of Worcester. Called to the Bar in 1630, he took up arms in the royal cause. Knighted, and served as Lieutenant Colonel in Lord Chandos' Horse, he was governor of Sudeley Castle, Gloucestershire, when it surrendered, and was imprisoned in the Tower of London for some years. After the war he returned to the Bar, was Recorder of Gloucester, and Counsel to the Dean and Chapter of Worcester (1662), and Judge on King's Bench (1663). In later years he lived in Kidlington, Oxfordshire, and built an almshouse there in memory of his wife and children, whose names are inscribed above the windows. He was buried in Temple Church, London.

MOSS, JOSEPH WILLIAM (1808-1862)

Eccentric doctor and biographer, born at Dudley (then in Worcestershire). His chief work, published before he was 20, was a large, closely-printed *Manual of Classical Biography*, for which he claimed to have consulted 3,000 different volumes. Critics pointed out many errors, but it was still a standard reference work a century later. Regarded as an eccentric recluse, he practised medicine at Dudley, and lived successively at Lichfield, Ross, and Wells, where he died.

MYATT, JAMES (1804-1879)

Champion of Worcestershire market gardening. Born at Loughborough, he was a market gardener at Camberwell, London, before taking a farm at Offenham (near Evesham), where he grew market garden crops on a large scale, especially asparagus, rhubarb, and strawberries. His innovative cultivation produced a number of new varieties, such as the British Queen strawberry, said never to be surpassed for flavour; Early Offenham cabbage; and Myatt's Early Ash-leaf potatoes. Together with his clever development of apple stocks, these pioneering innovations assisted in the substantial growth of cultivation in the Vale of Evesham. For many years he was a churchwarden of Offenham, and friends remembered him as a quiet, patient man.

NABBES, THOMAS (1605-1645)

Minor dramatist. He is supposed to have come from a humble Worcestershire family, but presumably with wealthier relatives since he attended Oxford and, despite leaving without a degree, entered the household of a Worcestershire nobleman. In 1630 he settled in London as a dramatist. His first comedy, *Covent Garden*, ridiculing the middle classes, was acted by The Queen's Servants in 1632, and his comedies and masques were popular – though not his tragedies. In 1628 he wrote an *Encomium of the Leaden Steeple at Worcester, repayred in 1628*, in which he expressed a wish to be buried in the cathedral. He was, however, probably buried in Temple Church, London. All his plays were reprinted in 1887.

NANFAN, SIR RICHARD (1445-1507)

Diplomat, statesman, and most famously, patron of Cardinal Wolsey. He was born at Birtsmorton Court (near Malvern), son of John, a faithful servant of Henry V in the French wars. He was appointed High Sheriff of Worcestershire (1485) and Commissioner of the

Peace for Cornwall, where his family had originated. He was knighted in 1488 and sent on a diplomatic mission to Spain and Portugal. In 1492 he attended the King in peace negotiations with France, and became governor of Calais, subsequently appointing Thomas Wolsey as his chaplain. He furthered the future cardinal's meteoric rise by securing him a position as a royal chaplain, probably when he retired to Birtsmorton. He had no children by his wife, so when he died his estates passed to his illegitimate son, John, though only after a lawsuit with the widow. His descendant Captain John Nanfan was Lieutenant Governor of New York, 1697-1705.

NASH, JOHN (1590-1662)

Wealthy Worcester clothier, of a family which originated at Ombersley (near Worcester), and owned mills along the River Salwarpe. He was Mayor (1633) and MP for Worcester (1640-8). Despite being an alderman in a city which stood out firmly for the King, he commanded a troop of horse for Parliament during the Civil War. He left money to establish Nash's Hospital almshouses, on the site of old almshouses in New Street, Worcester (where he had lived) and left legacies for clothing apprentices, and setting up young men in business. Buried at St Helen's, Worcester. His almshouses were rebuilt in the 1950s, but his imposing half-timbered home,

Wealthy clothier John Nash.

probably built by his grandfather, still stands. His younger brother, James, purchased an estate at Martley in 1660, and the family were squires there until 1937.

NASH, TREADWAY RUSSELL (1725-1811)

Worcestershire historian, born of a wealthy family at Clerkenleap, Kempsey. Aged 12 he attended King's School, Worcester, but three years later went to Worcester College, Oxford, graduating MA in 1747. His health weakened and he spent the next two years on a European 'grand tour'. He then remained at Oxford, tutor and Dean of Worcester College, and vicar of a nearby parish, until 1757. In 1758 he married and purchased an estate at Bevere (near Worcester). In 1761 he became Vicar of Warndon, and St Peter's, Droitwich. He was appointed Vicar of Leigh (near Malvern) in 1792, and then Rector of Strensham (1797). His great work was *Collections for the History of Worcestershire*, vol. I, 1781; vol. II, 1782; supplement, 1799. He also published an edition of <u>Samuel Butler</u>'s *Hudibras* in 1793. He died at Bevere and was buried at St Peter's, Droitwich. His only child, Margaret, married John Somers-Cocks, who in 1806 became Lord Somers.

NEVILLE, RICHARD, EARL OF WARWICK AND SALISBURY (1428-1471)

Major Worcestershire landowner, known to history as 'Warwick the Kingmaker'. Born probably at Bisham, Berkshire, eldest son of the first Earl of Salisbury; by marriage and inheritance he succeeded in 1449 to the Warwick earldom and estates, including castles at Worcester, Elmley Castle, Warwick, Cardiff, Glamorgan and Barnard Castle, and many manors in Worcestershire. Enormously wealthy and powerful, his undoubted political and military skills made him a key figure in the Wars of the Roses. In 1455 he joined a Yorkist rebellion against Henry VI, and distinguished himself at the first Battle of St Albans, becoming Captain of Calais, which gave him a European powerbase. In 1460 his father was defeated and executed, making him Earl of Salisbury. At the Battle of Northampton he captured Henry VI, then backed the claim of the young Yorkist Earl of March, who became Edward IV in 1461, though Warwick largely controlled the King. Edward's growing independence in the following years disrupted the relationship, however, and in 1470 Warwick drove Edward out of England, reinstating

Richard Neville, Earl of Warwick.

Henry VI. The change was short-lived; Edward raised an army and defeated and killed Warwick at the Battle of Barnet in 1471. He was buried at Bisham Abbey.

NICHOLAS (d. 1124)

Prior of Worcester, whose parents were friends of Wulfstan II, Bishop of Worcester. The future saint baptised him, and sent him to Canterbury to be educated. In 1133 he returned to be Prior of Worcester. He corresponded much with the historian Eadmer, and the monastery acquired a good reputation for learning in his time. He often quoted Wulfstan, and historian William of Malmesbury said the bishop miraculously arrested the tendency of Nicholas's hair to fall out. Within a week of Wulfstan's death Nicholas was bald!

NICHOLSON, GEORGE (1760-1825)

The work of this printer and author was envied and copied nationwide. Son of a Bradford printer, he also became a printer at Bradford, Manchester, and Shropshire, but chiefly at Bridge Street, Stourport. Though only a country bookseller, he revolutionised publishing, setting new standards in style and appearance of pocket volumes, and creating a taste for handy editions of favourite authors. He used the best artists and engravers for frontispieces and portraits, and his work was soon imitated by major London booksellers. In 1797 he started his *Literary Miscellany*, which ran to twenty volumes and is now much sought after. He was also an author, producing 'improving' moral books and tracts. The many local publications he produced at Stourport included Mary Southall's *Malvern* (1822, second edition, 1825) and John Crane's *Poems by a Bird of Bromsgrove*, which went through seven editions at least. He was buried in Stourport churchyard.

NOAKE, JOHN (1816-1894)

Newspaperman, local historian, and saviour of Worcester's historic Guildhall. Dorset-born son of a builder and surveyor, he came to Worcester by 1857, possibly having been a journalist in Birmingham, and worked successively on *Berrow's Worcester Journal*, as a sub-editor on the *Worcester Herald*, and then at the *Worcester News*. He lived at St George's Square between 1862 and 1879, and later at London Road. He married three times but still found leisure to write almost a dozen volumes of local history, and was Secretary of the Worcester Architectural and Archaeological Society for many years. A passionate enthusiast for preservation of local heritage, in the 1870s he fought his most important campaign when Worcester's ageing Guildhall needed substantial repairs, and there was a move to replace it instead. He strongly opposed this, and was Mayor in 1880 when the Guildhall was restored, at the substantial

Journalist John Noake.

cost of £22,000. He resigned from work in 1892, in his mid 70s, owing to increasing deafness. He was buried in Astwood Road Cemetery. Surprisingly, there is no portrait of him in the building that he saved for posterity.

NORRIS, WILLIAM (1821-1904)

Solicitor and great community activist. Youngest son of a Leicestershire clergyman, he purchased a practice in Tenbury, 1849, and spent his life in the town. He held various official appointments, but it was with the many voluntary organisations of his time that he really made his mark. The Tenbury Dispensary, the Cottage Hospital, the Benefit Societies, the Social Club, the cricket and football clubs, all found in him a generous and active supporter. He was one of the chief pioneers in the Volunteer Movement, 1859, in the building of the Corn Exchange, the founding of the Tenbury Agricultural Society, and especially in the promotion of Tenbury, Bewdley, and Woofferton Railway (1858). It was largely due to his tact and perseverance that many initial difficulties were overcome and the railway completed. He was also much involved with St Michael's Church. He took a leading role in the restoration of the church, served as churchwarden for thirty-two years, and was a life-long Sunday school teacher. It was largely due to his exertions that the National Schools at Tenbury were built, 1855. He died suddenly, aged 83. A memorial window in Tenbury church, and an alabaster plaque beneath, were placed there in his memory by his many friends.

NOTT, JOHN (1751-1825)

Worcester-born doctor, traveller and author. He studied surgery at Birmingham, London, and Paris, and in 1783 travelled to China as surgeon to an East Indian vessel. After 1793 he settled at Bristol where he remained for the rest of his life. He was a classical scholar, and wrote many books.

NYE, NATHANIEL (b. 1624)

Mathematician, author and Master Gunner at Worcester for Parliament during the Civil War. Baptised in Birmingham, possibly the son of a King Edward's School governor, he may well have attended there. In 1642 he published *A New Almanacke for the faire and populous Towne of Birmingham*, in which he was described as a 'Practitioner of Astronomy'. He also developed an interest in guns, Birmingham's major product at that time, and in gunnery. In 1645 he was Master Gunner of the Parliamentary garrison at Evesham, and in the following year successfully directed the artillery at the Siege of Worcester, relating his experiences in his 1647 book, *The Art of Gunnery, for the help of all such gunners and others that have charge of artillery, and are not well versed in arithmetic and geometry.* Published at Bromsgrove, it dealt with every branch of gunnery and sieges, even mixing gunpowder and curing gunshot wounds. There were two further editions in 1648 and 1670, but nothing further is known of his life.

Gunner Nathaniel Nye.

ODDA, EARL (c. 993-1056)

Powerful Worcestershire nobleman who became a monk. He may have been born near Pershore, though Deerhurst, Gloucestershire, is more likely. Son of Mercian Earl Aelfhere, who had taken Deerhurst and Longdon (near Malvern) from Pershore Abbey, it was apparently always Odda's intention to restore them. He held estates in Worcestershire, and acquired much additional land during the reign of his kinsman, Edward the Confessor. Late in life he was ordained as a monk by Bishop Aldred of Worcester. He died at Deerhurst, where he had built a chantry chapel, and was buried at Pershore Abbey. Chronicler John of Worcester said he was 'restorer of the poor, defender of widows and orphans, helper of the oppressed'. Since he died without an heir, his lands, including Pershore, were given to Westminster Abbey.

ORLETON, ADAM DE (c. 1275-1365)

Controversial Bishop of Worcester (1327-33), regarded as crafty, bold and unscrupulous by contemporaries. Probably born in Herefordshire, possibly a relative of powerful Marcher Lords the Mortimers, he was Doctor of Laws and the King's agent at the court of Pope Clement V from 1308. He was consecrated as Bishop of Hereford by the Pope in 1317, despite the King's opposition. Much involved with the barons' opposition to Edward II, he contrived the escape of one of the Mortimers from the Tower of London. He undoubtedly had a role in forcing the King's abdication, though the accusation of involvement in his murder is less certain. In 1327 he was 'provided' to Worcester by the Pope, though <u>Wulstan Bransford</u>, Prior of Worcester, had already been elected bishop. He was translated to Winchester in 1333.

OSBORN, JOHN (1584?-1634?)

Worcestershire-born worker in pressed horn and whalebone, who settled in Amsterdam, 1600. His medallion portraits in pressed horn of the Prince of Orange and his wife are in the British Museum, and that of Henry VIII in the Ryks Museum in Amsterdam. He left a son who carried on his business.

OSWALD, SAINT (d. 992)

Bishop of Worcester (961-92) and one of Worcester Cathedral's two saints. Of Danish parentage, he was brought up by his uncle Oda, Archbishop of Canterbury. Some years at the Benedictine Abbey of Fleury in France made him an ardent champion of monasticism. When he succeeded Dunstan at Worcester, he used persuasion – rather than the more brutal tactics used elsewhere – to turn secular clergy into monks at Worcester, Evesham, Pershore, Winchcombe and Deerhurst. He also founded monasteries at Wiltshire and Huntingdonshire. At Worcester he built the new monastic Church of St Mary, close to the old cathedral, and within ten years the old foundation was absorbed and the canons became monks. He is also believed to have established the Hospital of St Oswald in The Tything, making it one of the oldest charitable foundations in the country. In 972 Oswald became Archbishop of York, but still retained Worcester. He died at Worcester while washing the feet of the poor, which he did every day during Lent. He was buried in the monastic church he had built, though his remains were moved to the cathedral ten years later.

OSWEN, JOHN (fl. 1549-1553)

First Worcestershire printer. A printer at Ipswich in 1548, but was in Worcester early 1549, perhaps hoping his radical Protestant views would be better tolerated there. From his press in the High Street, on 30 January 1549, came *A Consultorie for all Christians*, the first book printed in Worcestershire. It included a copy of his royal licence, dated 6 January 1549, as official printer of Wales and the border counties of Shropshire, Herefordshire, Gloucestershire and Worcestershire. Over the next four years he printed twenty books in Worcester, including radical Protestant theological works and 'commissioned' works, such as Cranmer's New Testament (1550) and Book of Common Prayer (1552) and was said to have been patronised by Cardinal Wolsey.

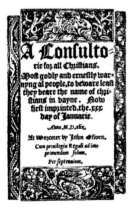

Title page of the first book printed in Worcestershire.

He was made a Freeman of Worcester in 1553. Soon after the accession of Catholic Queen Mary in July 1553, the Worcester press suddenly ceased to exist. No doubt, like many other radicals, he sold up – his types were in use in London in the late 1550s – and fled abroad. It was ordered that all his books be burnt and their owners treated as rebels, making these volumes extremely scarce, though a few copies were known in the county a century ago. Only three copies are known of the first Worcester book, two of them at Cambridge. There was no other printer at Worcester until <u>Stephen Bryan</u> arrived in 1709.

OTTLEY, ALICE (1840-1912)

Headteacher so revered that her Worcester school was named after her. Third of twelve children of a Yorkshire clergyman, she had no formal training or qualifications as a teacher, but was said to have gained her experience bringing up a tribe of younger brothers and sisters. On her father's death in 1861, the family moved to Hampstead, and opened a girls' school. In the early days of Cambridge Local Examinations she obtained a certificate in honours with five distinctions. After further experience at a school in Brondesbury, London, famous in its day, she was chosen in 1883 to become first headmistress of the High School for Girls at Worcester, founded by Dean <u>William John Butler</u>, at Britannia House on The Tything. She had furnished rooms, £250 per year, and £1 for every girl on roll over 150. By 1897 the

Alice Ottley in 1881.

roll had shot up to 205. During her twenty-nine years' work Miss Ottley exercised a strong influence on the school and public life of Worcester. She retired in 1912 due to ill health, and died on the day the school assembled for the first time under her successor. In recognition of her role in building the school, the governing council renamed it Alice Ottley School. It recently became part of Worcester Royal Grammar School.

OUSELEY, SIR FREDERICK ARTHUR GORE (1825-1889)

Composer, clergyman and founder of a Worcestershire college. London-born only son of a diplomat and baronet, he had the Dukes of Wellington and York as his godfathers. His musical skills were evident from an early age; he played Mozart and Beethoven on the piano aged 5, and composed an opera aged 8. He succeeded to the baronetcy in 1844, graduated MA in 1849, was ordained, and became curate at St Barnabas Church, Pimlico, London, where he met expenses of the choir from his own pocket. When, in 1851, religious troubles caused the break-up of the parish clerical team, he became concerned about the boys of the choir and opened an establishment near Windsor, subsequently moved to Tenbury Wells, where he set up

College founder Sir Frederick Ouseley.

St Michael's College for boys (1856) on an estate known as Old Wood. He also became Vicar of St Michael's. In 1855 he had become Precentor of Hereford and Professor of Music at Oxford, both of which posts he held until his death. At both college and university he laboured to make musical scholarship a respected form of learning, and filled the college library with many rare volumes and musical scores. He was a prolific composer of religious music. He died at Hereford. His college closed due to financial difficulties in 1985. An international school now occupies the site, and the college chapel has become a parish church. His library was transferred to the Bodleian Library, Oxford.

OWEN, NICHOLAS (*c.* 1562-1606)

Carpenter who saved many priests. Born in Oxfordshire, he was apprenticed to a joiner and in 1588 became servant to Jesuit superior Henry Garnett, who was tasked with hiding priests secretly ministering to Catholic families. Nicholas began using his craft skills to construct secret hiding places, especially at Harvington Hall, where he worked from around 1600. He was finally captured at Hindlip Hall (near Worcester), and tortured at the Tower of London, but died without revealing the location of any of his 'hides', and one at Harvington was not found for 300 years.

PADDOCK, TOM (1822-1863)

Bare-knuckle boxer, born at Redditch, hence his nickname 'The Needlepointer'. A skilful, courageous fighter who won ten out of his fifteen known bouts, and became Heavyweight Champion of England, but his violent temper often let him down. He first fought in 1844, and had seven bouts by 1847, winning all. But in 1850, he failed to take the title from William 'Bendigo'

Thompson, despite outclassing the ageing champion fighting his last match, because he angrily kicked Bendigo while he was down and was disqualified. In the same year he also fouled his way to defeat against Bill Perry, the 'Tipton Slasher'. In the following year a riot broke out during a bout against Harry Poulson in Derbyshire, and both boxers were jailed for ten months' hard labour. In 1854 he challenged Perry and Harry Broome of Suffolk, and when both declined he declared himself champion by default, though his title wasn't recognised until he beat Broome in fifty-one rounds in May 1856. He lost the title to Tom Sayers in his next bout in June 1858, and was beaten by Sam Hurst in a further title attempt in 1860. He died of heart disease in London in his early 40s, after a long illness.

Bare-knuckle boxer Tom Paddock.

PADMORE, RICHARD (1789-1881)

MP and businessman. Son of Thomas Padmore, of Ketley Ironworks, Shropshire. In 1818 he joined iron-founders Robert and John Hardy, with premises at Foundry Street, Worcester, and in 1829 they went into partnership as Hardy & Padmore. In 1823 he married Emma, the only daughter of John Jones, of Worcester, who had extensive iron-founding interests in the city, and the couple lived at Henwick Hall. He also became Chairman of the Worcester City and County Banking Company, and was busy with civic duties. He was Sheriff of Worcester (1845), twice Mayor, Justice of the Peace for Worcestershire and MP for Worcester (1860-8). He died aged 91. Hardy & Padmore produced

MP Richard Padmore.

street furniture castings which went all over the world, and many fine, decorative, iron castings – including the dolphin lamps on Westminster embankment, London, and a much-admired fountain, presented to Worcester by Richard Padmore in 1858, for use in the market hall, now in Cripplegate Park. The City and County bank merged with Lloyd's in 1889. Hardy & Padmore closed in 1967.

PAGANELL, GERVASE (c. 1127-1188)

Dudley, in Worcestershire until 1966, was demolished because of him. He was Lord of Dudley, and involved himself in the rebellion of Prince Henry in 1173. As a result, Henry II demolished the town. Paganell also founded a Cluniac priory about 1161, the ruins of which are in Priory Park, near Paganel Drive.

PAKINGTON, SIR JOHN (d. 1560)

The founder of the family fortunes was a lawyer, and eldest son of John Pakington by Elizabeth, daughter and heir of Thomas Washbourne, of Stanford (near Clifton-upon-Teme). In 1529 he was Treasurer of the Inner Temple, and clearly a favourite of Henry VIII, since he was granted the right to wear his hat in the King's presence. In 1532 he became Justice for North Wales, and lived chiefly at Hampton Court, Hampton Lovett (near Droitwich), which he purchased in 1524. Recorder of Worcester, he was knighted in 1545 and received Westwood (near Droitwich), the former Westwood Priory, from Henry VIII. At his death he held thirty-one manors, and many other lands. He was buried at Hampton Lovett. Hampton Court was destroyed during the Civil War.

PAKINGTON, SIR JOHN (1549-1625)

First baronet; great-nephew of Sir John Pakington; another lawyer. When Elizabeth visited Worcestershire in 1575, she was so struck by his wit and beauty that she invited him to court, gave him a knighthood and the nickname 'Lusty Pakington'. He also became a member of the Privy Council, but lived beyond his means in London, and ended up in debt. Elizabeth gave him the paid office of Bow-bearer of Malvern Chase, and offered him an estate in Suffolk, but when he went to see it, he was so moved by the distress of the late owner's widow that he begged the Queen to bestow it on her instead. More careful living, and a wealthy marriage in 1592, restored his fortunes, and he devoted much time to the improvement of Westwood, of which he built the central portion. He also formed the lake in the park, much to the annoyance of neighbours who claimed he had altered the boundaries. He angrily responded by destroying the dykes damming the water, and flooding the country for miles round. He also had property at Aylesbury, Buckinghamshire, where he entertained James I in 1603. He died and was buried there.

PAKINGTON, SIR JOHN (1621-1680)

Second baronet. During the Commonwealth he lost his lands three times! He was MP for Worcestershire before he was 20 (1640) and Aylesbury (1641), but as a Royalist he was ejected, and joined the King's army. Captured and imprisoned in the Tower of London in 1645, his estates were confiscated. His house in Buckinghamshire was levelled, and he only recovered his Worcestershire estates in 1648-9, on payment of £5,000. Two years later he lost them again, after he was captured at the Battle of Worcester (1651), bringing reinforcements to the future Charles II. This time he was cleared after two years because no one would give evidence against him, perhaps because he was captured by the Scots, but he was in constant trouble under the Commonwealth, and later lost his lands for the third time. After the Restoration, Charles II rewarded him for his loyalty. He was MP for Worcestershire from 1661 until 1679. Buried at Hampton Lovett. His wife was Lady Dorothy Pakington.

PAKINGTON, LADY DOROTHY (1623-1679)

Wife of second baronet, Sir John Pakington. She sheltered many of the clergy thrown out of their parishes under the Commonwealth, so that Westwood became the centre of the old High Church party. Her association with clergy, and her reputation for wide reading and deep thought, caused her to be regarded as the author of *The Whole Duty of Man*, a religious work published anonymously in 1658 – but it was more likely to have been written by Dr Richard Allestree, Provost of Eton. She died in the same year as her husband, and was buried with him at Hampton Lovett.

PAKINGTON, SIR JOHN
(1671-1727)

Fourth baronet. There is a long-established tradition that he was the inspiration for Addison's fictional Worcestershire baronet, Sir Roger de Coverley. He became MP for Worcestershire in 1690, before he was 20, and with one short break, remained so until his death. An opinionated High Church Tory, he frequently admonished the House on subjects such as the conduct of bishops. He was arrested for supposed complicity in a Stuart rising in 1715, but acquitted. In Worcestershire he quarrelled bitterly with Bishop Lloyd, whom he claimed had interfered in his election in 1702, though by 1706 they were on very amicable terms again, when the Pakington family paid a Sunday visit to

Fourth baronet Sir John Pakington.

the bishop at Hartlebury. He was buried at Hampton Lovett and the succession passed to his son, Herbert Perrott Pakington, Worcestershire MP, whose two sons, John and Herbert, were the sixth and seventh baronets. The title became extinct on the death of the eighth baronet, but was revived in favour of John Somerset Russell, his nephew.

PAKINGTON, SIR JOHN SOMERSET, FIRST BARON HAMPTON (1799-1880)

Politician and son of William Russell, of Powick Court (near Worcester). On succeeding in 1831 to the estate of his mother's brother, Sir John Pakington, he took that family name. He was created baronet in 1846. An MP for Droitwich (1837-74), he served in office under two Prime Ministers. He became a Privy Councillor in 1852, and was Secretary of State for War and Colonies in Lord Derby's first ministry, granting a representative constitution to New Zealand. In 1858, as First Lord of the Admiralty, he proposed building the first two iron-clad ships. In 1867 he became War Secretary under Disraeli. He also served as Chairman of Worcestershire Quarter Sessions (1834-58). Defeated in the election of 1874, he was made a peer, Baron Hampton of Hampton Lovett and Westwood. He died in London and was buried at Hampton Lovett. Descendants have continued to bear the title he first held, but the Westwood estate was sold by the family in 1900.

PARKER, GEORGE (1654-1743)

Disreputable astrologer, born at Shipston-on-Stour (part of Worcestershire until 1931). He went to London, aged about 15, either to become an apprentice cutler or to escape creditors, and later opened a tavern in 1698. He certainly became almanac-maker, astrologer, and quack doctor, at the Ball and Star (Salisbury Court, Strand), much to the disgust of rival John Partridge, who already carried on the same trade there – they frequently had violent quarrels. He was fined £50 for controversial content in one of his almanacs. He was said to be a Quaker, but married a zealous churchwoman, and it was said that they laboured so hard to convince each other of their views, that Parker ended as a High Churchman, and his wife a rigid Quaker. Not surprisingly they parted, and he became

Astrologer George Parker.

bankrupt. He later married again and visited relatives in Worcestershire to introduce his new wife. He died in London.

PARKES, DAVID (1763-1833)

Schoolmaster, draughtsman and antiquary, born at Cakemore, near Halesowen (then in Worcestershire). Apprenticed to a japanner (enameller) at Birmingham, he disliked the trade and set up a mercantile school in Shrewsbury. He spent his leisure travelling Shropshire making drawings of antiquities, a number of which no longer exist. He also collected books and prints of the county, and contributed to the *Gentleman's Magazine*. Prints of his detailed sketches are still much in demand. His biography was published in 1979.

PARKES, SAMUEL (1761-1825)

Chemist and author. Born at Stourbridge (then in Worcestershire), he settled in London as a chemical manufacturer. A colourful character and energetic champion for chemistry, he threw himself enthusiastically into the task of producing, between 1806 and 1815, a series of popular scientific manuals, which drew large numbers of students to pursue the chemical sciences by his lively writing style. His best known work was probably the *Chemical Catechism* (1806), which ran to twelve editions, and included poetical descriptions of chemical processes. His books also appeared in Europe and America, and

Chemist Samuel Parkes.

received many honours from learned societies. His scientific essays advanced the progress of chemical technology, and he was one of the key figures in the campaign to abolish salt duties, which had a major impact on salt production in Droitwich. He died and was buried in London.

PARRY, HENRY (1561-1616)
Bishop of Worcester, 1610-16. Previously chaplain to Queen Elizabeth I, for whom he read prayers on her death bed, and Bishop of Gloucester (1607). James I said he was the best preacher he had ever heard, and the King of Denmark gave him a valuable ring in appreciation of a sermon. Buried in Worcester Cathedral, where there is a memorial to him.

PAYNE, ERNEST (1884-1961)
Olympic champion and Worcester and Manchester United footballer. Born in a cottage at 221 London Road, Worcester, he became a carpenter but achieved fame as a sportsman. He made his sporting debut at a St John's Cycling Club event, on a bicycle he borrowed from his brother, and despite his short, stocky build, was quickly spotted by club officials as a potential champion. He joined the club in 1903 and was soon referred to in the cycling press as 'Ernie, the Worcester Wonder', winning 150 races in eight years. The highlight of his cycling career came at the London Olympics in 1908, when he was one of the four-man team which took gold for Britain in the Pursuit event, beating Germany by ten seconds. His football career began in 1908 or earlier. During the first half of 1909 he played several times for Manchester United, and also signed for Worcester City, having been a member

Olympic champion Ernie Payne.

of the team which won the Birmingham League in 1912. He lost his Olympic medal while serving in France in the First World War, but a replica is in Worcester Museum.

PEARSON, THOMAS (1774-1857)
Rector of Stockton-on-Teme (1808-28) and Witley (1828-57), and chaplain to Queen Adelaide at Great Witley. A very active county magistrate and administrator, he was involved with the building of the Shire Hall at Worcester. He founded, and for many years was secretary of, the Worcestershire Prisoners' Aid Society. A strong supporter of the Worcestershire Friendly Society and of the Worcester Infirmary, he was also the first to establish the allotment system in the county.

PENNETHORNE, SIR JAMES (1801-1871)

Architect who, over thirty years, planned and built much of Victorian London. Born in Worcester, he went to London in 1820 to study with the great architect John Nash. He was said to be the son of Worcester hop merchant Thomas Pennethorne, but it was claimed that James and his brothers were actually illegitimate offspring of the Prince Regent and Nash's new wife. Whatever the truth of this, James was treated almost as an adopted son by Nash and groomed as his successor. After studying drawing under Pugin and travelling in Europe to study architecture, he became Nash's chief assistant in 1828, and in 1839 was entrusted with two major urban redevelopment schemes, in which New Oxford Street and the docklands highway, Commercial Way, were created. From 1845 he was sole surveyor of the crown estate in London. His work included the Public Record Office, the ballroom at Buckingham Palace, the west wing of Somerset House, the Army Staff College at Sandhurst, and the design of Kennington, Victoria and Battersea parks. There are few Londoners who will not regularly come in contact with some aspect of his work. He retired and was knighted in 1870, and died in London the following year from heart disease. A major new study of his work, *Sir James Pennethorne and the Making of Victorian London*, was published in 1992.

PENNETHORNE, JOHN (1808-1888)

Architect and mathematician, younger brother of Sir James, he also entered Nash's office for a time. In 1830 he started a long working tour in Europe and Egypt. In 1837 he made observations at the Parthenon, which led to the reversal of the theory that Greek architecture was absolutely rectilinear. He found instead that classical architects had subtly curved lines to heighten the sense of proportion and symmetry of their buildings. He published details of his discovery in *The Elements and Mathematical Principles of the Greek Architects and Artists* (1844), but his major work was the superbly-produced folio edition, *The Geometry and Optics of Ancient Architecture* (1878), illustrated by examples from Thebes, Athens, and Rome. He never married. In later years he lived on the Isle of Wight, where he died.

PEROWNE, JOHN JAMES STEWART (1823-1904)

Bishop of Worcester (1891-1901) and previously an academic and Dean of Peterborough (1878-91). He was one of the leading academic theologians of the Old Testament Company for the Revision of the Authorised Version of the English Bible (1870-84). Amongst the books he wrote was one on Arabic grammar. He was buried at Hartlebury. A Worcester school named after him occupied the site on the corner of Barbourne Terrace, and later moved to Merriman's Hill Road. In 2002 Bishop Perowne C of E College became the first Worcestershire school to take Performing Arts status.

PERRINS, WILLIAM HENRY (1793-1867)

Chemist and sauce manufacturer. Born into a farming family at Chaddesley Corbett, educated at Worcester Royal Grammar School and trained as a chemist, he formed a partnership with pharmacist John Wheeley Lea at 68 Broad Street, Worcester in 1823. In 1837 they began producing Lea & Perrins Worcestershire Sauce. He was also a director of Royal Worcester Porcelain. He lived in Lansdowne Crescent, Worcester, and was buried at Claines.

PERROTT, GEORGE (1710-1780)

Yorkshire-born clergyman's son, who became a judge and settled at Pershore. He first became well known for prosecuting the fourth Earl Ferrers, who killed his servant and was the last peer to be hanged at Tyburn (1760). In 1759 he purchased the Lower Avon Navigation Rights, held by his descendants for almost two centuries, and built himself a house in Bridge Street, Pershore, now called Perrott House, where he died.

PHILLIPPS, SIR THOMAS (1792-1872)

Bibliophile Sir Thomas Phillipps.

Antiquarian and bibliophile. Born at Manchester, he was the illegitimate son of textile manufacturer Thomas Phillipps, of a Broadway family, who bought Middle Hill House there in 1794; High Sheriff for Worcestershire, 1801. While still at school he began the collection of manuscripts which almost certainly made him the greatest private collector of all time, though his hobby became a mania, and despite inheriting his father's substantial estate he spent a lifetime in debt. He scoured Britain and Europe, collecting charters, chronicles, chartularies, household books of kings, queens, and nobles, early English poetry, ancient Greek and oriental manuscripts, old Irish and Welsh collections, and many treasures from the libraries of famous monasteries. He collected 60,000 manuscripts, 40,000 printed books, plus coins and pictures. He filled hundreds of notebooks with detailed notes on collected items. He used these materials in many books. In 1822 he set up a private printing press at Broadway Tower, producing a constant stream of short-run books and pamphlets, though printers regularly left, complaining they hadn't been paid. He became a baronet in 1821, High Sheriff of Worcestershire in 1825, and was a Trustee of the British Museum. In 1826 he moved to Cheltenham, where he died and was buried at Broadway. He had allowed Middle Hill House to become ruinous – apparently to spite his eldest daughter, whose husband he violently disapproved of, though the couple completely refurbished it after his death. Broadway Tower was later the country retreat of William Morris. It took more than a century to dispose of his collection, the last sale taking place in New York in 1977.

PHILLIPS, THOMAS (1770-1845)

Distinguished portrait painter, born at Dudley (then in Worcestershire). He trained as a glass painter in Birmingham, and in 1790 was employed for the painted windows of St George's Chapel, Windsor, but turned to portrait painting and was quickly recognised as the pre-eminent portraitist of his time; his illustrious sitters included George Prince of Wales, William Blake,

Byron, Scott, Crabbe, Southey, Coleridge, and <u>Sir Thomas Phillipps</u>. He exhibited at the Royal Academy from 1808 and was Professor of Painting at the Royal Academy from 1825 to 1832. He died in London and was buried there.

PHILLIPS, CATHERINE (1727-1794)

Popular Quaker preacher. She was the youngest of six children of Quaker minister Henry Payton, of Dudley (then in Worcestershire), by Ann, daughter of Henry Fowler, of Evesham. A tall girl with what some saw as rather masculine features, she was educated mainly at home, and first ministered in 1748 in Dudley, 'in but a few words'. After this humble beginning she spent thirty years preaching throughout Britain, in Holland, and for three years in America. She first met her future husband, William Phillips, a widower from Bewdley, in 1749, when he was copper-mining in Cornwall, but was determined to pursue her ministry, and only finally agreed to wed him in Bewdley in 1772. After his death in 1785 she wrote a memoir, published after her death. She died at Redruth, Cornwall, where they lived.

POCHE, HENRY DE (d. 1289)

Little is known of his life, but his funeral was a riot. Apparently a leading Worcester citizen, it was claimed he had requested burial by the Grey Friars at their cemetery in Friar Street, but there was simmering resentment with the monks beside the cathedral, who also claimed the body. The monks violently attacked the friary on 1 March, and snatched the body for burial in their own cemetery, leaving a number of injured friars in their wake. The friars appealed to Archbishop of Canterbury John Peckham, and a rumour about the riot even reached the King. The archbishop backed the friars and ordered the body be returned, but Bishop of Worcester <u>Godfrey Giffard</u> backed the monks, and it took several strongly-worded letters from Peckham before the body was finally exhumed and handed over on 22 December. Despite their supposed promise that they would keep the handover quiet, the friars carried off the body in triumph, 'singing, amidst an uproarious scene', complained the monks.

POER, MARGARET LE (*c.* 1378-1454)

Heiress of Wichenford Court (near Worcester); a formidable lady. About 1400 she became second wife of John Washbourne, of Gloucestershire; Wichenford Court, then one of the largest mansions in the county, became the seat of the Washbournes. In 1405, during Owen Glendower's rebellion, a rebel army marched into Worcestershire. One party of Welshmen, reinforced by French soldiers of fortune, encamped on Woodbury Hill, and descended on the Court. No doubt her husband was away with the English Army, but Margaret was not dismayed. She lured the raiders' chief into the house, and while conducting him to the great panelled chamber on the first floor, stabbed him to death, and his followers were driven off. For centuries after, a dark stain on the floor was shown as the mark of his blood, and his ghost was supposed to haunt the scene of his death. A tomb, dated 1454, with recumbent figures of Margaret and her husband, was in Wichenford church. The Court that Margaret knew was rebuilt in 1712, and much reduced in size.

PRATTINTON, PETER (*c.* 1776-1845)

Important Worcestershire antiquarian. Born at The Redthorne, in Bewdley High Street, only son of wholesale grocer William Prattinton, he took a medical degree at Oxford in 1797, but used his inherited wealth to devote his life to antiquarian research. Though he transcribed much of the material left by Thomas Habington, he never published anything himself, but amassed a substantial collection of unique Worcestershire material. Each August he would leave Bewdley to travel the county for two months, transcribing deeds, rubbing brasses, and collecting books, pamphlets, notices, plans, letters, illustrations and portraits. Returning in October, he would work on his notes until February or March, then go to Worcester, Oxford or London for some months of research. He never married and was buried at Ribbesford. His collection was left to the Society of Antiquaries of London, where it is still preserved. An illustrated volume on the collection was published in Evesham in 1931. The Redthorne was a residential home in recent times.

PREEDY, FREDERICK (1820-98)

Hard-working architect and glass painter. He was born at Offenham, the third son of Evesham hosier William Frederick Preedy, who had been Mayor of the town, as had his father and grandfather. From about 1850 he was designing stained glass for George Rogers of Worcester, and in 1852 set up a practice in Worcester, but after they fell out the following year he taught himself to make stained glass, and his first windows were produced for Church Lench (near Evesham) about 1854. In 1859 he moved to London, where he remained for the rest of his life, though he must have travelled back to the county frequently since many of his commissions were here and in surrounding counties. He is believed to have made some 240 windows for more than 100 churches, but he also built twenty new churches, completely restored at least thirty others, and built at least six schools – and there may well be more of his work not yet identified. He died in Croydon and was buried in Wiltshire.

PRICE, WILLIAM (1780-1830)

Worcester-born assistant secretary and interpreter in Persia (now Iran), in 1811-12, to diplomat Sir Gore Ouseley, father of the founder of St Michael's College, Tenbury Wells. Born the son of a ladies' shoemaker, he initially took up the trade himself, but from 1807 concentrated on his study of languages, for which he had a remarkable facility. He later taught oriental languages in the seminary of his friend, Alexander Humphreys, at Netherstone House, possibly in The Tything, Worcester, and also published Persian books and translations.

PRIDEAUX, JOHN (1578-1650)

Bishop of Worcester, 1641-6. He was Regius Professor of Divinity at Oxford from 1615 to 1641, but as a committed Royalist, he was driven out in 1646, when Parliamentary troops captured the city. He then retired to the house of his son-in-law, Henry Sutton, Rector of Bredon, where he passed the rest of his days in cheerful poverty, and was buried in the chancel of the parish church. More than 600 of his books are in Worcester Cathedral library.

PYTTS, SIR EDWARD (1541-1618)

Eminent lawyer, son of Wilham Pytts, of the Perrie, a sixteenth-century farmhouse at Stoke Bliss (near Tenbury Wells). He had offices in Fleet Street, London, and in 1563 was Filacer – a lucrative legal office now extinct – of London, Middlesex, Huntingdon, and Kent. In 1575 he purchased the Kyre Park estate (near Tenbury), a medieval fortress of the Wyards and Marcher Lords the Mortimers, but by then ruinous. A detailed account of the substantial works he had carried out during 1588-1618 still exists, mostly in his own handwriting. He was knighted at the Coronation of James I in 1603 and made Sheriff of Worcestershire in 1612. He made a fine collection of early books at Kyre. Kyre Park was largely rebuilt in the eighteenth century and the grounds were remodelled by Capability Brown. The gardens are open to the public.

Lawyer Sir Edward Pytts.

RABAN, EDWARD (d. 1658)

Printer, born in Worcestershire. He joined the Netherlands Army in 1600 and, after much fighting and travelling, settled in Scotland as the first printer in Aberdeen (1662) and printer to the council. He issued many books there and married twice, but his home life may not have been entirely harmonious, since in 1638 he printed his own book entitled *The Glorie of Man, Consisting in the Excellencie and Perfection of Woman*, written, he said, 'to vindicate and deliver myself from the imputation of Sarcastick, bitter, too loose & liberall speeches, against the most noble worthie and transcendent sex of Women', though whether this was written entirely without sarcasm is open to question. He died in Aberdeen and was buried there.

RAINSBOROUGH, THOMAS (1610-1648)

Worcestershire MP. Son of an Admiral, his birthplace seems unknown. He first followed a naval career, commanding several vessels, but by 1645 was a Colonel in Cromwell's New Model Army, and took the surrender of Worcester on 19 July 1646. He was MP for Droitwich from 1647 to 1648. As a leading spokesman for the Levellers, a popular democracy movement ahead of its time, he was very popular with ordinary soldiers. When he was killed by Royalists at the Siege of Pontefract in 1648, thousands demonstrated in London. A fictionalised account of his life and death was included in the Channel 4 television series *The Devil's Whore*, 2008.

Thomas Rainsborough.

RALPH OF MANTES (*c.* 1027-1057)

Nephew of King Edward the Confessor; probably earl over Worcestershire. Born in the disputed Vexin on the border of Normandy, son of Edward's sister Goda, he came to England with his uncle in 1041. By 1050 he was an earl, probably of an old Anglo-Saxon tribal area which included Worcestershire and part of Warwickshire. He became Earl of Hereford, probably late 1051, but was in disgrace from 1055, after his dismal defensive failure led to the sacking of Hereford by Welsh raiders and rebel Mercians.

RICHARD (DE WYCHE), SAINT (1197-1253)

Droitwich-born bishop and saint. Younger son of a well-off family, he had no inheritance after his father's death, and may have farmed on the estate of his elder brother. He was offered the land and a good marriage, but preferred study and the Church. He had to attend Oxford as a poor scholar, but rose to be Chancellor of the University. He was Chancellor of the Diocese of Canterbury under Archbishop Edmund Rich, around 1235, and loyally accompanied him abroad in 1240. After the archbishop's death, he studied theology and was ordained at a Dominican house in Orleans. In 1245 he was requested to resume his duties as Chancellor of Canterbury, but in the same year was made Bishop of Chichester by the Pope. This greatly angered Henry III, who had his own candidate, and Richard could not fully take over the see for two years. He continued to oppose Henry over rights of clergy, but was also strict on religious duties. He died at Dover, the day after dedicating a new church to his old master, Edmund Rich, by then St Edmund. He was canonised in 1262, but his shrine at Chichester was destroyed at the Reformation.

RICHARDS, ALFRED BATE (1820-1876)

Newspaper editor, born at Baskerville House, Barbourne, Worcester, the eldest son of Knaresborough MP John Richards of Stourbridge (then in Worcestershire). At Oxford he took a degree (1841), but also produced an anonymous pamphlet, *Oxford Unmasked*, about abuses in the university, which rapidly went through five editions. When the author's identity became known, he thought it wise to move to London. Called to the Bar in 1845, he went on circuit briefly, but in 1848 entered journalism. He started a weekly paper in 1850, which subsequently failed, and in 1855 became first editor of the *Daily Telegraph*. He campaigned strongly for a volunteer rifle corps, and when the government agreed in 1858, he recruited 1,000 men to the 3rd City of London Rifle Corps, and became Colonel. In 1870 he became editor of pub trade newspaper, *Morning Advertiser*, then second only to *The Times* in circulation. He wrote poetry and five dramas, four unpublished. He died in London and was buried in Croydon.

ROBERTS, GEORGE EDWARD (1831-1865)

Amateur geologist and antiquary, born at Birmingham, brought up at Kidderminster. His first publication was on the 'Kidderminster Deposits' in an academic journal in 1857, and thereafter he contributed several papers annually to the *Geologist*, until his death at the early age of 34. His main work was *The Rocks of Worcestershire* (1860), and he also published *Habberley Valley and the Hill of Trimpley* (1857). He died at Kidderminster.

ROGER (1134-1179)

Bishop of Worcester, 1164-79. Son of Robert, Earl of Gloucester, and grandson of Henry I, he was educated with the future Henry II and was consecrated bishop by the ill-fated archbishop, Thomas Becket. He was much involved with the King's quarrel with Becket, but favoured neither side, which angered Henry. He was sent to Rome to express the King's remorse for Becket's murder in 1171, and again in 1178, but died, probably in France, during his journey home.

ROUS, SIR THOMAS (1608-1676)

Son of Sir John Rous of Rous Lench Court (near Evesham), he was Sheriff of Worcestershire in 1610 and 1636. He was created first baronet in 1641, was a Member of Committee for Worcestershire (1645), Assessment Commissioner (1656) and MP for Worcestershire (1654-5 and 1656-8) and Evesham (1660). He was a friend of minister <u>Richard Baxter</u>, and much of Baxter's book, *Saints' Everlasting Rest,* was written at Rous Lench, while Lady Jane Rous nursed him through a serious illness in 1647. The book was dedicated to Sir Thomas and his lady. He married twice more after her death. There were three more baronets until 1721 when the title became extinct. Rous Lench Court now serves as a luxury wedding venue.

ROUSE-BOUGHTON, SIR CHARLES WILLIAM (1747-1821)

Worcestershire baronet, of Poston Court, Herefordshire, born 'Boughton'. He spent some years of his early life in India, but under the will of Thomas (Phillips) Rouse, descendant of <u>Sir Thomas Rous</u>, he succeeded to the Rous Lench estate in 1768, and assumed the name Rouse. MP for Evesham (1780-90) and Bramber (1796-1800) and Secretary to the Board of Control (1784-91), he was created baronet in 1791. In 1782 he married Caroline, heiress of Downton Hall (near Ludlow), which has since become the family's principal residence. His son was MP for Evesham (1818-19 and 1820-6).

ROUTH, MRS MARTHA (1743-1817)

Teacher and preacher, born in Stourbridge (then in Worcestershire), the youngest child of Henry and Jane Winter. She became head of the Friends' boarding school in Nottingham, and in 1773 became a minister. On her marriage to Richard Routh of Manchester in 1776, she left the school and devoted herself to preaching, travelling throughout the British Isles and the United States. In three years she travelled 11,000 miles, and never failed at a single appointed meeting, whatever the difficulty of the roads. At the age of 70 she began to write her journal, which was partly published in 1822. She died and was buried in London.

RUDGE, EDWARD (1630-1696)

Successful businessman and son of William Rudge (Mayor of Evesham, 1661). He became a successful London merchant, and purchased the manor and site of the abbey lands of Evesham in 1664. He was MP for Evesham in 1681 and 1690-5. His son, John (1669-1740), was a merchant in Mark Lane, a Director of the Bank of England (1699) and Deputy Governor of the South Sea Company (1731-40). He was also MP for Evesham (1698-1701, and 1702-34).

RUDGE, EDWARD (1763-1846)

Landowner, amateur botanist and archaeologist; son of a Salisbury merchant who purchased a large portion of the Abbey estate at Evesham. He left university without a degree and turned to botany through the influence of his uncle, a retired barrister who formed a herbarium which he left to his nephew in 1817. Purchase of plants from Guiana led him to study the flora of that country, and publish a book on the subject (1805-7). Between 1811 and 1834 he conducted excavations in parts of the Evesham Abbey estate under his control, and sent the results to the Society of Antiquaries. He also published papers of botanical and archaeological interest. He was Sheriff of Worcestershire in 1829. In 1842 he erected an octagonal tower on the battlefield of Evesham to commemorate Simon de Montfort. He died at Evesham. His son, Edward, wrote *Some Account of the History and Antiquities of Evesham*, 1820.

RUSHOUT, SIR JOHN (1685-1775)

Sir John Rushout.

Whig politician. The son of Sir James Rushout (variously MP for Worcestershire and Evesham), and descendant of Mareschal de Gamaces (Grand Master of the Horse to Louis XI), who settled in London in the reign of Charles I. He was probably born at the Worcestershire estate the family acquired in 1683 – Northwick Park, at Blockley, near Moreton-in-Marsh (transferred to Gloucestershire in 1931). He succeeded as fourth baronet in 1711, and was MP for Malmesbury from 1713 to 1722. In 1722 he was also returned for Evesham and decided to take that seat, which he retained for more than forty years, until 1768. He was Lord of the Treasury (1742-3), Treasurer of the Navy (1743-4), Privy Councillor (1744) and Father of the Commons (1762). Worcestershire historian <u>Treadway Russell Nash</u> said of him: '... at 91 his memory, good humour, and politeness were then in their full bloom'.

RUSHOUT, SIR JOHN, BARON NORTHWICK (1738-1800)

Only son of <u>Sir John Rushout</u>, he was also MP for Evesham, 1761-96. He succeeded to the baronetcy on his father's death and in 1797 was created Baron Northwick of Northwick Park, a new title. He became a Fellow of the Society of Antiquaries in 1799. The title of Baron Northwick became extinct on the death of the fourth baron in 1887 and Northwick Park passed out of the hands of the Rushout family in 1912.

RUSSELL, JOHN (1796-1873)

Industrialist. Born in Worcestershire, his exact birthplace seems unknown, though he had links to the Worcester area, and married at Claines church in 1817. He owned the Worcester Pipe Works, but developed a wide range of business interests here and across the county borders in Gloucestershire and South Wales, including iron works and collieries. He amassed considerable wealth, and divided his time between homes in Cheltenham, Chepstow and London. A gas explosion in 1860 killed 146 miners and bankrupted the mining company, though not Russell personally. However, he had to sell his Monmouthshire estate to set up a trust fund for miners' families, and moved to Gloucestershire, where he died. He and his wife were both buried at St Clement's, Worcester. His four daughters were educated at Oakfield House, Claines, more recently River School.

RUSSELL, SIR WILLIAM (1602-1669)

Landowner and son of Sir Thomas Russell, of Strensham, where the Russells had their seat for centuries, latterly at Strensham Court, demolished in the 1820s. The family also inherited Witley Court, Great Witley, in 1498, and it must have been Sir Thomas who built a grand new house there between 1610 and 1620, the forerunner of the later mansion. William became first Baronet of Wytley in 1627, and lived at Witley Court during the Civil War. He fought under Prince Rupert at Worcester in 1642, and was Governor of the City and MP for the county in 1643. When the city surrendered in July 1646, Colonel Thomas Rainsborough insisted Russell should be exempt from the benefit of the treaty. Friends urged him to escape in disguise, but he insisted on surrendering for the public good, and Sir Thomas Fairfax agreed he should be treated as a prisoner. Fined £500 in 1644 for supporting the King, in 1649 he was imprisoned and lost much of his estates, though they were returned after the Restoration. He must have retained the Witley estate, since it was sold to the Foley family in 1655. He was buried at Strensham. The title Baronet of Wytley became extinct on the death of his son, Francis, last of the Russell male line in 1705.

RUSSELL, SIR WILLIAM OLDNALL (1784-1833)

Distinguished lawyer and legal author. He was son of Samuel Oldnall (Rector of St Nicholas, Worcester, and North Piddle, near Pershore) and of Mary (daughter of William Russell, of Powick), in accordance with whose will he took the name of Russell in 1816. Called to the Bar in 1809, he was appointed Chief Justice of Bengal, and knighted in 1832. He wrote a number of legal books, most notably, *A Treatise on Crimes and Misdemeanours* (1819), described as 'the best treatise on Criminal Law'.

SAEWULF

Eleventh-century Worcester merchant. He was in the habit of annually visiting his bishop, Wulfstan II, to confess much the same sins he had confessed the previous year, wrote twelfth-century historian William of Malmesbury. Wulfstan repeatedly advised him to remove himself from temptation by entering the monastic life. In old age he did become a monk at Malmesbury, and went on pilgrimage to Palestine, leaving a unique account of his journey and the places he visited. The account stopped abruptly after describing the return voyage to the Dardanelles, perhaps suggesting he died during the journey. The only known copy of his manuscript is in the library of Corpus Christi College, Cambridge.

SALWEY, RICHARD (1615-1685)

Fourth son of leading Parliamentarian MP Humphrey Salwey of Stanford Court, Stanford-on-Teme. He made a career as a London grocer and merchant, and was MP for Appleby (1645-53) and Worcester (1653). He was also a Major in the Parliamentary Army, member of many committees in London and Worcestershire, and Mayor of Worcester (1654). During 1654-9 he was English ambassador at Constantinople. President of the Council of State from September 1659. After the Restoration he was briefly imprisoned in Shrewsbury Castle and sent to the Tower of London, 1660 and 1663-4. He chiefly lived at Richard's Castle, in North Herefordshire, but also built a country house nearby at Haye Park in Shropshire.

SAMSON (d. 1115)

First Norman Bishop of Worcester, 1096-1115, successor to Wulfstan II. His qualifications were not impressive; he became a priest only the day before he became bishop, and was presumably a married man, since he had a daughter who had a liaison with the first Earl of Gloucester, and two sons, one of whom was made Archbishop of York in 1108. Nevertheless he was well-connected and a favourite at court, and was thus able to make rich grants to Worcester Priory. It has been suggested he was the scribe who oversaw compilation of Domesday Book. He was buried in Worcester Cathedral.

SANDYS, SIR EDWIN (1561-1629)

He helped found America, though he never went there. Born at Hartlebury, the second son of Edwin Sandys (Bishop of Worcester, 1559-70, and Archbishop of York). From 1586 he was MP for various constituencies, none local. He travelled in Europe between 1593 and 1599 and was knighted by James I in 1603. He was one of the founders of the Virginia Company of London, which in 1607 established the first permanent English colony in America, with its capital at Jamestown. Keen to expand English interests overseas, he also helped the 'Pilgrim Fathers' with a £300 interest-free loan. He helped create the first representative assembly in America, which met at Jamestown on 30 July 1619. By that date he was Treasurer of the Virginia Company, but was suspected of wishing to turn the colony into a republic, and the King forbade his re-election, saying, 'Choose the Devil if you will, but not Sir Edwin Sandys.' The company failed in 1624, and the Crown assumed government of the colony. He also held a senior position with the East India Company. He was buried in Kent, which he had lately represented as MP. His younger brother, George, was a pioneer settler, introducing industry and agriculture, and leading an expedition against marauding natives.

SANDYS, EDWIN (1613?-1642)

Second son of Sir Edwin Sandys, he matriculated at Wadham College, Oxford, at the age of 9! Colonel in the Parliamentary Army, he was wounded in battle at Worcester on

23 September 1642, and died soon afterwards. He was buried in Worcester Cathedral. His younger brother, Richard, also a Colonel in the Parliamentary Army, became Governor of the Bermuda Company in 1647, and purchased Down Hall, Kent, where he settled.

SANDYS, SAMUEL, BARON SANDYS (c. 1695-1770)

Samuel Sandys.

Born in London, eldest son of Edwin Sandys, MP for Worcestershire, he also occupied that position for twenty-five years, from 1718 until 1743. His political reputation was based on his vigorous opposition to Walpole. In 1742 he was appointed Privy Counsellor and Chancellor of the Exchequer, and on losing that position was created Lord Sandys, Baron of Ombersley in 1743, and was Speaker of the House of Lords (1756-7). He was responsible for building the present Ombersley Court, which was re-fronted with stone in the nineteenth century. He died in London from injuries received when his carriage overturned on Highgate Hill and he was buried at Ombersley. His title became extinct on the death of his son in 1797, but was revived in 1802 for a female relative and has continued since.

SAVAGE, HENRY (c. 1604-1672)

Born at Dobs Hill, Eldersfield, south of Malvern, he was master of Balliol College, Oxford from 1651. He was appointed chaplain to Charles II in 1665 and married Mary, sister of Lord Sandys, by whom he had seven children. He wrote a number of books, including a history of Balliol, which was the first history of an Oxford college. He was buried in Balliol Chapel.

SCOTT, WILLIAM (1760-1834)

Manufacturer and local historian, and eldest son of John Scott, of Stourbridge (then in Worcestershire). He and his brother, John, ran a very successful cloth manufacturing business in Stourbridge, from which they retired in 1808. He was a leader of the Presbyterian (now Unitarian) body in Stourbridge, and transcribed the Register of Baptisms from 1709, and also wrote *Records of the Congregation from 1662*, and other local subjects. His chief work was *History of Stourbridge and its Vicinity* (1832).

SEBRIGHT, WILLIAM (d. 1620)

Born at Blakeshall, Wolverley, where his family had lived since at least the early fourteenth century,
he was MP for Droitwich (1572-84) and Town Clerk of London (1574). In 1606 he purchased
the Besford estate (near Pershore) from Edmund Harewell, whose family had owned
it for generations, after he ruined himself through the expense of his many public
offices. He also had a London estate at Bethnal Green which he left for the foundation
of Wolverley Grammar School, for repairing the church and four bridges, and for the
poor of Kidderminster, Bewdley, and surrounding areas. He had no children and left the
Besford estate to his nephew Edward, who was made a baronet in 1626. The estate was
held by descendants until 1885, and the baronetcy continued until 1985. The half-timbered,
sixteenth-century Besford Court that William knew was largely incorporated into a stone
mansion built in 1912. Wolverley Grammar School continued on a site in the centre of the
village until 1931, when it moved to a new site, renamed Sebright School. It closed in 1970
and reopened as Wolverley High School.

SEBRIGHT, SIR JOHN SAUNDERS (1767-1846)

Famed livestock breeder who influenced Darwin. He was the seventh baronet, of Besford Court
(near Pershore), and Beechwood, Hertfordshire; his mother was Sarah, daughter of Edward
Knight, of Wolverley. He is best remembered for the Sebright, one of the most popular
bantam breeds of chicken, and the first poultry breed to have its own enthusiasts' club, set
up about 1810, but he also applied his selective breeding skills to cattle, dogs and pigeons.
He wrote several influential pamphlets including, *The Art of Improving the Breeds of Domestic*
Animals (1809), *Observations upon Hawking* (1826), *Observations upon the Instinct of Animals*
(1836). The first of these, with observations on the failure of weaker animals to reproduce,
attracted the attention of Charles Darwin, and their correspondence through a mutual
friend influenced Darwin's theory of natural selection. When Darwin's famous *On the*
Origin of Species appeared in 1859, it cited Sir John's work extensively. He was independent
MP for Hertfordshire for many years from 1807. He died in Middlesex. Besford Court was
converted into apartments in 2002.

SEWARD, THOMAS (1708-1790)

Clergyman and father of a poet. Born at Badsey (near Evesham), he was Rector of Eyam,
Derbyshire, and Kingsley, Staffordshire, before obtaining posts in Lichfield and Salisbury
Cathedrals in 1755. At Lichfield he made the acquaintance of Dr Johnson, and was described
by Boswell as a 'genteel, well-bred dignified clergyman, who had lived much in the
world'. He evidently had literary interests, having edited the plays of seventeenth-century
dramatists Beaumont and Fletcher, and his daughter Anna became a well-known author
and poet, often called 'the Swan of Lichfield', whose poems were edited after her death by
Sir Walter Scott.

SHELDON, RALPH (1623-1684)

Landowner and antiquarian. Born at Beoley (near Redditch). He formed a fine library at
Weston, Warwickshire, collected curios, and was learned in the history and antiquities

of the county. The family suffered much during the Civil War. Their home at Beoley was burnt by Royalists, and although his father pleaded he had taken no part in the fighting, Parliamentarians confiscated the Beoley estate and sold it. It was reinstated to Ralph after the Restoration. Worcestershire historian Treadway Russell Nash said he was a man 'of such remarkable integrity, charity, and hospitality as gained him the universal esteem of all the gentlemen of the county; insomuch that he usually went by the name of The Great Sheldon'. His chief work was *A Catalogue of the Nobility of England since the Norman Conquest*. He died at Weston. He was childless, and his brother, Edward, had become a monk, so the Beoley estate passed to an Oxfordshire relative, and was sold in the eighteenth century.

SHERIFF, ALEXANDER CLUNES (1816-1878)

Eminent ironmaster and Worcester businessman, son of Alexander Sheriff, of Perdiswell Hall, Droitwich Road, Worcester. He lived variously at the Hall and Shrub Hill House. He was Chairman of Worcester Royal Porcelain Co., and Worcester Engine Works Co., and Director of the Metropolitan Railway, and the Russian Vyksounsky Iron Works Co., amongst many other appointments. Sheriff of Worcester and twice Mayor, during which friends presented him with an 18-carat gold mayoral chain that he presented to the city, 'to be worn by all future Mayors', which it was, although in February 2009 the

Ironmaster Alexander Clunes Sheriff.

council decided it was too valuable to be taken outside the Guildhall. He was MP for Worcester from 1865 until his death. A street in Worcester is named after him.

SHERWOOD, MARY MARTHA (1775-1851)

Best-selling nineteenth-century children's author, born at Stanford-on-Teme, the eldest daughter of Dr George Butt (Vicar of Kidderminster and Rector of Stanford). Though she remembered her childhood as happy, she had to wear an iron collar and wooden back boards from 6 to 13 to cure a slouch! In 1790 she attended Abbey School, Reading, where Jane Austen had been a pupil. Her first book, a romantic novel called *The Traditions*, appeared in 1794. After her father's death in 1795, the family moved to Bridgnorth and her religious views became more evangelical, as shown in *History of Susan Gray*, which darkly emphasised innate human sinfulness and inevitable damnation. In 1803 she married her cousin, Captain Henry Sherwood, and accompanied him to India, where she taught classes for

Author Mary Martha Sherwood.

children and founded an orphanage, while turning out many more stories, as popular abroad as in England; *Little Henry and his Bearer* (1814) went through 100 editions during the century, including translations in French, German, Hindustani and Chinese. When the family returned after eleven years, she opened a school at Henwick, Worcester, and a girls' boarding school at Lower Wick (near St Johns) and lived in Britannia Square. In 1849 the family moved to Middlesex, where she died. In total she wrote more than 400 stories, tracts and best-selling books which were particularly popular in America, where a sixteen-volume edition of her 'works' appeared in 1855. But as the century progressed there was greater emphasis on childhood innocence, and her books fell out of fashion.

SHRIMPTON, MOSES (1820-1885)

Vicious police killer. Shrimpton was a poacher, frequently in prison. On 28 February 1885, PC James Davis, 33, stationed at Beoley (near Redditch), failed to return from night duty, and before 9 a.m. his body was found by a farmer in Eagle Street Lane, Alvechurch, with more than forty stab wounds. Police found chickens had been stolen from nearby Weatheroak Hill Farm, and footprints at the scene suggested Davies had apprehended the poultry thief, who unexpectedly turned on him. Shrimpton, 66, was well known to raid poultry farms. Police cornered him in a squalid Birmingham back-street flop house, where they found bloodstained clothing, boots matching prints from the scene, and a probable murder weapon – a pocket-knife. They also traced a watch, recently sold by Shrimpton, which belonged to the dead man. Shrimpton denied the offence, but the jury quickly returned a 'guilty' verdict and he was hanged at Worcester, 25 May. The dead police officer left a widow and four small children.

SIDDONS, SARAH (1755-1831)

Greatest tragic actress of her day, with important connections to Worcester. Born in Brecon, eldest of twelve children of actor/manager Roger Kemble of Hereford, whose small theatrical company toured the Marches. She was educated at a private school at Thorneloe House, Barbourne, Worcester, later the eye hospital. Nineteenth-century writer Edward Bradley was fortunate to find a centenarian schoolfellow, who recalled that initial disdain for the daughter of players was overcome by Sarah's cheerful, kindly disposition and excellent performances in school entertainments. Around the age of 11 she made her first recorded theatrical appearance, as Ariel in *The Tempest*, at the 'Worcester Theatre', a stable in the yard of the King's Head Inn, opposite the Town Hall on the site of the present Guildhall. Playing the Duke of Richmond was a young man named William Siddons, and when she was 16 they became engaged. Her parents disapproved, but relented in 1773. The couple were married and she resumed work with the Kemble company as Mrs Siddons. A first engagement at Drury Lane, London, in 1774, was not well received, but her re-engagement in 1782 was the first of many triumphs which won for her the title the 'Incomparable Siddons'. Fêted by society, and painted by leading artists of the day, including Gainsborough and Reynolds, she was regarded as a great tragic actress, especially for her Lady Macbeth. Her private life was not happy however; she and her husband eventually parted, and she outlived five of her seven children. She died and was buried in London.

Tragic actress Sarah Siddons.

SIDNEY, MARY, COUNTESS OF PEMBROKE (1561-1621)

Perhaps the greatest female writer of Tudor England. Born at Tickenhill Palace, Bewdley, the daughter of Sir Henry Sidney (President of the Marches and Lord Lieutenant of Ireland) and Mary (daughter of the Duke of Northumberland). Her only brother and childhood companion was Elizabethan poet Sir Philip Sidney. She was well educated, acquiring knowledge of Latin, Greek, and probably Hebrew, and in 1576 attended court. In 1577 she married Henry Herbert, Earl of Pembroke, and became mistress of Wilton House (near Salisbury). They had four children, the eldest of whom, William Herbert, may have been the young man described in Shakespeare's Sonnets, and both of her sons were praised as patrons in Shakespeare's First Folio. In 1580 her brother Philip stayed for some months at Wilton, and at his sister's suggestion began his *Arcadia*, which she edited and added to

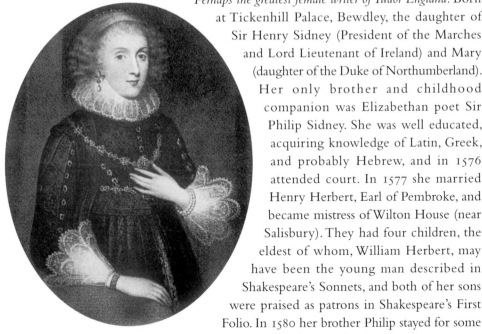

Elizabethan writer Mary Sidney.

after his death in 1586, and published in 1590. She was a generous patron to many poets. She produced translations of many European works and a version of the Psalms, as well as poetry and drama. She died in London and was buried beside her husband in Salisbury Cathedral.

SKEY, FREDERIC CARPENTER (1798-1872)

Distinguished surgeon, born at Upton, the second son of George Skey, a Russian merchant. He became Lecturer on Anatomy at St Bartholomew's Hospital, London, 1843-65: Professor of Human Anatomy, and afterwards President of the Royal College of Surgeons. For his services as Chairman of the Committee on contagious diseases he was made C.B. (Companion of the Bath). He wrote on surgery and hysteria. He died and was buried in London.

SLEATH, ROBERT (d. 1805)

The man who achieved national notoriety by 'stopping the King' at Worcester. He was gatekeeper of the Ombersley Road turnpike tollgate in the late eighteenth century. It was situated some distance north of the junction with Droitwich Road, perhaps roughly where St Stephen's Street is now; the later tollhouse, which still exists at the junction of the two roads, was only built about 1814, and the gates were taken down in 1877. On Saturday, 2 August 1788, George III and the royal family, with a large entourage, passed through the gate on their way to visit Bishop Hurd at Hartlebury – but the substantial toll was not paid. So when Robert saw the entourage returning that afternoon, he locked the gate and refused to let the King through until all the tolls had been paid in full. According to one version of the story, George III had to wait several hours while a courtier was despatched to the city to get the money. Had Robert tried this sort of thing on Henry VIII he would probably have quickly lost his head, but times had changed and he was never brought to account for his 'defence of Barbourne gate'. When he died in Birmingham seventeen years later, this epitaph appeared in the local press:

> On Wednesday last old Robert Sleath,
> Passed through the turnpike gate of death.
> To him would Death no toll abate,
> Who stopped the King at Worcester gate.

SMITH, EDMUND (1672-1710)

Poet, much praised by Dr Johnson. Son of a successful London merchant who died when he was young, he was born either at Tenbury Wells or Hanley Castle – the home of his grandfather, Sir Nicholas Lechmere. Brought up by an uncle and educated at Westminster and Christchurch, Oxford, where he wrote excellent Latin verses, but was apparently expelled in 1705 for 'riotous conduct'. He went to London and was helped by the essayist, poet and politician, Joseph Addison. In 1707 his tragedy *Phaedrae and Hippolitus*, translated from Racine, was acted at the Haymarket Theatre, but not well received. His *Poem on the death of Mr. John Philips* (1708) was described by Dr Johnson as 'among the best elegies which our language can show'. He was buried at Hartham, Hertfordshire. His *Works* was published in 1714, and Johnson included him in his *Lives of the English Poets* (1781).

Clergyman Miles Smith.

SMITH, MILES (d. 1624)

Very learned and long-serving Worcestershire clergyman; Hereford-born son of an arrow-maker. He attended two Oxford colleges and became a great Latin and Greek scholar, and was unsurpassed in Hebrew. Rector of Hartlebury (1589-1624) and Upton (1604-24), he was one of the leading translators of the old Authorised Version of the Bible, for which he also wrote the preface. He became Bishop of Gloucester (1612-24), but retained his Worcestershire parishes.

SNELL, HANNAH (1723-1792)

Disguised as a man she served in both the army and navy. Born in Friar Street, Worcester; one of the six daughters of a hosier and dyer. Perhaps inspired by the military exploits of her grandfather and brother, both killed in action, she often formed up her youthful playmates and marched them around the city. Orphaned at 17, she lived with a married sister in Wapping, London, and in 1743 married a Dutch sailor, but he left when she was seven months pregnant and their child lived only a few months. In 1745, vowing to find her errant husband, she dressed in her brother-in-law's clothes and enlisted in a regiment under his name, James Gray. Soon deserting over some grievance, she walked to

Hannah Snell – joined the Marines in disguise.

Portsmouth and enlisted as a marine, serving five years on several ships and seeing action in India, where she was wounded. She was also flogged twice, but her true sex was never discovered. Sadly her search was in vain; she received word her husband was hanged for murder aboard a Dutch ship. On her discharge in 1750, she revealed her true identity and created a sensation. The romantic tale of her courageous search for her lost love captured the public imagination. She performed in uniform on the London stage singing humorous and patriotic songs, receiving a royal pension of one shilling a day for life. She married twice more and kept a pub. At the end of her life she became a pensioner at Chelsea Hospital, where it was said she died insane.

SOMERS, JOHN, BARON SOMERS (1651-1716)

Brilliant lawyer who rose to be Lord Chancellor of England. Born and brought-up at Whiteladies, the former convent site now the Worcester Royal Grammar School. The son of a Worcester attorney of the same name, he attended King's School, and was called to the Bar in 1676, quickly making a name for himself as an orator in high-profile cases. In 1689 he was MP for Worcester, appointed Solicitor General and knighted, and presided over the Committee which drew up the Declaration of Rights – regarded as the basis of our modern democratic system of government. He was also credited with being the chief architect of the treaty with Scotland, which turned Britain into the United Kingdom. In 1694 he supported the

Lawyer and Lord Chancellor John Somers.

King in his refusal to renew the Licensing Act, thus securing the liberty of the press. Within eight years of entering Parliament, Somers was appointed Lord Chancellor and created Baron Somers of Evesham. A generous supporter of the arts, he granted Addison a pension and Swift's *Tale of a Tub* was dedicated to him. His career declined under Anne, but recovered somewhat under George I. If, as tradition tells us, Somers commissioned architect <u>Thomas White</u> to build Britannia House in The Tything, later the home of Alice Ottley School, then he probably did so about 1714 and may have intended it as his retirement home, but sadly he died in Hertfordshire before he could occupy it. He never married.

Sir Humphrey Stafford and his wife Eleanor.

STAFFORD, SIR HUMPHREY (1400-1450)

Born at Grafton Manor, Bromsgrove, home since the thirteenth century of one of the most wealthy and influential families in the Midlands. He was Governor of Calais in the 1430s. He supported Henry VI in 1450 against a Kentish uprising led by Jack Cade, protesting against unfair taxation and corruption, but was bludgeoned to death in a clash with the rebels, and his brother William was also killed. They feature as characters in Shakespeare's *Henry VI, Part Two.* He was buried in Bromsgrove church, where alabaster figures of he and his wife, Eleanor, surmount the tomb. He had no children and the estate passed to a nephew who was later executed under Henry VII, and Grafton Manor passed to the Talbot family. The house was destroyed in a fire in 1710, but was rebuilt in the 1740s and is now a hotel.

STEYNOR, EGBERT (fl. 1690)

He sank two salt pits on his land at Droitwich in 1690, thus challenging the monopoly of the ancient saltworks, which was based on a charter from King John. After various expensive law suits in the Court of Chancery, it was finally decided that he had the right to sink the pits, and the old monopoly was broken. New salt pits were rapidly dug and the price of salt plunged, from two shillings a bushel to fourpence. But he was ruined by the lawsuits, and was obliged to accept a pension of seventeen shillings a week from the parishes of St Andrew and St Nicholas, Droitwich.

STREET, SIR THOMAS (1625-1696)

Distinguished lawyer, the son of a Worcester family which had long lived at Greyfriars in Friar Street. He was at the Inner Temple in 1646 and qualified as a barrister. He was Town Clerk and Recorder of Worcester and Droitwich, as well as Counsel to the Worcester Dean and Chapter. He was MP for Worcester (1659-81), despite fruitless early Puritan efforts to unseat him because, they claimed, he used profane language and had borne arms for the King – charges of which he was cleared. He was Justice for South Wales (1677), a Serjeant-at-law and King's Serjeant, and Judge in the Court of Common Pleas (1681). He achieved national fame, and much admiration, for being the only one of twelve judges to oppose James II but, perhaps because of this, William III

Lawyer Sir Thomas Street.

would not even grant him an audience in 1688, and he retired to Worcester. Buried in the cathedral, where there is a memorial to him. The lease of Greyfriars was sold after his death. The property is now managed by the National Trust and is open to the public.

STRICKLAND, HUGH EDWIN (1811-1853)

One of the first people to explore the geology of Worcestershire. Born in Yorkshire, his family subsequently made their home at Cracombe House (near Evesham). As a boy he collected fossils and invented a wind gauge, and later spent his university vacations exploring the railway cuttings that were then being dug. After university he began to study the geology of the Vale of Evesham, and presented papers to the Geological Society of London. He worked on the first geological map of Worcestershire, and assisted with the geological ordnance map – which led to an invitation to join an expedition to 'Asia Minor' (Anatolia and Armenia). Later he lived at Apperley Green (near Worcester) and helped explore the New Red Sandstone formation of Gloucestershire, Worcestershire, and Warwickshire. Appointed Deputy Reader in Geology at Oxford in 1849, he was killed while examining a railway cutting in Nottinghamshire.

STURGE, CHARLES (1802-1888)

Gloucestershire-born younger brother of eminent Quaker philanthropist and Birmingham alderman Joseph Sturge, he was a corn factor and lived for many years at Wribbenhall (near Bewdley). He is credited with persuading John Bright to stand as MP for Birmingham in 1858. Joseph and Charles both went on a peace mission to Tsar Nicholas in Russia before the Crimean War, and were well received, though unsuccessful. On their return, Queen Victoria gave them an audience to hear about their mission. When asked afterwards whether, as a Quaker, he minded kissing the Queen's hand, Charles replied – no doubt with a smile – that he did not, since she was a comely young woman.

SWAN, BECKY

Witch who lived in Worcestershire Street, Kidderminster, in the mid-nineteenth century. A 'white' or good witch, she was said to possess healing powers and a knack for finding lost property – but locals were apparently in some awe of her, and concocted a fantastical account of her death. Supposedly a large black cat, from which dogs fled howling, arrived at her door, at the sight of which she turned white with fear. Four days later, when neighbours plucked up the courage to enter the cottage, all that remained of Becky was a pile of ash on the floor.

SYMONDS, WILLIAM SAMUEL (1818-1887)

Clergyman, author and amateur geologist. Herefordshire-born curate of Offenham (near Evesham) and Welland (near Malvern), before becoming Rector of nearby Pendock (1845-77). While at Offenham he met Hugh Edwin Strickland, whose acquaintance sparked a lifelong interest in geology. A founder of the Herefordshire Woolhope Naturalists' Field Club (1851) and the Malvern Naturalists' Field Club (1853), he published many papers and essays on Worcestershire geology from 1855 onwards. He also wrote a series of books, including *Notes for Young Naturalists* (1859) and two locally-set popular historical novels, *Malvern Chase*, set during the Wars of the Roses, and *Hanley Castle*, set in the period of the Civil War. He was buried at Pendock.

TALBOT, SIR GILBERT, (d. *c.* 1516)

Ancestor to two earldoms. Born the third son of John (second Earl of Shrewsbury), he came to prominence with his support for Henry Tudor, Earl of Richmond, who became Henry VII after the Battle of Bosworth Field in 1485, which effectively ended the Wars of the Roses. Gilbert commanded the right wing of Henry's army at Bosworth, and was rewarded with the grant of Grafton Manor (near Bromsgrove) and other lands at Upton Warren, Kidderminster, Kings Norton, Kenswick and Westbury. He was one of the commanders at the Battle of Stoke, a final Yorkist insurrection, in 1487. A favourite of the King, he was appointed steward of Feckenham Park (1493), knighted and made Governor of Calais (1495). He was buried at Whitchurch in Shropshire. On the death of Edward, eighth Earl of Shrewsbury in 1618, the earldom came to a descendent of Sir Gilbert, after which the title has continued to the present day, with their seat formerly at Alton Towers, until that estate was sold. He was also the ancestor of the Earls Talbot.

TANGYE, JOSEPH (1826-1902)

Industrialist who retired to the county. Born into a Cornish farming family, he developed considerable mechanical ability, and with his four brothers set up Cornwall Works, Birmingham, in 1855, which developed into a massive industrial concern, making engines and hydraulic rams. A member of the Society of Friends, Joseph was encouraged in his early efforts by Joseph and <u>Charles Sturge</u>. In 1857 the brothers had a great opportunity when Brunel needed to launch SS *Great Britain*, the largest ship ever then built. Tangye Brothers' powerful hydraulic jacks did the trick, and also launched the company's rise to fame. In 1864 the business moved to massive works at Smethwick and by 1870 was employing 800 people. Joseph retired in 1872 and purchased Tickenhill Palace, Bewdley, in 1873 from the Crown, for £4,600. He installed a steam engine driving a dynamo which provided electric light and pumped up well water. His study, where he spent several hours daily working on new mechanical inventions, was fitted with a lathe worked by electricity. In the 1920s his daughter, Alice, and her husband, opened a large collection of country craft and life exhibits to the public at Tickenhill, which was transferred to Hartlebury in the 1960s to form the basis of the County Museum collections. Tangye equipment was used in the installation of Cleopatra's Needle (1878), construction of Sydney Harbour Bridge (1932), sections of Birmingham's Spaghetti Junction (1972), and London's Thames Barrier (1974-84) and is still manufactured by a company in Lancashire.

TAYLOR, ISAAC (1730-1807)

Engraver, part of a gifted family. Born in the parish of St Michael in Bedwardine, Worcester, son of William and Ann Taylor, he first helped his father in his business as a brassfounder, silversmith, and engraver. The young Isaac showed a particular gift for the last, engraving a Triumphal Arch to commemorate the re-election of the local MP in 1747. In 1752 he went to London and began engraving plates for the popular *Gentleman's Magazine*, and for many books. The high quality of his work was much admired, and he acquired many friends amongst the capital's artistic and literary community, including Italian engraver Francesco Bartolozzi, writer Oliver Goldsmith, actor David Garrick, and painter Henry Fuseli. He died and was buried in London. His brother James, also Worcester-born, became a leading London china-painter and magazine-illustrator. Isaac's descendants settled in Essex, several becoming writers, including poet Jane Taylor who wrote *Twinkle, Twinkle, Little Star*.

TEMPLE, SIR RICHARD (1828-1902)

Politician and colonial administrator, of The Nash, Kempsey (near Worcester). He entered the Indian Civil Service in 1847, rising to become Lieutenant Governor of Bengal (1874-7) and Governor of Bombay (1877-80). He was a tireless administrator, but was criticised by his superiors for 'extravagance' in importing large amounts of rice to feed the starving during a famine in Bengal in 1874, and has been accused in modern times of consequently making too little effort to relieve suffering during a famine in Madras in 1877. Created Baronet of The Nash, Kempsey, in 1876, as the descendant of an ancient title. In 1880 he returned to England to pursue a political career, becoming Tory MP for Evesham (1885-92), Vice Chairman of London School Board (1885-8) and MP for Kingston (1892-5). He died in London and was buried at Kempsey. The Nash is now used as a wedding venue.

THACKWELL, SIR JOSEPH (1781-1859)

Distinguished soldier, of Birtsmorton Court (near Malvern). He joined the Light Dragoons in 1800, became Captain in 1807, and fought in the Peninsular War. He was in the retreat to Corunna (1808) and fought at Vittoria and the Pyrenees (1813). At Waterloo in 1815, he had two horses shot from under him, was promoted to Major during the battle and lost his left arm. Afterwards he served with distinction in India. He received the thanks of Parliament three times. In 1854 he was appointed Inspector General of Cavalry and Lieutenant General. He died in Ireland.

THOMAS, WILLIAM (1670-1738)

Clergyman and local historian. He was born at Sidbury, Worcester; grandson of Bishop of Worcester William Thomas (1683-9), and William Bagnall, who provided a horse ready-saddled for the future Charles II after the Battle of Worcester. He became Rector of St Nicholas, Worcester in 1723. He published books on the antiquities of Malvern in 1725, and Warwickshire, in 1730, and *Survey of the Cathedral Church of Worcester* in 1736. He collected materials for a history of Worcestershire, which were used by Treadway Russell Nash in his history of the county. St Nicholas Church is now a bar.

THORNBOROUGH, JOHN (1551-1641)

A long-serving but controversial Bishop of Worcester (1616-41). He had been a chaplain to Queen Elizabeth; also Bishop of Limerick (1593-1603) and Bristol (1603-17). However, he had divorced around 1595 and quickly got remarried – supposedly then illegal – to a lady who was rumoured to be pregnant. Though clearly a clerical careerist, he was also independent, taking a tolerant attitude to Puritans, and – most oddly for a senior churchman – dabbling in alchemy, a 'dark art' combining primitive chemistry with mysticism, and often associated with quackery. He was known to have employed Simon Forman, a popular but controversial London astrologer and occultist, and perhaps Robert Fludd, a physician, astrologer and mystic who dedicated a book to the bishop in 1623. The bishop himself wrote an alchemical book, *Lithotheorikos*, which was published in 1621. He died at Hartlebury and was buried in the cathedral.

Bishop John Thornborough.

THROCKMORTON, SIR JOHN (d. 1445)

Lawyer and landowner; of a family who had held lands in Worcestershire since at least the twelfth century, and took their family name from a manor at Fladbury (near Pershore). In 1415 he was granted land and property at Throckmorton, Fladbury, by the Bishop of Worcester. In 1417-18, he attended the Earl of Warwick at Caen, and in 1431 was appointed one of the earl's attorneys. He was MP for Worcestershire in 1414, 1420, 1422, and 1432. Through his marriage, land at Coughton, Warwickshire, came to the family. In 1439 he was appointed one of Warwick's executors, joint custodian of his castles and estates during his son's minority. At his death he was Under-Treasurer of England. He was buried at Fladbury. In 1444 the incoming bishop, John Carpenter, took such exception to the 1415 grant to Sir John that he threatened to excommunicate the prior and monks of Worcester over it! This was eventually resolved by his son, Thomas, who became so friendly with the bishop that he was appointed steward of all his castles and manors.

THROCKMORTON, FRANCIS (1554-1584)

Either a plotter against Queen Elizabeth I, or a victim of her fearsome espionage machine. Son of Sir John Throckmorton (one-time Recorder of Worcester), of Feckenham (near Redditch). After studying at the Inner Temple, he toured Europe talking to English Catholic exiles, doubtless learning details of plots to restore Catholicism in England. He settled at Paul's Wharf, London, in 1583, allegedly organising correspondence between Mary, Queen of Scots, and her political friends, including the Spanish Ambassador. He was soon arrested, incriminating papers were allegedly found at his house, and he confessed on the rack. However, he denied his guilt at his trial at the Guildhall in 1584. Forced into another confession, he again pleaded his innocence on the scaffold.

TILLEY, VESTA (1864-1952)

Music hall star. Born Matilda Alice Powles in the now-vanished Blockhouse slums of Worcester; second of thirteen children of china gilder turned music hall artiste Harry Powles and wife Matilda. Nicknamed Tilley by her family, she began her performing career before she was 5 as 'The Great Little Tilley'. Her full-time career began when she was probably only about 7, with an engagement in Birmingham as a male impersonator – an act said to have been developed after trying on her father's coat and hat. At 10 she was performing twice nightly in London, and began to use the name Vesta – a common term then for a match – after the brand Swan Vesta. In 1890 she married theatrical entrepreneur William de Frece, who wrote many of her songs. She was famous in Britain and America – where she toured very successfully – for her characters Monte from

Music hall star Vesta Tilley.

Vesta Tilley as one of her famous male music hall characters.

Monte Carlo, Algy the Piccadilly Johnny, and especially Burlington Bertie: all 'swells' whose manners were humorously parodied. They made her probably the highest-earning woman in Britain. She returned to Worcester several times for performances at the Alhambra music hall, Lowesmoor, and the Cornmarket Public Hall. During the First World War she entertained troops and visited hospitals. Her husband was knighted in 1919 for contributions to the war effort, making her Lady de Frece. She gave her last performance in 1920, then concentrated on helping her husband's new career as an MP. She was widowed in 1935 and died in London. A memorial plaque was unveiled in 2009 in Wylds Lane, Worcester, where her family also lived.

TOMBES, JOHN (1603-1676)

Controversial clergyman, born at Bewdley and educated at the grammar school, he entered Magdalen Hall, Oxford, aged just 15, and was a lecturer by 21. He developed a reputation as a preacher, and after leaving university preached briefly at Worcester, before becoming Vicar of Leominster until 1643. His Presbyterian views were increasingly unpopular and he moved to Bristol, but when the city was taken by Royalists he escaped to London, and became a minister. He was soon dismissed for refusing to baptise infants on theological grounds, and became preacher of the Temple – on condition he did not preach on infant baptism – but was dismissed four years later for publishing his views. Returning to Bewdley, he was chosen to be minister of the Baptist St Anne's Chapel. Still controversial, in January 1650 he had a famous theological debate in the chapel at Bewdley with Richard Baxter, of Kidderminster, which lasted for eight hours. It drew a massive crowd from the universities and far afield, which became so rowdy that the local magistrate had to intervene. Baxter later claimed it was the ambition of Baptists like Tombes 'to baptise all the maids of Bewdley naked'. Tombes was later at Ross, Ledbury and Leominster again, but after the Restoration he married a rich widow at Salisbury, and declined all further Church offices. He died and was buried at Salisbury.

TOY, JOHN (1611-1663)

Worcester-born clergyman, schoolmaster and author. Initially chaplain to the Bishop of Hereford, he became headmaster of the Worcester Free School, now the grammar school, but moved to the King's School in 1643, where he remained until his death. He also held the parish of Stoke Prior (near Bromsgrove). He wrote *Worcester's Elegie and Eulogie* (1638), a long poem describing the plague which raged in Worcester (1637-8) and a book of Latin poetry (1662). He was buried in the cathedral. The Toy family were long settled at Kidderminster.

TURNER, BENJAMIN BRECKNELL (1815-1894)

Great early photographer. Born in London, where his family had a chandlery business at Haymarket. In 1847 he married Agnes, the daughter of Henry Chamberlain of the Worcester porcelain manufacturing family. His father-in-law had retired in 1837 and purchased Bredicot Court (near Worcester), where the young couple spent holidays. When Turner took up photography in 1849 – only a few years after its invention – he became the first person to record Bredicot and many other rural Worcestershire locations. He exhibited at the world's first photographic exhibition in London in 1852, and was highly praised. He continued to exhibit into the 1880s. He died in London. Though probably best known nationally for his images of Crystal Palace (which was later destroyed in a fire), his rural studies are probably his finest work. Though his equipment was cumbersome compared with modern cameras, his pictures were and still are regarded as some of the greatest ever taken of the English countryside. Many of his originals are in the Victoria and Albert Museum, and prints are still in demand.

TURNER (WILKES), MARY (1762-1808)

Convict transported to Australia in the first convict fleet in 1787. The daughter of Pershore farmer William Turner and his wife Betty, she worked as a servant, but appeared at Worcester Assizes on 5 March 1785, accused of stealing a black silk cloak and other clothing, worth forty-two shillings, from Nancy Collins, the daughter of her Pershore employers. She was sentenced to death, but this was later commuted to seven years transportation. When she arrived in Australia she had begun to use the surname Wilkes – perhaps the name of a lost love, though there is no evidence that she had married. On 5 March 1789, she and another convict were accused of stealing and sentenced to fifty lashes. On 25 March she gave evidence, perhaps in revenge, at the trial of seven marines accused of stealing from the stores, six of whom were hanged two days later. She was subsequently arrested, suspected of perjury, but the charge could not be proved. By 1794 she had formed a relationship with convict David Batty and they had three children, but never married, and she was buried in Australia under the name Wilkes.

TURNER, THOMAS (1747-1809)

Early porcelain manufacturer. Son of clergyman Richard Turner of Elmley Castle and Little Comberton (near Pershore), he got his early training at the Worcester Porcelain factory, where he became a skilful draughtsman and designer under the guidance of <u>Robert Hancock</u>. He married Dorothy Gallimore, whose father had an estate at Caughley (near Ironbridge, Shropshire), where in 1775 they started a porcelain works, with which Hancock was briefly associated. Initially the wares and patterns were very similar to those of Worcester, and during 1789-94 most Caughley products were decorated in Worcester. Thomas subsequently changed the type of porcelain used, and introduced Chinese-style under-glaze willow pattern, which proved very popular. The Caughley factory was sold to Coalport in 1799. He was Freeman of Worcester, Much Wenlock and Bridgnorth.

URSE D'ABITOT (*c.* 1040-1108)

First Norman Sheriff of Worcester. Not prominent in Normandy, he may not have been at the Battle of Hastings, but became an important landowner in England after the invasion; appointed sheriff over Worcestershire in 1069, probably living in Droitwich. He quickly built a castle at Worcester, to the south of the cathedral, and the encroachment of the bailey on a cathedral graveyard began the first of a series of disputes with the only man in Worcestershire whose power rivalled his own – <u>Wulfstan II</u>, Bishop of Worcester. An acquisitive man, he was accused more than once of purloining Church property – though he did assist in the foundation of a hermitage at Great Malvern. The Domesday survey (1086) showed him holding substantial lands in Worcestershire, but also Herefordshire, Gloucestershire and Warwickshire. Under William II and Henry I he achieved some national prominence as a constable of the royal household. It is not known where he died or was buried. His son succeeded as sheriff but was exiled around 1110. Through his daughter he became ancestor of the Beauchamps of Elmley Castle (near Pershore), whose heraldic symbol was a bear – *ursa* in Latin. Worcester Castle ceased to be of military significance after the thirteenth century, but was the county prison until 1814 when a new prison was built in Castle Street, after which the motte was dismantled by 1846.

VELLERS, ROBERT (1743-1815)

Born at Worcester, he made a fortune as a silk mercer, with premises 'in the College Church-Yard'. His press advertisements boasted that ladies could see 'every new colour in silk, the same as at mercers in London'. By his will he bequeathed £6,000 to the Worcester Infirmary, and £100 to each parish in the city, to maintain the poor. He was buried in the Cloister Green.

VERNON, THOMAS (1654-1721)

Leading lawyer. Probably born at Hanbury Hall (near Droitwich), his great-grandfather was Rector of Hanbury in 1580, and his grandfather purchased the manor in 1631. Called to the Bar in 1679, he practised in the Court of Chancery for forty years. He was reputed to be the ablest man in his profession, and became wealthy as a result, investing a good deal in Worcestershire property. In the early eighteenth century he rebuilt Hanbury Hall as an elegant William-and-Mary style mansion, added to the family estate with land in Hanbury and Shrawley, and left £20,000 cash for future purchases. He was MP for Worcestershire in 1715 and two years later he was elected to be the Treasurer of the Inn – the most senior position. He continued in legal practice almost until his death. He was buried at Hanbury, where there is a memorial. His reports of cases in Chancery were posthumously printed in several volumes. Hanbury Hall remained the home of the Vernons until 1940, and is now a National Trust property, open to the public.

WADLEY, THOMAS PROCTER (1826-1895)

Clergyman and local historian. Warwickshire-born Rector of Naunton Beauchamp from 1874, he spent many years studying genealogy and the local history of Worcestershire and

Gloucestershire. His chief work, published in 1886, was an abstract of almost 450 county wills held at Bristol covering the period 1381-1595. He also published details of Worcester marriage licences from 1660, and rescued from possible loss large numbers of abstracts of parish registers held at Edgar Tower, Worcester, for the period 1600-1700. He was a frequent contributor to genealogical publications, and also wrote poetry and collected historical prints connected with Shakespeare.

WAKEMAN or WYCHE, JOHN (d. 1549)

Son of William Wakeman, of Drayton (near Belbroughton). He was the last Abbot of Tewkesbury and the first Bishop of Gloucester. He became a Benedictine monk, using the name Wyche and was elected Abbot of Tewkesbury in 1534. In July 1535 he entertained Henry VIII and Thomas Cromwell. At the Dissolution in 1539, he surrendered the monastery and received an annuity of 400 marks, which he had to give up when he was consecrated first Bishop of Gloucester in 1541, reverting to the name Wakeman. While abbot, he set up a splendid tomb for himself at the abbey, but he was actually buried in Gloucester Cathedral.

WALCOT, JOHN COTTERELL PHILLIPPS (1849-1901)

Sailor who played an important role in founding the Australian Navy. Born at Kempsey, the second son of Revd John Walcot (afterwards Rector of Ribbesford) and Mary Sophia (daughter of Sir Thomas Phillipps, of Middle Hill, Broadway), he joined the navy in 1863, and in 1867 served five months as midshipman on Nelson's *Victory*. After a varied service, he retired in 1882 with the rank of Commander, but in 1884 accepted the new post of Commandant of the South Australian Naval Forces, and sailed on the force's first warship, *Protector*, for Adelaide where he received a warm welcome. He became a tireless campaigner for naval defence, giving evidence on the subject before the Select Committee of the House of Assembly, while also fulfilling various community roles as a Justice of the Peace, and 'Juror on Naval and Military Armaments and Ship Models' at the Adelaide Jubilee International Exhibition in 1887. He also took charge of the fledgling lifeboat service and effected improvements through regular inspections. In 1893, having played an important part in founding the Australian Navy, he retired to Pirton Court (near Worcester). He was buried at Bitterley (near Ludlow).

WALKER, JOHN SEVERN (d. 1875)

Keen student of county architecture, and especially church-building. He lived at Malvern Wells and played a major part in forming Worcester Architectural Society, being Treasurer and Honorary Secretary for many years. He acted as a guide on many excursions, and fostered interest in neglected old buildings, publishing *A Guide to the Churches of Bredon, Kemerton, and Overbury* in 1835, and *Architectural Sketches, Ecclesiastical, Secular, and Domestic, in Worcestershire and its Borders* in 1862-3.

WALL, SAINT JOHN (1620-1679)

Priest executed for his work in the county. Born in Lancashire, he trained abroad as a Catholic priest and secretly worked in the county and Warwickshire from 1656. He had a particular association with Harvington Hall (near Kidderminster) where he said mass illegally for <u>Lady Mary Yate</u>, and doubtless hid at times in some of the most secure 'priest holes' in England. His undoing was the panic surrounding the 'Popish Plot': a supposed Catholic conspiracy to assassinate Charles II, fabricated by convicted perjurer Titus Oates. Wall was arrested at Rushock Court (near Harvington Hall), lodged in the prison at Worcester Castle, and tried in London. Cleared of the plot but sentenced as a Catholic priest, he was put to death at Red Hill, Worcester on 22 August; the last English priest to be executed. He was buried in St Oswald's churchyard, The Tything, Worcester, where there is a memorial plaque; another memorial, at the rear of 4 Whittington Road, marks the execution site. In 1879 a memorial crucifix was erected in the graveyard at Harvington. He was canonised in 1970. Harvington Hall is now open to the public and its 'priest holes' are a particular attraction.

WALL, JOHN
(1708-1776)

Doctor, chemist, artist, civic leader. Born at Powick (near Worcester), of a well-connected county family, he began to practise as a Worcester physician in 1736, and in 1745 was concerned with Bishop <u>Isaac Maddox</u> in the foundation of Worcester Infirmary on Silver Street. Always an innovator, he wrote many medical and scientific papers. Around 1750, with apothecary William Davis, he conducted experiments in porcelain-making at Davis's shop in Broad Street, Worcester, and in the following year they joined with local businessmen to set up what would become

John Wall – doctor and porcelain manufacturer.

Worcester Royal Porcelain Company, creating badly-needed employment. The venture had a site for stone extraction and crushing at Shrawley, and was based at Warmestry House, Worcester – the former Severn-side mansion of the Warmestry family – whose quartered device, a crescent, was the original Worcester porcelain mark. The take-over of a Bristol works brought in skilled workers, enabling the factory to meet the doctor's aims of making Worcester wares distinctive and high quality, and the venture prospered and employed 1,000 at its height. He laid the foundation for the nineteenth-century 'water cure' development of Malvern with his work *Experiments and Observations on the Malvern Waters* (1756) and was also an accomplished artist and portrait painter. In 1761 he built himself an 'out of town' house in Foregate Street, where there is a plaque, but in 1774 he retired to Bath, where he died. The porcelain works eventually became the oldest in England, but closed in June 2009, though the on-site museum is still open.

WALSH, JOHN HENRY (1810-1888)

Surgeon who became the leading national field sports authority. Born in London, he may have had family connections with Worcester, where he practised for some years from 1844 at Foregate Street and in The Tything. He wed Margaret Stevenson of Claines in 1833, and Susan, daughter of Dr Malden of Worcester, in 1835, though both women died within a year of the marriage. When he married again in 1852 his wife outlived him. In that year he settled in London, and continued to practise as a surgeon, but gradually abandoned the profession as his books on rural sports achieved success. His comprehensive *Manual of British Rural Sports* first appeared in 1855, under his pen-name 'Stonehenge'. In that year he joined the staff of periodical *The Field*, and within two years became editor. He produced many books and was the acknowledged authority on rural sports. He died and was buried in London.

WALSH, WILLIAM (1662-1708)

Poet, critic, and MP. He was born at Abberley Hall, on an estate given to an ancestor by Henry VIII. He went to Oxford but took no degree, becoming MP for Worcester between 1698-1702, and Richmond, Yorkshire, 1705-8. In 1705 he became only the second person to hold the royal post of Gentleman of the Horse. In 1691 he published *Dialogue Concerning Women, Being a Defence of the Sex.* He collaborated with Sir John Vanbrugh and William Congreve on an adaptation of a Molière farce, and his poetry was published in *Dr Johnson's Miscellany* in 1716, and several other collections. He is perhaps best remembered as a friend of poet Alexander Pope, who visited him at Abberley in 1707, and dramatist William Wycherley, who benefited from his criticism. He was buried at Abberley. After his death Abberley Hall passed to the Bromley family, who sold it in 1836; since 1916 it has been a school.

Poet William Walsh.

WALTON, ELIJAH (1832-1880)

Landscape artist, associated with Bromsgrove. Son of a Birmingham tailor, he studied art and married there in 1867. After further study in London he settled at The Forelands (near Bromsgrove). He was an eminent painter of mountain scenery in oils and watercolours, chiefly from sketches made in Switzerland, Norway, Egypt, Syria, and Greece. His wife's death in 1872 much affected his health, and his own death, a few years later, left their three sons, all pupils at different boarding schools, as orphans. His home was later purchased by Birmingham Education Department and opened about 1920 as The Forelands Convalescent School, an open-air school which closed in 1967. Since then the site has been redeveloped. His paintings are still popular when they appear in auctions.

WALWYN, WILLIAM (1600-1681)

Early campaigner for democracy and equality, born at Newland (near Malvern); grandson of a Bishop of Hereford. He started his working life apprenticed to a silk merchant in London, becoming a master weaver and setting up in the trade himself. In 1627 he married Anne Gundell, with whom he had twenty children. An advocate of religious toleration, he backed Parliament in the Civil War, but in the 1640s became a leader of the Leveller social and political reform movement. In 1645 he published *England's Lamentable Slaverie*, protesting the imprisonment of Leveller leader John Lilburne, and in 1646, with Richard Overton, wrote *A Remonstrance of Many Thousand Citizens*, regarded as a founding document of the Leveller movement. He tirelessly petitioned Parliament for reforms, and in 1647 co-authored *An Agreement of the People*, the Leveller manifesto. After the second Civil War broke out, he called for a constitutional monarchy. After Charles I's execution he published nothing more, but was imprisoned for some months in 1649. On release he returned to family life and interested himself in medicine, beginning to practise as a physician during the 1650s, and publishing several medical tracts and handbooks. He died and was buried in London.

WARD, WILLIAM, EARL OF DUDLEY (1817-1885)

Born in Suffolk, of a family which traced their origins to a wealthy goldsmith and jeweller to Charles I. He inherited a vast fortune in Black Country industrial holdings from a distant relative in 1833, while still a minor. In 1837 his trustees purchased the Worcestershire estates of the Foley family, following a fire at Witley Court, Great Witley. His wealth rested on iron works, chemical factories, more than 200 mines, and large landholdings in the West Indies and England, including more than 14,000 acres in Worcestershire. In the 1850s large sums were spent in improvements at the Court, engaging architect Samuel Daukes to remodel the house in Italianate style, and William Andrews Nesfield to transform the gardens and create two massive fountains. In the 1850s he helped rescue from destruction the Kidderminster carpet industry, then still reliant on hand looms, by erecting 'Lord Ward's Shed', which provided steam power to local carpet manufacturers renting part of the premises, enabling the industry to compete with national rivals. A cloister in the parish church was erected to his memory. He was created Earl of Dudley in 1860, a re-creation of an old title. An 1860s restoration of Worcester Cathedral was largely due to his generosity.

He married twice and had six sons and a daughter. He died in London and was buried at Great Witley. A monument in Worcester Cathedral was funded by public subscription. His widow survived him by more than forty years, dying in 1929.

WARD, WILLIAM HUMBLE, EARL OF DUDLEY (1867-1932)

William Humble Ward.

Son of William Ward, Earl of Dudley. He inherited his father's title and vast wealth while still a teenager, though he did not come into it until later, and did not take up residence at Witley Court until the age of 21, in 1888, when there were three days of celebrations with large numbers of guests from the gentry, estate workers and tenants, and local and London tradesmen – all entertained separately of course. Similar celebrations were held in 1891 for his marriage to Norfolk banking heiress Rachel Anne Gurney. The young earl became part of the racy circle surrounding the Prince of Wales, and in the 1890s, the heyday of Witley Court when there were more than 100 servants, the future Edward VII was a frequent visitor to the lavish house parties. The earl sat on the Conservative benches in the House of Lords, and was Parliamentary Secretary to the Board of Trade (1895-1902), Lord Lieutenant of Ireland (1902-5) and Governor General of Australia (1908-11). His extravagant spending in these appointments outstripped even his massive resources, and his marriage was also under strain; a separation was agreed in 1908, with Lady Dudley getting Witley Court. When she drowned in 1920, he sold the estate and married former Gaiety girl Gertie Millar. Witley Court was sold to a Kidderminster carpet manufacturer, but was left derelict after a fire in 1937. It was sold for £4,000 in 1939 and has since passed through various hands, having been offered for sale on Internet auction site eBay in 2003, but the Court has been managed by English Heritage since 1984 and will continue to be open to the public. The title of Earl of Dudley is still held by his descendants, and the actress Rachel Ward is his great-granddaughter.

WARMESTRY, GERVASE (1604-1641)

Official and poet. Born into an old Worcester family who made their home at Warmestry House, which was built by the beginning of the seventeenth century on the site where the College of Technology now stands. He was the son of William Warmestry, Chief Registrar of Worcester – a role held by members of the family since 1544. Educated at Worcester Grammar School and Oxford, in 1630 he succeeded his father as Registrar. He also wrote political poems, the best known of which was *England's Wound and Cure* (1628). He was buried in the cathedral.

WARMESTRY, THOMAS (1610-1665)

Younger brother of <u>Gervase Warmestry</u>, *he attended King's School and Oxford*. He was Rector of Whitchurch, Warwickshire (1635-46), and Clerk to the Worcester Diocese. In 1646 he was appointed to negotiate terms of surrender of the city with the Parliamentary Army, and afterwards fled to join the King, but was deprived of all his Church preferments and threatened with loss of his lands at Blockley (then in the county, but transferred to Gloucestershire in 1931). At the Restoration he was made master of the Hospital of the Savoy, London, and Dean of Worcester (1661-5). A Royalist trooper wrote that he 'was bro't into Worcester as Dean by above 100 horse; a clergy band stood ready to receive him in the City; the King's Scholars at the College gate'. His chief work as dean was the erection of a 'great organ', over which he experienced many difficulties, chiefly because he was, said Bishop Skinner, 'utterly ignorant of music'. In 1662 he was appointed Vicar of Bromsgrove, and held both offices until his death. He was buried in the cathedral.

WATSON, JOHN (1520-1584)

Cleric and doctor. Born at Evesham, where his family lived until the 1540s when his father built the Mansion House, Bengeworth, now the Evesham Hotel. He graduated from Oxford in 1544 and became Prebendary of Winchester (1551), Chancellor of St Paul's (1557), and Archdeacon of Surrey (1559). In 1573 he took a degree in medicine at Oxford, and until 1580 was master of the Hospital of St Cross, Winchester, and dean of that city. In 1580 he was made Bishop of Winchester. Apparently a modest man, he paid £200 to the Queen's favourite, the Earl of Leicester, to lobby Elizabeth not to make him bishop – but when she heard this, she said a man was more worthy 'who will give £200 to decline, than he who will give £2,000 to attain it', and immediately appointed him. Buried in Winchester Cathedral, he left a legacy for the benefit of Evesham scholars.

WEAVER, THOMAS (1616-1662)

Born in Worcester, of a family connected with London publishers. He attended Christ Church, Oxford, and became chaplain at the cathedral in 1641. However, he was ejected by Parliament, presumably for having Royalist sympathies, and for some years 'lived by his wits' writing humorous works and political skits, some of which got him into trouble with the government. One, called *Zeal Over-heated*, resulted in a charge of treason, but he was acquitted by the judge, who, after reading the verses, was loath 'to condemn a scholar and a man of wit'. After the Restoration he was employed by the Excise at Liverpool, where he died.

WHISTON, ENOCH (1858-79)

Cold-blooded murderer, hanged at Worcester in 1879. The 21-year-old labourer and horse driver shot and robbed Alfred Meredith, an ironworks clerk carrying more than £300 for wages, at a quiet spot between Dudley and Woodside. Whiston was quickly apprehended and executed on 10 February.

WHITE, JAMES (1775-1820)

Pioneering advertising man, born at Bewdley and educated at Christ's Hospital School, London, with poet and essayist Charles Lamb who became a life-long friend. In 1790 he was apprenticed as a clerk at the school, but in 1800, at a base in Warwick Square, East London, he founded an advertising agency credited with pioneering the use of professional copywriting services, with some 'puffs' written by Lamb. The agency prospered, and in 1808 moved to Fleet Street, in the heart of the publishing district. Always a colourful character, he had a fascination for Shakespeare's Falstaff, often dressing the part, and in 1796 published a humorous book, *Letters of Sir John Falstaff and His Friends.* Lamb wrote an account of a feast which White held every year for the chimney sweeps' boys, and said when White died 'he carried away half the fun of the world'. His agency continued under descendants until 1962. The Arthurian author T.H. White was his great-great-grandson.

WHITE, alias BRADSHAW, JOHN (1576-1618)

Much-respected monk, born probably at Henwick (near Worcester). He was educated at Jesuit colleges in Europe, but during an illness in 1600 he vowed to become a Benedictine monk if he recovered. In 1603 he returned to England as a Catholic missionary working in Worcestershire. At a time when Catholic priests were hunted down and executed, his open and honest character helped him obtain a government promise that no Benedictine should suffer for ministering in England. This sparked Jesuit jealousy and intrigues against Benedictines in Europe, but in England he established all Benedictines in one congregation – which was not persecuted. He was also successful in reformation of several French monasteries, and died at Longueville, as he visited a monastery.

WHITE, THOMAS (d. 1738)

Important Worcester-born architect. Apprenticed to a statuary and stonecutter in Piccadilly, London, he also studied art. Sir Christopher Wren, architect of St Paul's, London, took him to Rome where he carried on his sculpture, and also made measurements of St Peter's Basilica. He is said to have assisted Wren with the model of St Paul's Cathedral, and was offered the post of superintendent of the building. But he preferred to return to Worcester, where he had property, and was architect of a number of important buildings in the city. Amongst his first work must have been Britannia House in The Tything, recently Alice Ottley School, traditionally believed to have been commissioned by <u>John Somers</u>, whom White may have met in London. The commission would have had to date from between 1714, when Somers' fading career recovered somewhat, and 1716 when he died. The Guildhall was completed 1721-3. The statues of Queen Anne and the two kings are of his design, and apparently partly of his execution. The corporation were so appreciative that they gave him a pension of £30 a year for life. St Nicholas Church, with its finely conceived west front, was begun by White in 1726. St Swithin's, except the old tower, was rebuilt in 1736; the pulpit has been considered a splendid example of its kind. He died unmarried.

WILLIAMS, SIR EDWARD LEADER (1828-1910)

Born at Worcester, eldest of the eleven children of Edward Leader Williams and brother of artist <u>Benjamin Williams Leader</u>. He followed his father into civil engineering, becoming Engineer to the River Weaver Trust, and the Bridgewater Navigation Co., but his chief distinction was as designer of the Manchester Ship Canal, for which he was knighted in 1894. He died at Altrincham.

WILLIAMSON, GEORGE HENRY (1845-1918)

George Henry Williamson.

Industrialist who helped create modern Worcester. Born in London, the second son of an Irish 'tinman' who started a small japanning (enamelling) business in Lowesmoor, Worcester, and built it into a large concern. The company moved to the new Providence Works in the Blockhouse area in 1858. George, who lived off Bath Road, invented the 'lever lid' – which is still used on paint tins. On his father's death, in 1878, he took over the business, first with elder brother, William, and alone from 1890, increasing the staff from 400 to 1,000, making a wide range of tinplate products. For forty years he was a leading member of the city corporation, and as Chairman of the Streets Committee was credited with replacing the medieval alleyways of the city centre with wide, attractive thoroughfares, lit by electricity, for which he facilitated the building of the first municipal power station. He also raised Hylton Road to try to avoid flooding, improved the riverside, and pressed private landlords across the city to improve their properties, especially in poor areas. He was Mayor of Worcester in 1893. He was not, however, successful in national politics. He became Tory MP for Worcester in 1906, but was soon disqualified over allegations that his supporters had bribed voters. He was exonerated personally, but the scandal led to a royal commission, and it was not until 1908 that a by-election could be held to choose a new MP. His son, also George, took over the business after his death, and it became part of Metal Box in 1930, but the Providence Works continued to produce tinplate products until 1963. A telephone exchange now stands on the site.

WILLIS, RICHARD (1664-1734)

Son of William, a tanner at Ribbesford (near Bewdley), he rose high in the Church. Educated at Bewdley School and Oxford, he made a reputation as a preacher at St Clement's, Strand, London, and in 1694 went to Holland as chaplain to William III. He was Prebendary of Westminster in 1695, and in 1699 became one of the founders of the Society for Promoting Christian Knowledge – which has a chain of bookshops. He became Dean of Lincoln (1701), Bishop of Gloucester (1715), Salisbury (1721), and Winchester (1723). He died in London and was buried at Winchester.

WILLIS-BUND, JOHN WILLIAM (1843-1928)

Historian, born at Wick Episcopi (near Worcester). The son of a judge who came to Worcestershire after an unhappy career in colonial jurisprudence, he attended Eton and Cambridge, and was called to the Bar. He made a career in county administration and was Chairman of the Severn Fishery Board, but is best remembered as an historian and researcher. He was very active with the Worcestershire Historical Society and the Worcester Diocesan Architectural and Archaeological Society, regularly reading research papers and editing historical documentation for publication. He wrote *The Civil War in Worcestershire* (1905), edited *Trials for Treason*, in three parts (1879-82) and wrote extensively on the Welsh Church, including *The Celtic Church of Wales* (1897) and *Black Book of St David's* (1902) – though these were not well reviewed. He also edited the *Victoria County History of Worcestershire*.

WILSON, JOSEPH BOWSTEAD (1841-1911)

Genial Cumberland-born clergyman who made his mark through public service in Worcestershire. After Cambridge, where he was a distinguished oarsman and rowed in the University Boat Race in 1863, he was assistant master of Bromsgrove School (1865-72), Rector of St Helen's, Worcester (1873-81), and later Rector of Knightwick with Doddenham, west of Worcester (1881-1909). Regarded as a man endowed with quiet energy, great tact, and a genius for friendship, he filled many public positions, including county councillor and President of the Farmers' Association. He reinvigorated the old-established Worcestershire Archery Society, and in 1893 was a founder of the successful Worcestershire Historical Society, of which he was Honorary Secretary for the rest of his life, doing much to build the membership. He was also active in the search for valuable historical material, and published details of entries in the registers of his parishes. He accumulated what was said to be the most complete collection of Worcestershire books in the county. He retired in 1909 and moved to Oakfield, Claines, more recently River School. He died there and was buried at Knightwick.

WINDSOR, ANDREWS, FIRST BARON WINDSOR (d. 1543)

Worcestershire landowner – though he didn't want to be! Eldest son of Thomas Windsor, of Stanwell, Middlesex, he was a staunch supporter of Henry VIII and a valiant soldier, first commanding a troop of horse at the age of 15. He fought for Henry in the French wars, attended him at the Field of the Cloth of Gold (1520), and was one of the commanders under the Duke of Suffolk in the French War of 1524, for which service he was created Baron Windsor (1529). Whether he fell out of favour is not clear, but when Henry visited him at Stanwell in 1542, he took a liking to the estate and demanded Windsor exchange it for one in Worcestershire. Thus, though Windsor protested, he became the owner of the manor of Tardebigge, a possession of the former Bordesley Abbey (near Redditch), with his seat at Hewell Grange, where the family settled for many generations. Hewell Grange was rebuilt several times, the last in 1884-91. It was purchased by the Crown and opened in 1946 as a borstal, which became HMP Hewell Grange in 1991. HMP Blakenhurst and Brockhill prisons have since been built there.

WINDSOR, THOMAS, SIXTH LORD WINDSOR (d. 1642)

Probably born at Tardebigge, the only son of Henry, fifth Lord. He was knighted in 1610, and became Rear Admiral of the Fleet, sent in 1623 to bring Prince Charles from Spain – he is said to have spent £15,000 in entertainments on that occasion. He attended Charles I at York in 1639. He married Catherine, daughter of Edward, Earl of Worcester – but they had no children, and on his death his title went into abeyance, though it was revived in 1660. He was buried at Tardebigge.

WINDSOR-HICKMAN, THOMAS, EARL OF PLYMOUTH (1627-1687)

Sole heir to his uncle Thomas Windsor, he raised a troop of horse for Charles I and fought valiantly at Naseby in 1645. He also raised the Siege of High Ercall, Shropshire, but was imprisoned and fined by Parliament. At the Restoration he was reinstated as seventh Baron Windsor, and made Lord Lieutenant of Worcestershire in 1660. Governor of Jamaica (1661-4), he defeated the Spaniards in Cuba, but returned home through ill health. He was Master of Horse to the Duke of York (1676), and Governor of Portsmouth (1681) and Hull (1682). He was created first Earl of Plymouth in 1682, and a Privy Councillor in 1685. Buried at Tardebigge. The title of Baron Windsor is still held by the Earl of Plymouth.

WINDSOR, THOMAS, LORD MOUNTJOY (1669-1738)

Distinguished soldier and MP. Second son of Thomas Windsor-Hickman (first Earl of Plymouth), he was Page of Honour to James II. He became MP for Droitwich aged 17 (1685-7). Cornet of his father's Troop of Horse, raised in Worcestershire in 1685, he became Captain in 1687, distinguished himself in the Irish and Flemish wars of William III, and became Honorary Freeman of Worcester in 1685. He was created Viscount Windsor (1699), promoted Lieutenant General (1709), and created Lord Mountjoy (1711).

WINNINGTON, SIR FRANCIS (1634-1700)

Lawyer, born in Worcester, called to the Bar in 1660. Knighted, he became Attorney General in 1672 and Solicitor General in 1674. His second wife was Elizabeth, one of three daughters of Edward Salwey, of Stanford Court, between whom that estate was split. Eventually the whole estate devolved to her, beginning Winnington ownership of the estate. By 1675 his annual income from the law exceeded £4,000, and he used some of it to purchase the leasehold of the Crown manor of Bewdley for 140 years. He became MP for Windsor

(1677), Worcester (1678-81), and Tewkesbury (1692-8). Any hopes of political preferment ceased when he supported the Exclusion Bill in 1678-9, which would have removed from succession the future James II, a Catholic, and he was refused a judgeship in 1689. He was buried in the old church at Stanford-on-Teme.

WINNINGTON, THOMAS
(1696-1746)

Politician, born at Stanford Court, Stanford-on-Teme. The second son of Salwey Winnington, MP for Bewdley, he became MP for Droitwich (1726-41) and Worcester (1741-6). A Whig and chief supporter of Walpole, he became a Lord of the Admiralty (1730), then of the Treasury (1736-42). In 1741 he was made a Privy Councillor and Cofferer of the Household (1741-3) and then Paymaster General of the Forces (1743-6). He died due to incorrect medical treatment and was buried in Stanford church under a marble monument by Roubiliac. He had no heir and the Stanford Court estate passed to his cousin Edward Winnington, the first of a line of baronets with their seat at the Court.

Politician Thomas Winnington.

WINSLOW, EDWARD (1595-1655)

Pioneering American colonist, born at Droitwich. The son of a prosperous salt boiler, he was apprenticed to a London printer, but favoured a Puritan sect and went to Leiden, Holland, in 1617, where he married and printed pamphlets which were illegal in England for religious reasons. In 1620 he sailed on the *Mayflower* with the 'Pilgrim Fathers' to found the colony of Plymouth, Massachusetts – the earliest permanent settlement in New England, and one of the earliest in America. His wife died soon after their arrival in December 1620, and in 1621 he married Susannah, a widow and fellow passenger: the first marriage in the colony.

Edward Winslow – US pioneer.

His brother, Kenelm Winslow from Kempsey, joined the colony in 1624. Accounted the most able and active man amongst the settlers, he successfully negotiated with Native Americans and served three terms as colony governor. His fame spread so far that Barbadians petitioned that he should be appointed their governor. He was sent three times on missions to England, bringing back the first cattle seen in the colony in 1624. From the last of these missions in 1646 he never returned, having impressed Cromwell, who provided him employment in his government at generous remuneration. In 1655 he commanded an expedition to the West Indies, but died of a fever and was buried at sea. He wrote four books and a journal, which have been eagerly seized on by historians as evidence for the early years of the Plymouth colony. His statue was unveiled in St Andrews Shopping Centre, Droitwich, in 2009.

WINTOUR, ROBERT (*c.* 1566-1606)

Gunpowder plotter. Elder brother of Thomas Wintour, he married Gertrude, daughter of prominent recusant John Talbot of Grafton, and in 1594 inherited the Huddington Court estate (near Droitwich). Reluctant to be implicated in the Gunpowder Plot, he was finally persuaded by his brother in February 1605. His role was to provide funding and gather arms for an insurrection in the Midlands after Parliament had been blown up. Before Holbeche House was besieged, he and Stephen Littleton slipped away and hid for two months in the countryside, on one occasion fleeing when surprised by a drunken poacher. Robert was supposed to have held secret trysts with his wife, possibly while he hid in woods around their home; in the glass of their bedroom window is etched a despairing message, said to have been scratched by Lady Wintour with her diamond ring, perhaps while awaiting a signal from the woods. They eventually took refuge with Littleton's uncle at Hagley Park, but were betrayed by a servant. He was executed, 30 January 1606, at St Paul's churchyard, London. John Wintour – a half-brother who was also involved – was executed at Red Hill, Worcester, 7 April 1606. Surprisingly, the Wintours were not immediately deprived of their estate, but Lady Wintour forfeited it for recusancy in 1607, though her son regained it.

Gunpowder plotter Robert Wintour.

WINTOUR, THOMAS (1572-1606)

Thomas Wintour – gunpowder plotter.

Leading gunpowder plotter, of Huddington Court (near Droitwich). A close friend of chief plotter Robert Catesby, he was involved from the start in the 1605 plot to blow up James I and Parliament. A Catholic convert and well-educated soldier, who spoke several languages and had fought with the English Army in the Netherlands, he went to Spain, 1603, on an unsuccessful mission to persuade the Spaniards to invade England and restore Catholicism. In 1604 he went to Flanders to try again, and recruited Guy Fawkes to the plot. He also recruited his somewhat reluctant elder brother, Robert Wintour. When the plot was discovered he fled to Holbeche House, on the Staffordshire border, which was the home of another plotter, Stephen Littleton. There they were besieged by the Sheriff of Worcestershire, Richard Walsh, with 200 men. Catesby was shot dead; Wintour was wounded and taken to the Tower of London, where he confessed. At his trial he begged, in vain, for his brother's life. He was hung, drawn and quartered, 31 January 1606, at Old Palace Yard, Westminster, opposite the building he had planned to blow up.

WOOD, ELLEN (1814-1887)

Author Ellen Wood.

Best-selling Victorian novelist. She was born near Worcester Cathedral, the daughter of Thomas Price, who had inherited a large glove factory from his mother, Elizabeth Evans, of Grimley. She was brought up by paternal grandparents until the age of 7 and developed severe curvature of the spine as a child, making her an invalid, but she still lived a full life. In 1836 at Whittington she married Henry Wood, head of a large banking and shipping business, by whom she had three sons and two daughters. She is often known in literature as Mrs Henry Wood. For twenty years they lived in the South of France and she began writing stories for monthly magazines, the first published in 1851. But this idyll was interrupted in 1856 when the business failed and they moved to London, short of money. Learning of a £100 book prize, she dashed off *Danesbury House*, her first novel, and won the money. It persuaded a magazine editor to serialise her novel *East Lynne* in 1860, and an enthusiastic *Times* review launched her into a highly successful career. Probably her most popular book, it was a best-seller in Britain and abroad, and was dramatised as a lurid Victorian melodrama. After that, no year passed without a book or two from Mrs Wood, many of them featuring the Worcester scenes and people she had known. Her father was said to be the original Ashley in *Mrs. Halliburton's Troubles.* Her books were often either shocking thrillers or tales of families in despair, and she gave full vent to the moralising and overwrought emotions so popular in fiction of the time. She produced more than thirty novels and hundreds of short stories, writing in a reclining chair with the manuscript propped on her knees. She died and was buried in London, but there is a monument to her at Worcester Cathedral.

WOODWARD, HERBERT HALL (1847-1909)
Composer, youngest son of Robert Woodward of Arley Castle (near Bewdley). He took holy orders and in 1881 was appointed Minor Canon of Worcester Cathedral, and from 1890 Precentor. He was the composer of many well-known services and anthems and took a large share in the founding of the Cathedral Choir School, greatly improving cathedral music.

WOODWARD, THOMAS (1801-1852)
Victorian artist who received royal patronage. Born at Pershore, son of a solicitor, at an early age he became a pupil of Royal Academician animal painter Abraham Cooper, and was a constant exhibitor at the Royal Academy from 1822 until his death. His work won high praise from Landseer, and Queen Victoria and Prince Albert employed him to paint their favourite animals. He died from consumption (tuberculosis) and was buried at Pershore Abbey where there is a memorial to him.

WULFSTAN I (d. 1023)
Bishop of Worcester, 1003-16, also Archbishop of York at the same time. Danish raids caused great distress in this period and he was noted for trying to rally the people to resistance. He was unpopular with the monks of Evesham and Gloucester, who called him 'the reprobate' and claimed he plundered Church lands. This may partly have been in retaliation for the harsh discipline he enforced on them, but when his sister married she was endowed with monastic lands at Ribbesford and Knightwick. His nephew, Brihteag, was bishop after him, and he was the maternal uncle of Wulfstan II.

WULFSTAN II, SAINT (*c.* 1008-1095)
Last, and perhaps greatest, of the Anglo-Saxon bishops. Son of a Warwickshire vicar, and nephew of former Worcester bishop Wulfstan I, he was educated at the monastic schools of Evesham and Peterborough, ordained in 1038, and joined Worcester monastery as a schoolmaster. He finally became prior, much improving the position of the monastery. Always an ascetic, he was said to have become a vegetarian after being distracted during a service by the smell of roasting goose. He was a friend of Harold Godwineson (later King Harold), and was favoured by Bishop Aldred (who had to give up the see in 1062, but wanted to hang on to a number of the bishop's manors), and they ensured that the election fell on Wulfstan. In 1066 he supported Harold against the Normans, but after Harold's death he accepted the inevitability of the conquest, and William the Conqueror was so impressed with him that Wulfstan was the only Anglo-Saxon bishop to remain in office. A much-loved bishop, he was also a tireless builder, founding Great Malvern Priory and building a new Worcester Cathedral and many parish churches, fearlessly scaling the builders' scaffolding to check on progress. He was canonised in 1203, his tomb attracted many pilgrims.

WYATT, GEORGE (1886-1964)

First World War hero. Born in Worcester, the son of a groom, he went to Holloway School, Droitwich, and served for several years in the Coldstream Guards before joining Barnsley Police. At the outbreak of the First World War he was called up as a reservist and joined the British Expeditionary Force. At the Battle of Mons he twice displayed outstanding bravery and was awarded the Victoria Cross. He later said modestly of one of these incidents: 'I got hit on the head and went on firing. That's all.' He was twice wounded, but survived the war and returned to the police, retiring in 1934 to take up farming. He was buried near Doncaster.

George Wyatt VC.

WYLDE, JOHN (1590-1669)

Lawyer and MP, son of George Wylde, of Kempsey (a Serjeant-at-Law, or senior barrister, and MP for Droitwich). He followed his father into law and politics. He was called to the Bar in 1612, became Serjeant-at-Law in 1636, and was MP for Droitwich (1624-6, 1628-9, 1640, and 1659) and MP for Worcestershire (1640-8). Nationally he was a member of many committees and held several posts including Chief Baron of the Exchequer (1646-53). Locally he became Under Steward of Kidderminster by a new Charter on 4 August 1636, was recommended as Deputy Lieutenant of Worcestershire (1642) and was Recorder of Worcester (1646). In 1653 he fell out of favour with Cromwell and retired to Worcestershire, becoming Justice of the Peace and a commissioner for the county. He died at Hampstead and was buried in Hampshire.

WYLDE, THOMAS (d. 1558?)

Wealthy Worcester clothier or cloth-maker, son of Simon Wylde, of The Ford, Droitwich. A leading Worcester citizen, he was bailiff in 1547 and MP 1549-52 and 1558. In 1544 he bought the former religious house The Commandery for £498, and it remained the family home for 250 years. With <u>Robert Yowle</u>, he refounded what was then known as the Old Trinity School, and has since become Worcester Royal Grammar School. He gave land at Pitchcroft to the corporation on condition that they should erect a Free (non-denominational) School in the city, 'to bring up youthes in their a.b.c., mattens, evensong, and other lernynge'. The school, which had been supported for centuries by the Trinity Guild, had closed in 1553, but was re-established in a room at St Swithin's Church, and moved to The Tything in 1868.

WYRE, THOMAS (1858-1888)

Killer who murdered his own small son. An agricultural labourer from Wolverley (near Kidderminster), Wyre had two children but his marriage was unhappy. On 3 March 1888 his wife walked out, taking their eldest child and telling him he should look after the youngest, a boy aged 4. Wyre said he would take the boy to his parents, but the child was never seen alive again. Three months later, workmen at Castle Hill, Wolverley, found his body in a well. Wyre was convicted at Worcester Assizes and hanged in the city on 18 July.

WYSHAM, SIR JOHN DE (1295?-1332)

Trusted royal official and soldier, of a knightly family of Woodmanton Manor, Clifton-upon-Teme.
In 1311 Edward II made a grant to him for life of the Castle of St Briavel's, Gloucestershire, and the Forest of Dean, possibly as constable of the forest. Shortly after the Battle of Bannockburn, in 1314, he was entrusted with an investigation into corruption in procurement of army supplies: a certain Ralph de Benton had received good victuals for the army at Berwick-upon-Tweed, but had them exchanged for bad victuals at Newcastle-upon-Tyne, no doubt to his considerable profit. Two years later Sir John had custody of the castle and town of Berwick. In 1322 he was charged to survey the array of fighting men in West Yorkshire, and in 1326 was appointed one of the supervisors of array in the counties of Worcester and Hereford. As Steward of the King's household (1328), he secured a grant to Worcester for bridge building or repair. In 1330, perhaps by influence of Roger Mortimer (Earl of March) he was appointed Justice of North Wales, and subsequently, in conjunction with Thomas, Earl of Warwick, was keeper of the County of Worcester. In 1332 he was given leave to crenellate or fortify his manor house, but he died the same year. A farmhouse was later built to replace the manor house.

YARNOLD, WILLIAM (1855-1905)

A former soldier hanged at Worcester for murdering his unfaithful wife. Yarnold, 48, was a veteran with twenty-six years' service. While he was on duty in South Africa during the Boer War, his wife, Annie, 42, left him for another man, but kept pocketing her husband's pay. On his return to Worcester he tried repeatedly for a reconciliation, but without success. On 4 October 1905, he visited her home at The Moors and stabbed her in the back, almost severing her spinal cord. She died a few days later. He was convicted of murder, but there was considerable local sympathy for him, and 6,000 people petitioned the Home Secretary for leniency. Nevertheless he was hanged at Worcester on 5 December. The couple seem to have been childless, and in the condemned cell he made a will leaving a £30 insurance policy to Worcester Infirmary, where his wife had died.

YARRANTON, ANDREW (1619-1684)

Soldier, ironmaster, engineer and imaginative entrepreneur, born at Larford, Astley (near Stourport), where his family owned land. He was apprenticed to a Worcester linen draper, but left, and at the outbreak of the Civil War joined the Parliamentary Army, and rose to be Captain, at one time governor of Hartlebury Castle. He discovered slag from Roman ironworks at Pitchcroft, Worcester (probably after the battle in 1651) and for at least a decade from 1652 shipped large quantities of it to Astley for re-smelting in his more efficient blast furnace. As a Parliamentary officer he was treated with suspicion after the Restoration, and imprisoned several times, though probably on trumped-up charges. When free he was busy supplying farmers with seed for growing clover, which provided animal fodder and fertilised the soil. A self-taught navigation engineer, he produced plans to make the River Salwarpe navigable from the Severn to Droitwich, and to make the Stour navigable for Black Country coal – but neither plan was carried out for a century or more. More successful was his scheme for the River Avon, which made it navigable above Evesham for two centuries and below Evesham to the present day. In 1675 he was living at Larford (near Stourport), perhaps in semi-retirement. In 1677 he published a book packed with further fascinating ideas ahead of their time, including one to end unemployment and another to pay debts without money. According to John Aubrey (author of *Brief Lives*), he met a violent end, being beaten and drowned in a tub of water.

YATE, LADY MARY (1610-1696)
Landowner, daughter of Humphrey Pakington, of Harvington Hall (near Kidderminster), where she grew up. Being from a Catholic family, she was involved from an early age in the covert actions of priests who secretly said mass or took refuge at the hall. At 20 she married Catholic Sir John Yate and they lived at his Berkshire estate, but must have regularly visited the hall, since two of her five children were christened at Chaddesley Corbett. On her father's death she inherited the Harvington estate, and on her husband's death, 1659, she returned to the Hall and lived there for almost forty years. During that time Catholic priests were always welcome, and a number of 'priest holes' have been found. A regular visitor was priest St <u>John Wall</u>, executed in Worcester in 1679, who is depicted in a stained-glass window in the nursery, giving communion to Lady Yate. She was said to be a lady of great piety and benevolence, whose good deeds included endowment of three almshouses for widows, and support for village lad <u>Sylvester Jenks</u>, who became chaplain to James II. However, she was sued in 1668 for allegedly trying to cheat her mentally ill nephew, who had taken refuge with her, out of £3,000 worth of jewels and money. She was buried at Chaddesley Corbett. Harvington Hall is now open to the public.

YOUNG, FRANCIS BRETT
(1884-1954)
Best-selling writer, born at The Laurels, Halesowen (then in Worcestershire). He was the son of Dr Thomas Brett Young (later Medical Officer of Health for the area). In Birmingham he qualified as a doctor and met his wife, Jesse, a physical education student and singer, for whom he composed songs. After a spell as a ship's doctor, he bought a medical practice in Devon. During the First World War he served as a doctor in East Africa, but was invalided out in 1918, unable to practise, and began developing a career as a writer. In 1932 he settled at eighteenth-century Craycombe House, Fladbury (near Pershore), and gradually renovated it with money from his successful 'Mercian' novels, set in Worcestershire

Novelist Francis Brett Young.

151

and surrounding areas. It was requisitioned by the Red Cross in 1939 and he moved to Cornwall. In 1944 he published *The Island*, a stirring epic poem of Britain's history, which immediately sold out and had to be reprinted. After the war, for the sake of his health he moved to South Africa, where he died. His ashes are in Worcester Cathedral. The Laurels is now a private members club.

YOWLE, ROBERT

Elizabethan Worcester clothier, a contemporary of Thomas Wylde. He gave £100 towards the re-foundation of a Free School, and bound the 'maister and skollers' to go yearly to the place where he was buried and pray for the souls of himself, his parents, his wife and children, and all 'Chrysten sowles'. He bought the great Trinity Hall, in what is now The Trinity, formerly belonging to the Trinity Guild, and presented it to the Company of 'Weavers, Walkers [fullers] and Clothiers' about 1540. Around that time land at The Greyfriars was let to him, where he created a home for himself and built a row of houses on Friar Street, which he let out. He was MP for Worcester (1547-52, 1554-5, 1558) and one of the two Bailiffs of the City (1548, 1552, 1559). He established a charity administered by the corporation.

WORCESTERSHIRE
BOUNDARY CHANGES

The table below shows some of the most important changes to have taken place in the county's boundaries in past centuries. A more detailed list, covering the period to 1959, is held by Worcestershire Record Office.

DATE	CHANGE
1542-3	Bewdley, which was usually regarded as part of Worcestershire in the fourteenth century, had become part of Shropshire by the fifteenth century, and was not transferred back until the mid-sixteenth century.
1844	Some detached parts of counties transferred. Worcestershire gained Halesowen and Oldbury from Shropshire, and Clent from Staffordshire.
1891	Balsall Heath, part of Kings Norton, transferred to Birmingham.
1893	Edvin Loach transferred to Herefordshire.
1897	Acton Beauchamp transferred to Herefordshire.
1909	Quinton transferred to Birmingham.
1911	Northfield, Kings Norton and Yardley transferred to Birmingham.
1931	The town of Shipston-on-Stour and the parishes of Alderminster, Tidmington and Tredington transferred from Worcestershire to Warwickshire. The parishes of Redmarley D'Abitot, Staunton, Blockley, Daylesford and Evenlode transferred to Gloucestershire.
1966	Dudley ceded to Staffordshire. Oldbury, Smethwick and Rowley Regis became part of the Worcestershire borough of Warley, which merged with West Bromwich in 1974 to form Sandwell Metropolitan Borough.
1974	Halesowen and Stourbridge ceded to Dudley which became part of West Midlands County. Worcestershire became part of the County of Hereford and Worcester until 1998.

Index *of*
WORCESTERSHIRE
PLACE NAMES

Other titles published by The History Press

Haunted Worcestershire
ANTHONY POULTON-SMITH

Anthony Poulton-Smith takes the reader on a fascinating A-Z tour of the haunted hotspots of Worcestershire. Contained within the pages of this book are strange tales of spectral sightings, active poltergeists and restless spirits appearing in streets, inns, churches, estates, public buildings and private homes across the area. They include tales from Worcester, Bewdley, Droitwich, Bromsgrove, Tenbury Wells and Stourport-on-Severn.

978 0 7524 4872 5

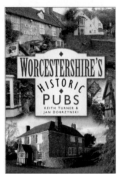

Worcestershire's Historic Pubs
KEITH TURNER & JAN DOBRZYNSKI

Within this book is information on sixty of Worcestershire's historic pubs, including prime examples of riverside pubs – the famous Severn mug houses – wayside inns, canal and railway pubs, and home-brew pubs, as well as the mainstay of every community, the local. All are fully recommended to anyone in search of good beer, cider and food, a great atmosphere, a slice of Worcestershire history – and the odd quirk, curiosity, witch and ghost or two.

978 0 7509 4421 2

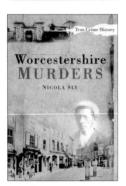

Worcestershire Murders
NICOLA SLY

Worcestershire Murders brings together numerous murderous tales, some of which were little known outside the county, and others which made national headlines. They include the murders of the entire Gummery family at Berrow in 1780, and Maria Holmes, slain by her husband at Bromsgrove in 1872. Cases from the twentieth century include two unsolved murders. Nicola Sly's carefully researched and enthralling text will appeal to anyone interested in the shady side of Worcestershire's history.

978 0 7524 4898 5

England's First Castle: The Story of a 1000-Year-old Mystery
TERRY WARDLE

In early September 1051, the *Anglo-Saxon Chronicle* recorded that 'the French had built a castle', the first Norman castle in England. Yet for centuries the circumstances behind the construction of this castle and its actual location have remained a mystery – until now. In the first ever account of this subject, Terry Wardle looks at the history behind the building of the castle and the man who built it, the Norman soldier Osbern.

978 0 7524 4797 1

Visit our website and discover thousands of other History Press books.

www.thehistorypress.co.uk